Columbia University

Contributions to Education

Teachers College Series

No. 851

AMS PRESS
NEW YORK

SOME RESTRICTIONS AND LIMITATIONS TO THE FREE INTERSTATE MOVEMENT OF TEACHERS

BY WILLIAM D. STRATFORD, PH.D.

TEACHERS COLLEGE, COLUMBIA UNIVERSITY
CONTRIBUTIONS TO EDUCATION, NO. 851

Published with the approval of
Professor Willard S. Elsbree, Sponsor

BUREAU OF PUBLICATIONS
TEACHERS COLLEGE, COLUMBIA UNIVERSITY
NEW YORK · 1942

Library of Congress Cataloging in Publication Data

Stratford, William D 1909-
Some restrictions and limitations to the free interstate movement of teachers.

Reprint of the 1942 ed., issued in series: Teachers College, Columbia University. Contributions to education, no. 851.
Originally presented as the author's thesis, Columbia.
Bibliography: p.
1. Teachers--Legal status, laws, etc.--United States. I. Title. II. Series: Columbia University. Teachers College. Contributions to education, no. 851.
KF4175.Z9S8 1972 344'.73'078 79-177811
ISBN 0-404-55851-8

Reprinted by Special Arrangement with Teachers College Press, New York, New York

From the edition of 1942, New York
First AMS edition published in 1972
Manufactured in the United States

AMS PRESS, INC.
NEW YORK, N. Y. 10003

ACKNOWLEDGMENT

It is a pleasure for the author to express his appreciation to Professor Willard S. Elsbree, sponsor, whose encouragement and critical judgment have made this study a rich experience. The author is happy also to acknowledge his indebtedness to Dr. Walter E. Hager, Professor George D. Strayer, Professor Nickolaus L. Engelhardt, and Professor Clarence Linton for their interest in him and his work during three and a half years of graduate study in Teachers College. Professor Carter Alexander, Professor Irving Lorge, and Professor Ralph Spence helped greatly with their analytical and critical suggestions. The cooperation of the staffs in the Teachers College, the South Hall, and the Law Libraries at Columbia University, and the Congressional Library in Washington, D.C., was unstinted and most helpful.

More than five hundred busy state educational executives, certification directors, and city school superintendents provided data for this study. To them appreciation is due. Dr. Frank Hubbard, of the Research Division of the National Education Association, and Dr. Benjamin W. Frazier, Senior Specialist in Teacher Training of the United States Office of Education, helped with valuable bibliographic material and suggestions. To the national administrative officers of five other professions the author extends his cordial thanks for their cooperation. Especially is a debt acknowledged to Everett S. Elwood, Executive Secretary of the National Board of Medical Examiners, who spared neither time nor energy to assist the writer. A valued friend, Harold Snyder, of the American Council on Education, helped to formulate the data sheets used jointly in connection with the community study.

The author wishes most of all to express his appreciation to his parents, whose example and sacrifices through the years have made the good life more nearly possible.

WILLIAM D. STRATFORD

CONTENTS

TABLES AND FIGURES

FIGURES

SOME RESTRICTIONS AND LIMITATIONS TO THE FREE INTERSTATE MOVEMENT OF TEACHERS

CHAPTER I

INTRODUCTION

IN fulfilling its responsibilities for education as one of its legal functions, each American commonwealth has had to meet the problem of developing requirements that would ensure adequately trained teachers for its schools. Underlying such development in all the states was originally the same tacit assumption: the commonwealth is primarily concerned with seeing that its teachers meet its requirements for certification and not with their residential status. But as each state has been free to develop its certificates under its own definition of "adequacy," obvious fundamental differences[1, 2] among the states have produced correspondingly great variations in certification requirements and procedures. Specifically, a legally certificated teacher in one state is often unable to meet the corresponding requirements of another, either technically or actually. The result is a welter of restrictions and interference with the free interstate movement of teachers. Of the magnitude, quality, incidence, or effects of such restrictions, no one can claim to have even approximate knowledge. Still less is known with respect to their significance for public welfare or for the teaching profession.

NEED FOR THIS STUDY

The need for this investigation is indicated by the following factors:

1. *The literature on teacher certification reveals a widespread criticism of present state restrictions.*

The American Council on Education listed this problem of restric-

[1] Lyle Ashby, *The Efforts of the States to Support Education.* National Education Association, Washington, D. C., 1936. Pp. 63.

[2] John K. Norton and Margaret A. Norton, *Wealth, Children and Education.* Bureau of Publications, Teachers College, Columbia University, New York, 1937. Pp. 100.

tions as one of the major issues in teacher education.[3] In speaking of interstate variations in certification, the Council added:

> . . . While supply and demand stand in different ratios in different states, and while the movement of teacher population is not equal in all directions, a common approach should have been found in this matter.[4]

Gildersleeve, discussing the difficulties encountered by a liberal arts college that attempts to prepare students to meet the certification requirements in more than one state, says:

> . . . it seems to be rapidly becoming impossible for graduates of our best liberal arts colleges to teach in the public schools of this country.[5]

Kendall treats a similar problem in the New England States. Writing of the extension of the authority of the state departments of education and the restrictions in certification requirements, he adds:

> . . . examination of the certification regulations of these six states indicates clearly that some high barriers are in the making. . . .
>
> The state . . . having developed such a teacher-training program at public expense, the state board must justify the expenditure *by utilizing its own product.* In one fashion or another it does so. The implications of such a centralized authority to teacher-training colleges elsewhere become apparent.[6] *

Holmes refers to the "sorry business of meeting state requirements" and poses the problem:

> Can any reform be proposed which will . . . counteract the localism and inbreeding which is another blight on American preparation for teaching? [7]

[3] American Council on Education Studies, *Major Issues in Teacher Education,* February, 1938, p. 20.

[4] *Ibid.*

[5] Virginia C. Gildersleeve, "And Sadly Teach. State Requirements That Discourage Educated Persons from Teaching," *The American Scholar,* Vol. 5, Number 4, September, 1936, p. 426.

[6] Raymond L. Kendall, "The Closing Door," *Journal of Higher Education,* IX, No. 5 (May, 1938), 258–259.

* Italics are the author's.

[7] Henry W. Holmes, "The English Teacher and Educational Theory: The Sorry Business of Meeting State Requirements," *School and Society,* XLVIII (August 6, 1938), 177–179.

Valentine, deploring present certification practices and requirements as part of a system which perpetuates mediocrity, makes an even broader criticism of certain of the limiting and restricting aspects of certification:

> *Certification authorities should make their requirements less rigid.** They could study to advantage the experience of college admissions officers, who have found that flexibility in admissions requirements produces better material for college than rigid adherence to detailed requirements for admission. . . .[8]

He then continues, pointing out the effect on students of the rigid requirements:

> A saner system of certification would draw into school teaching many students admirably qualified to teach, who now choose other careers. *They are repelled by the present rigid professional requirements,* or wisely do not wish to take the necessary time from education to meet them. . . .[9] *

By way of example, Valentine continues:

> . . . And is it not likely that professional skill itself is being interpreted too narrowly along lines of uniform techniques? The measure of professional skill in a teacher is ability to teach successfully. Professors Whitehead, Bliss, Perry, Kittredge, and Tinker possess professional skill —*yet not one of them could or would qualify professionally today to teach in the public schools of their states.*[10] *

He then says that young people of high intellectual and personal qualifications do not choose to elect school work as a career because they sense the mediocrity of the present system and react unfavorably to its inflexible requirements.[11]

These writers are typical of many who challenge the wisdom of present variations in state certification policies and practices as well as of the restrictions imposed.

[8] Alan Valentine, "Teacher Training *versus* Teacher Education," *The Educational Record,* XIX (July, 1938), 340.

[9] Valentine, *op. cit.,* p. 340.

* Italics are the author's.

[10] *Ibid.,* p. 336.

[11] *Ibid.,* p. 345.

2. *Certain states are trying to solve this problem by group action.*

Two groups of states, one in the Midwest[12, 13] and the other in the South,[14, 15] are attempting to solve the problem of certification variations and restrictions in a cooperative way. The General Education Board considered the second of these attempts of sufficient importance to merit a grant of funds.[16]

3. *The changing requirements for certification afford an opportunity for well-founded suggestions.*

The certification requirements of the states are constantly changing,[17, 18] with some trends in opposite and often doubtful directions. Certain changing standards indicate a lack of critical analysis and foresight on the part of those who plan them and enact them as statutes or regulations. This conclusion is reached also in a report of the American Council on Education:

> In general, there is no scientific basis for teacher certification requirements. There is, therefore, great confusion and much disagreement as to the validity of present certification practices. Such a situation constitutes more than a deficiency. It is a serious indictment against our entire program of teacher education.[19]

This same type of criticism is made by Valentine, who then queries:

> Wherein lies the sacredness of these requirements? They were not formulated, after thorough study and hard thinking, by a conclave of serious and representative educators. They are not even a frequently revised product of continued trial and error. In most states they represent a compromise, made by "experts" . . . between various political, economic, and educational interests. They can be called a narrowing down from pressure group to pressure group.[20]

[12] "The Midwest Conference Certification," *School and Society* (December 10, 1938), pp. 746–747.

[13] Russel E. Jonas, "Progress Report, Midwest Regional Conference on Certification," Des Moines, Iowa, November, 1939 (mimeographed report).

[14] Richard E. Jaggers, Director of Teacher Training and Certification, Department of Education, Frankfort, Kentucky, letter to the author, December 5, 1938.

[15] Richard E. Jaggers, "The Education and Certification of Secondary Teachers"; in the South Carolina Association of Collegiate Registrars, *Report of the Eleventh Annual Meeting,* May 12, 1939, pp. 22–29. [16] *Ibid.,* pp. 22–29.

[17] State Boards and Departments of Education, Rules and Regulations Governing the Certification of Teachers, 1936–1941.

[18] Robert C. Woellner and M. Aurilla Wood, *Requirements for Teaching Certificates, For Junior High School, Senior High School, Junior College.* 1936, 1937, 1938, 1939, 1940. Chicago: University of Chicago Press (mimeographed).

[19] American Council on Education Studies, *Major Issues in Teacher Education,* February, 1938, p. 21. [20] Valentine, *op. cit.,* pp. 344–345.

Plainly there is lack of critical analysis and foresight in the planning and enacting of certification standards. The right kind of study should provide such analysis, without which the desired foresight cannot be expected.

4. *Any regulations drafted in terms of a particular set of conditions without due regard to long-time planning are dangerous.*

There is always a tendency for regulations to linger in force past the time when they are needed or desired. The tendency to draft regulations during any particular set of circumstances must be guarded against. Recent economic conditions have aggravated restrictions in some commonwealths and many communities. Educational officials need to be even more careful about enacting legislation that will later prove dangerous.

5. *The present lack of agreement on restrictions might be removed by an investigation that would establish a basis for thoughtful consideration of the issues involved.*

Considerable disagreement exists in both lay and professional groups regarding restrictions, their existence, causes, trends, and implications. This disagreement will never be removed except through pertinent facts properly interpreted. A study is needed to bring the facts into the open and to indicate their implications so that thinking on the problem can be clarified.

6. *The absence of a similar study during the past three decades leaves the field open for one now.*

Since Ellwood P. Cubberley's study of 1906,[21] the problem of interstate restrictions has been considered by several writers. Cook's researches[22, 23] and McMullen's[24] study treat phases of interstate reciprocity. Frazier discusses the matter of restrictions.[25] The National

[21] Ellwood P. Cubberley, *The Certification of Teachers;* in National Society for the Scientific Study of Education, Fifth Yearbook, Part II. The University of Chicago Press, Chicago, 1906.

[22] Katherine M. Cook, *State Laws and Regulations Governing Teachers' Certificates.* U. S. Bureau of Education, Bulletin No. 22. Government Printing Office, Washington, D. C., 1921. Pp. 244.

[23] Katherine M. Cook, *State Laws and Regulations Governing Teachers' Certificates, 1928.* U. S. Bureau of Education, Bulletin No. 19. Government Printing Office, Washington, D. C., 1928. Pp. 296.

[24] Raymond F. McMullen, "Reciprocity Among the States in the Certification of Teachers." Unpublished Master's thesis, Ohio State University, 1932. Pp. 162.

[25] Benjamin W. Frazier, *Development of State Programs for the Certification of Teachers.* U. S. Office of Education, Bulletin No. 12. Government Printing Office, Washington, D. C., 1938. Pp. 166.

Education Association treats the different ways of obtaining interstate mobility in six professions.[26] Although the problem has been discussed, the factual information regarding restrictions is lacking. It seems an opportune time for making a study of restrictions that will supply this factual information.

Definitions Used in This Study

It was found necessary early in this investigation to define accurately the terms "restrictions" and "limitations." The definitions that proved most serviceable follow. Each definition is made clearer by several illustrations.

1. *A "restriction" is any requirement, policy, procedure, or factor in certification or employment that can be satisfied only within the restraining state or community.*

To illustrate: Residence within the state or community for a specified period of time may be required. Again, certification may require courses that are offered *only within the respective state.* Sometimes the candidate for certification or employment may be required to go to the particular state or community to take an examination, no matter how thorough his previous preparation.

2. *A "limitation" is any requirement, policy, procedure, or practice in certification or employment that favors residents of the restraining state or community.*

For example: A state may have a peculiar course requirement freely offered by colleges within that state, but seldom by colleges in other commonwealths. Then again, a state may require an unusual number of semester hours or clock hours of a subject, a requirement which tends to favor in-state persons. While such peculiar requirements may be met in any state in which corresponding courses are available, in the main the residents of the particular state are favored. An unusual sequence of courses may also fall within the limits of this definition. Any variation in course requirements between or among states would provide limitations. Thus one state may have a three-hour course requirement, while in an adjoining state the requirement may be four semester hours for the identical course. The

[26] National Education Association, *Statutory Status of Six Professions,* September, 1938, pp. 192–194, 196–197, 200–202, 204–206, 209–210.

difference in requirements would be a limitation for teachers in the state requiring the lower number of semester hours.

Aims of the Study

This study aims to find and interpret restrictions and limitations to the free interstate movement of high school teachers of academic subjects. Specifically, this aim comprises four major purposes:

1. To trace briefly the historical development of certain phases of restrictions and limitations, as found in 1906 and 1938.
2. To set forth the restrictions and limitations involved in the certification requirements, policies, and practices of the forty-eight states in 1938 and in the requirements for 1941.
3. To set forth the restrictions and limitations in the employment policies and practices of city boards of education and school superintendents in the communities of selected sizes in 1938.
4. To suggest possible ways of solving certain of the problems of restrictions and limitations in view of the findings of this investigation.

Limitations of the Study

It was early found necessary to establish certain limitations to this investigation in order to avoid numerous by-paths. Specifically, this study has no reference to restrictions in any country except the United States. Furthermore, only restrictions for high school teachers of academic subjects are considered; no reference is made to restrictions for elementary school teachers, supervisors, administrators, or high school teachers of non-academic subjects, such as music, fine arts, or household arts. The historical treatment of restrictions had to be limited from the standpoint of expense, time, and possible contribution to this study, and therefore includes a discussion of restrictions only since 1906.

In the study of restrictions in employment policies of communities, it was not feasible to send data sheets to all cities; such sheets were sent only to cities between 15,000 and 100,000 population. The number of communities[27] in this range is great enough, however, to provide a large sampling of employment restrictions.

In any study the problem chosen must be considered in relative isolation from many related factors. For example, in this study it was not feasible to do more than allude to the economics of restrictions, the relative financial background of the states, the supply of and demand for teachers, population trends, and other deeply set social factors.

This study could not include an investigation of teacher retirement plans, which definitely are a factor in restrictions. In almost one-half of the commonwealths there are state retirement provisions of various types. Usually teachers pay regularly a certain amount of money into retirement funds. If a teacher, however, wishes to leave the state to teach elsewhere, practices vary as to whether he might take all or part of the money set aside by him or for him in the retirement fund. Obviously, whether a person can take this portion of the retirement fund with him when he leaves a state influences his decision to go or remain. Although this study could not consider this problem, there are given in Appendix E two tables briefly listing the various state practices in this regard.

This study could not discuss the possible restrictive or restraining effects of salary differentials, tenure plans, and similar factors which conceivably might affect a person's desire to leave or stay within a commonwealth. It was found necessary to adhere strictly to a discussion of restrictions in requirements, policies, and practices of certification and employment of high school teachers of academic subjects.

Although this study includes an investigation of many administrative policies and practices in certification and employment, there are some unwritten or extra-legal practices that cannot be ferreted out by research techniques. Whether good or bad, from any standpoint, such practices remain without objective evidence of their existence. That they are powerful is not to be denied. For example, a registrar of a large Midwestern college has said: "Sometimes it seems to me that state certification officials are in office to *prevent* certification rather than to *help* carry it on." Even if one were able to obtain such

[27] 539 communities are in this range between 15,000 and 100,000 population. Cf. *United States Fifteenth Census,* 1930. Three additional cities that had reached this size were also included.

information, it could hardly be documented or proved; consequently, this is one area that could not be included in this study. Though these unwritten restrictions are powerful, they are tenuous and unmeasurable.

Basic Assumptions of the Study

Several assumptions are made in this investigation with regard to the research methods used, the matter of certification itself, and the entire study.

In any research method, certain assumptions are warranted. In the case of the particular research methods employed in this investigation it is assumed that the techniques are reliable and valid; that the information needed could be obtained by the methods followed; that a true and unbiased picture could be obtained of present practices; that the key people from whom responses were needed knew what was wanted and were willing to give accurately the information through the means of the techniques employed; and that the results of the methods followed, or the data, could be interpreted adequately.

Underlying present certification procedures is the assumption that present methods are better than other alternatives to obtain the teachers desired. Another assumption is that training in colleges, as now constituted, makes a teacher good or better than would otherwise be the case.[28] It is important to note, however, that this is a study of restrictions and limitations, not primarily a study of certification itself.

Certain assumptions are made in the study itself. These are:

1. The expression "Making the best possible educational conditions available to all children" includes teacher personnel as well as physical surroundings.
2. The best possible teacher will be provided when he is selected from the best teachers available for the particular position *on the basis of merit,* as it is usually considered, and *not on the basis of residence.*
3. Free interstate movement of teachers is desirable.

[28] Henry W. Holmes, "The English Teacher and Educational Theory: The Sorry Business of Meeting State Requirements," *School and Society,* XLVIII (August 6, 1938), 177–179.

This last concept grew out of a comprehensive study of available educational literature and a survey of prevailing practices and authoritative opinions. It is in harmony with the opinions of recognized students of the certification and employment problems, as evidenced by the following typical quotations.

Ellwood P. Cubberley, in 1906, then Professor of Education at Leland Stanford Junior University, expressed this concept of the desirability of interstate freedom of movement of teachers as follows:

> There should be as little restriction as possible on the ability of a good teacher to move about, either from county to county or from state to state. Such freedom of movement is in the interest of the schools. On the other hand, barriers, as such, are bad. . . .[29]

Twenty-one years later, after considerable change had occurred in certification, Cubberley added:

> Interstate recognition of equivalent training should be extended, with a view to making it easy for the successful and properly trained teacher to cross state lines and engage elsewhere in what is in reality a national service.[30]

Several other authorities, in presenting various plans by which interstate freedom of movement of teachers might be accomplished, thereby support the concept of the desirability of such mobility. Barrett, then State Superintendent of Public Instruction for Iowa, reporting at a meeting of the National Education Association on "Reciprocity in Licensing Teachers," said:

> . . . reciprocity in licensing teachers between states is desirable, and . . . a united effort should be made to bring about uniformity of requirements and reciprocal relations. The American teacher should be so in fact as well as in name. The crossing of the boundary line of any state should no longer be assumed to nullify the qualifications of the skilled teacher. . . .[31]

[29] Ellwood P. Cubberley, *The Certification of Teachers,* p. 17; in National Society for the Scientific Study of Education, Fifth Yearbook, Part II. The University of Chicago Press, Chicago, 1906. Pp. 88.

[30] Ellwood P. Cubberley, *State School Administration,* p. 368. Houghton Mifflin Co., Boston, 1927. Pp. 773.

[31] Richard C. Barrett, "Reciprocity in Licensing Teachers," *National Education Association Journal of Proceedings and Addresses,* 1902, p. 305.

According to Switzer, who studied the trends in the certification of teachers in the United States in 1936:

> As the problem is Nation-wide in importance, national cooperation with the various States in making the rules for certification is highly desirable.[32]

Pittenger, Chairman of the Committee of the American Association of Teachers Colleges in 1931, said in regard to restrictions in community employment:

> Nothing should be done to interfere with the employment of teachers from other States, provided their standards of academic and professional training are equal to those required by the laws of the State.[33]

McMullen, superintendent of schools and formerly a graduate student at Ohio State University, who made a study of reciprocal relations among the states, gave several reasons why the interstate freedom of movement of teachers should be encouraged. Such freedom, according to McMullen, would equalize the supply of teachers among the states, avoid provincialism and inbreeding of ideas in local school systems, and promote the raising of local standards in the selection of teachers. Furthermore, he said that interstate freedom would assist in the dissemination on a national basis of new educational ideas.[34]

According to Frazier, Senior Specialist in Teacher Training in the United States Office of Education, and a recognized student of certification problems:

> The interstate migration of teachers should not be hindered by certification regulations or requirements based upon any considerations other than the professional competency of such teachers.[35]

[32] Edna Switzer, "The Trends in the Certification of Secondary School Teachers in the United States." Unpublished Master's thesis, Washington University, 1930. Pp. 144.

[33] L. A. Pittenger, "Raising Certification Requirements," *National Education Association Journal of Proceedings and Addresses,* 1931, p. 910.

[34] Raymond F. McMullen, "Reciprocity Among the States in the Certification of Teachers." Unpublished Master's thesis, Ohio State University, 1932. Pp. 162.

[35] Benjamin W. Frazier, *Development of State Programs for the Certification of Teachers.* U. S. Office of Education, Bulletin No. 12. Government Printing Office, Washington, D. C., 1938. Pp. 166.

Bowers, Supervisor of Certification of the State Department of Education in Ohio, in naming ten principles of teacher certification, lists as one of them:

> Certification regulations should provide for a free movement of teaching talent across state lines.[36]

He continues with the following comment:

> . . . We have been too prone to foster the spirit of localism in the employment of teachers. This practice cannot be condemned when it is placed on the basis of equal ability. It should not be tolerated if ability is sacrificed for home talent, for in so doing, we encourage an inbreeding of ideas and customs which makes for isolation of communities and hinders progress. Flexibility and broadmindedness in certification policy is the keynote of this principle.[37]

These statements are in harmony with the final assumption made by this study, namely, that the free interstate movement of teachers is desirable. It is perhaps equally significant that, as far as the author has been able to find, *no recognized authority in certification, teacher employment, teacher training, or closely related fields has stated at any time that free interstate movement of teachers is undesirable.*

Research Methods and Procedures Used in This Study

Both historical and present practice survey research methods were used in this study. The survey investigation inherently demanded a national picture of contemporary practices. Since it was not possible to see personally the people from whom the responses were necessary, data sheets were used for this purpose.

After the literature in the pertinent areas had been read, the general plan of the investigation was outlined and techniques were prepared for the survey of present practices. The data sheets[38] were formulated, and then were criticized by several competent persons.[39]

[36] Harold J. Bowers, "Ten Principles of Teacher Certification," *American School Board Journal,* 96 (June, 1938), 41–42, 92–93.

[37] Bowers, *op. cit.,* p. 92.

[38] Copies of data sheets and letters accompanying them are presented in Appendixes A and B.

[39] Students in the Advanced School of Education, Teachers College, Columbia University.

Trial copies were sent to some state officials and city school superintendents to discover weaknesses or factors that could be corrected. Changes were made in each instance as a result of these precautionary measures.

For the state certification survey, the requirements for certification, taken from the state regulations, were typewritten directly onto the face of the data sheet. An additional complete list of the certification requirements was sent for verification to each state education department, thus making possible a triple check on the requirements which were fundamental in this study. In every instance, the data sheet received from a state education department or board was later returned to that body for verification.

Because of the nature of the data sheets sent to the city school superintendents, anonymity in print was promised the superintendents. Correspondence with both state and city officials helped to clarify details and to furnish additional information regarding their practices.

The data received were grouped, tabulated, and put into chart and written form. An interpretation of these data provided the rest of the investigation with several possible solutions to the problem presented in the conclusions.

Sources of Data for the Study

At least four sources of data were involved in this study. The secondary sources included the general literature on certification, as well as the researches on this subject. The primary sources included the state statutes, the official state education department or board rules and regulations on certification, and the data sheets used in the original investigations.

Earlier research studies and publications of the United States Office of Education furnished most of the information used in the historical discussion, together with an appreciable proportion of the facts used in the later topics of the study. For the analysis of the certification requirements, both the 1938 and the 1941 rules and regulations governing certification were used. A large part of the study is based upon the materials which were obtained from the data sheets.

Validity of Materials and Techniques

Returns were received from all the forty-eight states with regard to certification requirements, procedures, and policies, making a 100 per cent response. In addition, each data sheet was verified by a second check by an official in each of the state education offices.

The community employment policy data sheets were sent to 542 city school superintendents. Of these, 338 were returned, thus providing a 62.4 per cent response. In every instance the official to whom the data sheets were sent was in a position to know about the facts or policies concerned and was also in a position of responsibility in connection with the answers given. With the data sheets verified by a check and supplemented by correspondence, all based on a thorough study of the pertinent statutes and the literature in the field, it is thought that the materials in this study constitute a valid basis for this investigation.

CHAPTER II

HISTORICAL STUDY OF PHASES OF CERTIFICATION: RESTRICTIONS AND LIMITATIONS

To reveal clearly certain trends in certification, restrictions, and limitations between 1906 and 1938 is the purpose of this chapter. Only after these trends are known is it possible to make a critical analysis and interpretation of the restrictions and limitations in 1938 and in 1941.

Five Categories of Restrictions

In the first decade of the twentieth century, Ellwood P. Cubberley, then Professor of Education at Leland Stanford Junior University, made a study of the certification of teachers. This investigation was published in 1906 as Part II of the Fifth Yearbook of the National Society for the Scientific Study of Education.[1] After a thorough and critical analysis of certification requirements and administrative practices, Cubberley indicated what restrictions to the free mobility of teachers were present. When his findings were grouped and compared with the results of the present investigation, it was found that most of the topics pertaining to restrictions of both studies, more than three decades apart, could be placed in five main categories:

1. Administrative units of certification.
2. Examinations and training courses as bases of certification.
3. State recognition of *diplomas* issued by *institutions* of learning in *other* states.
4. State recognition of *certificates* issued by *other commonwealths.*
5. Specific state requirements and courses.

[1] Ellwood P. Cubberley, *The Certification of Teachers;* in the Fifth Yearbook of the National Society for the Scientific Study of Education, Part II. The University of Chicago Press, Chicago, 1906. Pp. 88.

After consideration of possible alternatives, it seemed best to use Cubberley's findings as a starting point for the first four of these categories and to trace them from 1906 to 1938. The requirements in the fifth category developed, in the main, after 1906, so this last area will be traced historically from just prior to 1906 to 1941 by the use of other sources. In conclusion, a few additional factors with regard to interstate teacher mobility will be given.

1. *Administrative units of certification have become largely centralized from local and county units in 1906 to state units in 1938.*

As late as 1906, in fifteen states the certification of teachers was almost wholly in the hands of the county superintendent alone; in fifteen other states the certification of teachers was controlled by a county board of education or examiners and in the remaining states the certificating authority was the state, the town, or some combination of the state and the locality.[2] In reference to the county plan, Cubberley said:

> . . . it is gradually being discarded in favor of higher standards and a more liberal method of certification. . . .
>
> . . . The strict county plan has so many disadvantages from the point of view of a satisfactory system that the continuance of its use is defensible only where the standards of the state are so low or so widely divergent that a change to any more liberal system would be certain to lead to even worse results. . . .[3]

He added further:

> . . . *The strict county system too often perpetuates the rule of the weak by shielding them from the competition of the strong.* . . .[4] *
>
> . . . In a number of our states there is no recognition of certificates from one county to another within the state. Many of these barriers are indefensible. . . .[5]

Then, in speaking of restrictions due to the great diversity of administrative units of certification, Cubberley stated:

[2] Cubberley, *op. cit.*, p. 65.
[3] *Ibid.*, p. 17.
[4] *Ibid.*, p. 73–74.
* Italics are the author's.
[5] *Ibid.*, p. 74.

Among the plans in use in the different states there is so great a diversity in standards and procedure that the ability of a teacher to transfer from one county to another or from one state to another is in many cases most unnecessarily restricted. Many of these restrictions are unwarranted by any educational standard and serve no useful educational purpose. . . .[6]

. . . It is . . . an unfortunate condition of affairs when the schools of each county in a state are protected from the teachers of every other county in the state by a system of artificial barriers. . . .[7]

. . . Localism . . . in the aim of education has been and still is one of the most serious defects of our system of free public education. . . .[8]

As the foregoing quotations indicate, there were in 1906 great variations in requirements and practices among the communities and counties constituting the administrative units for certification. The almost utter lack of comparability of standards was intensified by many small administrative units, each with its own requirements and restrictive policies. Some idea of the wide variety of certificating units and requirements can be gained from the fact that in 1900, there were 2,836 counties[9] in the nation, many of them having some certificating authority, many different requirements, and varied certification practices. A teacher who attempted to obtain certification and employment in another city or county experienced difficulty in moving across the barriers provided.

The requirements were made more restrictive by the fact that certification was not administered by comparable officials. In one county, the board of education administered certification, in another the board of examiners, and in still a third the county superintendent.[10] Similarly, non-comparable officials administered local and state certification. Further lack of comparability was brought about because different groups prepared the examination questions, administered the examinations, and corrected the papers.[11] Lack of understanding by the officials in one administrative unit of the procedures, require-

[6] *Ibid.*, p. 11.
[7] *Ibid.*, p. 23.
[8] *Ibid.*, p. 17.
[9] U. S. Twelfth Census, 1900, Vol. I, p. XXXVII.
[10] Harlan Updegraff, *Teachers' Certificates Issued under General State Laws and Regulations.* U. S. Bureau of Education, Bulletin No. 18. Government Printing Office, Washington, D. C., 1911. Pp. 269.
[11] *Ibid.*, pp. 143–144.

ments, and policies of another also contributed to the wide variations of practices.

In 1906, however, certain factors were operating that were later to spell the doom of the dominant county plan and the local character of certification, and still later even to change the entire administration of certification. Of some of these trends, which had been going on for over a century, Cubberley wrote at the time.[12] Specifically, permission was being given by the state to one county to have its examination papers corrected in another county; uniform examination papers were being prepared by the state and sent to all the counties within the state; papers were being forwarded by the counties to the chief state school officials for endorsement, thus giving them more general validity; and inter-county recognition was being given teachers' certificates. Other forces tending to break down the strict county system were the establishment and development of coordinate systems of state examinations and state certification; the issuing of certificates of wider validity; the increase in educational and professional standards which has led to the abolition of the lower grades of county certificates; and the growing force of professional opinion as the teaching profession has come to express itself more forcibly on questions of public educational policy.[13] These factors gave more general validity to the certificates by obtaining more inter-county recognition.

These trends reveal a centralization of certification that was indicative of the centralizing tendencies in public administration in general. Fairlie[14] and Webster[15] had earlier pointed out some of these centralizing tendencies, the latter with particular reference to teachers' examinations. Later, Strayer showed the development of centralizing tendencies in specified areas, including certification as one.[16] Cook[17]

[12] Cubberley, *op. cit.*, pp. 19–24.

[13] *Ibid.*, p. 23.

[14] John A. Fairlie, *The Centralization of Administration in New York State.* Columbia University, New York, 1898. Pp. 207.

[15] William C. Webster, *Recent Centralizing Tendencies in State Educational Administration.* Columbia University, New York, 1897. Pp. 78.

[16] George D. Strayer, Jr., *Centralizing Tendencies in the Administration of Public Education.* Bureau of Publications, Teachers College, Columbia University, New York, 1934. Pp. 123.

[17] Katherine M. Cook, *State Laws and Regulations Governing Teachers' Certificates.* U. S. Bureau of Education, Bulletin No. 22. Government Printing Office, Washington, D. C., 1921. Pp. 244.

has presented this dominant centralizing trend in a tabulation, which is reproduced here in Table I.

TABLE I

Tendency Toward Centralization of Certificating Authority in State Departments of Education, 1898–1937 (From Cook's and Frazier's Studies) [1,2,3,8]

Kind of System	Number of States [4]						
	1898 [5]	1903 [6]	1911 [7]	1921	1926	1933	1937 [8]
1	2	3	4	5	6	7	8
State systems (state issues all certificates)	3	5	15	26	36	39	41
State-controlled systems (state prescribes rules, gives questions, and examines papers; county authorities issue some certificates)	1	[e]	2	7	4	3	3 [a]
Semi-state systems (state makes regulations and gives questions; county authorities issue certificates and correct papers)	17	[e]	18	10	5	3	1 [b]
State-county systems (both issue certificates; county retains full control over examination for 1 or more certificates)	18	[e]	7	3	2	2	2 [c]
State-local systems				2	1	1	
County system (county grants all certificates	4	4	1				1 [d]

[a] Arkansas, Illinois and Missouri.

[b] Mississippi.

[c] California and Wisconsin.

[d] Massachusetts.

[e] No data.

[1] Katherine M. Cook, *State Laws and Regulations Governing Teachers' Certificates.* U. S. Bureau of Education, Bulletin No. 22. Government Printing Office, Washington, D. C., 1921. Pp. 296.

[2] Katherine M. Cook, *State Laws and Regulations Governing Teachers' Certificates.* U. S. Bureau of Education. Bulletin No. 19. Government Printing Office, Washington, D. C., 1928. Pp. 296.

[3] State departments of education. Rules and regulations governing certification, 1933.

[4] Temporary and emergency certificates and permits not included.

[5] See also James H. Blodgett, *Legal Provisions of the Various States Relating to Teachers' Examinations and Certificates.* U. S. Bureau of Education. Report of the Commissioner of Education, 1897–98. Vol. 2, pp. 1659–91. Government Printing Office, Washington, D. C., 1899.

[6] See also William R. Jackson, *The Present Status of the Certification of Teachers in the United States.* U. S. Bureau of Education. Report of the Commissioner of Education, 1903, Vol. 1, pp. 463–519. Government Printing Office, Washington, D. C., 1905.

[7] See also Harlan Updegraff, *Teachers' Certificates Issued Under General State Laws and Regulations.* U. S. Bureau of Education, Bulletin No. 18. Government Printing Office, Washington, D. C., 1911. Pp. 12–135.

[8] See also Benjamin W. Frazier, *Development of State Programs for the Certification of Teachers.* U. S. Office of Education, Bulletin No. 12. Government Printing Office, Washington, D. C., 1938. Pp. 166. See page 16.

This tendency toward centralization of authority to certificate teachers is further indicated in Figure 1.

The centralizing trends were actually developing to a greater extent than is revealed by Table I and Figure 1. These data show only the *number* of states of each type and give no indication of the developments *within* each state. Great centralizing changes were occurring *within* each commonwealth. Just how this centralization of certification took place in a typical state is also indicated elsewhere in a study by Cook.[18]

By 1937 the centralization of certification had developed so far that forty-one states were completely administering their certification activities through the state education department or board. In six of the seven states not yet completely centralized, strong tendencies in that direction were evident. For example, of a total of 4,944[19] certificates issued in one year in California, only thirty were issued on the basis of examinations in the counties.[20] Only six-tenths of one per cent of all the certificates issued in that state were given by the counties, yet because of this small percentage, California cannot yet be called completely centralized as to certification.[21] Similarly, but not in an identical manner, five other states indicate strong centralizing tendencies in certification. Massachusetts alone still retains a decentralized system of certification, with the state education department certificating teachers only in the thirty small state-aided high schools.[22] In all the remaining towns and cities in this common-

[18] Katherine M. Cook, *State Laws and Regulations Governing Teachers' Certificates,* p. 6–8. U. S. Bureau of Education, Bulletin No. 22. Government Printing Office, Washington, D. C., 1921.

[19] Annual Report of the Division of Teacher Training and Certification, California State Department of Education, Division of Teacher Training and Certification, Sacramento, California, May 15, 1937. Mimeographed report, pp. 2, 10.

[20] For 1935–36, county examinations were given in eleven counties to forty-seven persons who were not certificated. Thirty of these candidates passed and were granted elementary certificates in nine counties.

[21] While the situation is gradually being adjusted, the fact remains that as long as the constitutional provision of county examinations is made effective by statutory regulation, there is no hope that California can secure to all the schools adequately prepared teachers.

[22] Four-year high schools: Ashby, Ashfield, Berhardston, Brimfield, Brookfield, Charlemont, Charlton, Chester, Essex, Huntington, Mendon, Millis, New Marlborough, New Salem, Northfield, Norwell, Pembroke, Plainville, Rutland, Sheffield, Stow, West Newbury, Williamsburg. Less than four-year high schools: Bedford, Cumminton, East Brookfield, Princeton, Sterling, West Brookfield, Westminster. (See footnote 23.)

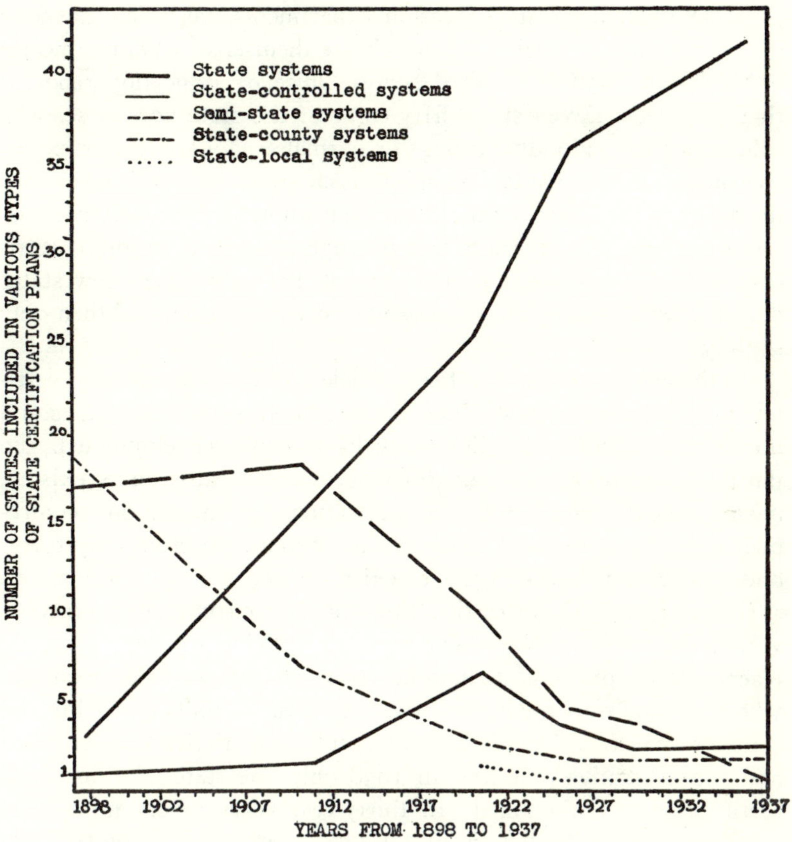

FIGURE 1. Tendencies toward Centralization of Certificating Authority into State Systems of Certification, 1898–1937

wealth, each school district sets its own certification or employment standards.[23]

Aside from the state education departments, very few agencies give certificates or credentials which are themselves legal certificates to teach. In 1938 the United States Office of Education reported that in at least eleven states fifty-eight of the state normal schools, college boards, individual college or normal school boards, or executive officers of the institutions might issue teaching certificates under the delegated authority of the state.[24] This number is rapidly decreasing, however. It is thus seen that by 1938 the centralization of certification had developed to such an extent that only a very few states deviated from a complete state system of certification, and then only slightly.

As the heterogeneous practices, policies, and requirements of certification of the early 1900's have been reduced, some restrictions and limitations described by Cubberley have also been eliminated. To illustrate, where in 1906, 2,836 county administrative units existed, most of them with their own organization, administration, requirements, and practices, with many of these being restrictive, only forty-one central certificating agencies existed in 1938 in as many states.

Greater simplicity in certification and fewer contrasting practices within the states were present in 1938, making the mobility of a teacher from one unit to another somewhat freer. For example, where in 1906 over ninety county administrative units existed in one commonwealth, each with its own peculiar restrictive examinations and administrative practices, in 1938 only one state administrative certification unit remained. In thirty-two years ninety units have

[23] Letters to the author from A. Russell Mack, Supervisor of Secondary Education, Department of Education, Commonwealth of Massachusetts, December 6, and December 14, 1937.

A Massachusetts law gives the following: "No person shall be eligible to teach in a high school on account of which reimbursement is made by the commonwealth . . . who does not hold a high school teacher's certificate issued by the department. . . ." General Laws, Commonwealth of Massachusetts, Section 12, Chapter 71.

Certificates are issued only to teachers holding positions in state-aided high schools or to candidates who are assured of election to such positions. Certificates from this Department are not required in the remaining high schools of the state nor in the elementary schools. From Circular of Information, The Commonwealth of Massachusetts, Department of Education, 1937, *Certification of Teachers in State-Aided High Schools.*

[24] Benjamin W. Frazier, *Development of State Programs for the Certification of Teachers.* U. S. Office of Education, Bulletin No. 12. Government Printing Office, Washington, D. C., 1938. Pp. 166.

become supplanted by one. Differences in certification policies and practices exist now in most instances *between and among the commonwealths.*

As centralization of certificating authority has taken place, it has separated the *certificating* responsibility from the *employing* authority. The combination of both was formerly notoriously restrictive. Forty-one commonwealths have taken over the entire certificating burden in as many states; others share a large part of the duties.[25] The communities, on the other hand, have taken over the employing responsibilities. It remains to be seen later in this study whether or not the community employment policies have tended to reduce the employment restrictions.[26]

Centralization has made it possible for certification officials to become better informed with regard to the requirements and practices in other states. Formerly, each certification department had to deal with as many as ninety county administrative units in its own state and a varying number of units in other states. Now, however, each of forty-one state education departments usually deals directly with only one main certification group in each of forty of the other states, and to a degree is its own authority in its own commonwealth.

Some contrasting and divergent sources of administrative opinion were eliminated by certification centralization. However, with this decrease has come an increase in responsibilities for the centralized staffs and a greater need for critical thinking and long-term planning on the part of the policy forming and administering bodies. This centralization of certification in the state education departments between 1906 and 1938 implies basically that in the present study of restrictions in certification only the state education departments are concerned, not the counties or communities. Restrictions and limitations *in certification* exist between and among the forty-eight states.[27] However, because of the separation of the employing function of the communities from the certification power of the state, a formerly restrictive combination, the present study will need to consider restrictions in both *state certification* and *community employment*

[25] In Massachusetts a person must still meet the standards of any particular community except those with the state-aided high schools and the superintendency unions.

[26] Chapter VI.

[27] Chapters III, IV, and V.

policies and practices. The problem of the present survey will therefore need to be bifocal in order to include these two distinct phases of the problem.

2. *The basis of certification has changed from examinations to the acceptance of evidence of professional training.*

Commenting on the fact that examinations constituted the basis of most certification in 1906, Cubberley said:

> In the matter of examinations, there is great need of our decreasing the emphasis which we now place on the written test. . . . As fast as can be done, the periodical written examination ought to be diminished in importance as a means of recruiting our teaching force. . . .[28]

Examinations were used in all the certificating systems in the different states. Though differing much in minor details, these systems are reducible to a very few types:

The *Town System* was represented by Massachusetts and Connecticut, which still maintained the local examination plan—a survival of the old colonial system.[29] Normal school diplomas were accepted in lieu of the examination in both states.

Then there was the *County System,* about which Cubberley said:

> In the strict county examination and certification plan, the county superintendent, or the county examining board if such a body has been provided for, prepares the questions, gives the examinations, grades the papers, and grants the certificates of the different grades to those who pass, and the certificates, when granted, are not valid outside the county where issued. . . .[30]

Illinois, Maryland, North Carolina, Oklahoma, and Wisconsin were good examples of the strict county plan. In commenting on this type, Cubberley added:

> . . . it is . . . an unfortunate condition of affairs when the schools of each county in a state are protected from the teachers of every other county in the state by a system of artificial barriers which place the emphasis on a written examination, and neglect the much more impor-

[28] Cubberley, *op. cit.,* p. 76.
[29] *Ibid.,* p. 12.
[30] *Ibid.,* p. 16.

tant evidence of professional training for the work of successful experience as a teacher. . . .[31]

City certificates also were given on the basis of examinations. Either the cities were directed or permitted to examine and certificate their own teachers or, while required to accept the county or state certificates, could provide for an extra or supplementary examination.[32]

Finally there were the *State Systems,* in which examinations by the state more or less supplanted the local examining systems or existed in a coordinate relation to them.[33] Arizona, Alabama, and South Dakota are examples of the state system. Although examinations were used in every commonwealth as a basis for issuing one or more certificates, in more than a fourth of the states examinations were the *only* basis for certification. Cubberley remarked about this condition as follows:

> . . . In fourteen states there is no admission to the teaching profession except on examination. In eleven of these states forty or more subjects are required to secure the highest certificate granted, and all must be secured by examination. . . .[34]

It is apparent that examinations constituted a major role as a basis for certification in 1906. Although as early as 1898, twenty-nine states issued one or more certificates on the basis of professional training without an examination, by and large the emphasis was still on examinations.[35]

Where the county and local examination plans were used, a person legally qualified to teach in one community or county *would be unable to teach in another city or county without taking additional examinations,* which were given in from one to thirty-seven subjects.[36]

Examinations, however, were gradually falling into disrepute as a basis for admitting persons into the teaching profession. It was evident that examinations did not measure the factors they were

[31] *Ibid.,* p. 23.
[32] *Ibid.,* p. 24.
[33] *Ibid.,* pp. 47–51.
[34] *Ibid.,* p. 74.
[35] Katherine M. Cook, *State Laws and Regulations Governing Teachers' Certificates,* p. 13. U. S. Bureau of Education Bulletin No. 22. Government Printing Office, Washington, D. C., 1921.
[36] Cubberley, *op. cit.,* p. 28.

supposed to measure. The questions were often discriminatory and the methods of correcting the examination papers varied widely. Furthermore, the rise and development of normal schools had been bringing into existence a new basis for establishing certification that was more and more being used.

After the establishment of the first normal schools, it was not long before those trained in these institutions were asking for county and state certification without the necessity of taking the examinations usually required. As a consequence, the states very early began to recognize professional training as a basis for certification. The recognition given to this type of training grew rapidly. Table II indicates this growth but does not tell the complete story, giving only the number of states granting certificates on the basis of professional training and not the number of certificates granted on such a basis within a state.

It is important for the purposes of this study to note that as evidences of professional training became recognized as a basis for

TABLE II

Growth of Recognition of Academic and Professional Attainments in Requirements for Certification of Teachers (*From Cook's Study*) [a,b]

States in Which:	1898	1903	1911	1919
Professional training is recognized as basis for granting one or more certificates	29	33	42 [a]	47
Professional subjects are included in examination for all grades of certificates or the lowest grade	17	40	42	46
Professional training is prerequisite for certificates of lowest grades	0	0	2	17
Graduation from standard high school [c] is prerequisite for certificate of lowest grade			1	11
Graduation from high school and some additional professional training is prerequisite for lowest grade certificate			1	4

[a] Katherine M. Cook, *State Laws and Regulations Governing Teachers' Certificates*, p. 13, Table 2. U. S. Bureau of Education, Bulletin No. 22. Government Printing Office, Washington, D. C., 1921. Pp. 244.

[b] Emergency or temporary certificates are not considered in this table. Certificates deemed of this nature include a third grade "special" certificate in Wisconsin, where the regular third grade certificate requires six weeks of professional training, and a third grade "special" certificate issued in Idaho.

[c] Missouri and Kansas require high school graduation for some but not the lowest county certificates. The New Jersey law requiring high school graduation (4 years) did not become effective until 1914, though it was passed in 1911.

certification, there occurred a slow decrease in certification by examination. This decrease was due partly to the rapid growth of teacher-training institutions and classes and partly to the general distrust of the reliability of examinations. This decrease in the use of examinations was accompanied by a decrease in the restrictions which Cubberley had indicated were present *in the examination system.* More and more the increase in the acceptance of professional training for certification was due to the recognition by leaders that greater professional competence could thereby be obtained.

One implication of this trend was that when evidences of professional training were accepted by a certificating body, this acceptance meant that a person could take courses in some institution of higher learning and apply for a certificate *on that basis* alone without taking an often expensive and possibly unreliable examination or without being required to travel to the respective city, county, or state to obtain certification. A person could apply in several counties or states for certification *on the basis of identical courses* taken in any acceptable teacher-training institution. Where, in the examination system, a person was required to take examinations every time he wanted a certificate in another city, county, or state, now the *same courses could be used as the basis for one or more certificates.* This change swept away some of the restrictions and limitations present in the older examination system.

Not only could the same courses be used to obtain certification over a wide area geographically, but they also could be used chronologically over a wide span of time. Evidences of having taken the courses could be kept for use from month to month or from year to year. Of course, certification changes had to be taken into account by the applicant. Then too, after a period of years, less and less credit could be given by the state for certain courses or training.

The acceptance of evidences of training for certification by cities, counties, and states provided an impetus to the growth and development of teacher-training institutions. As these developed and improved their offerings, the acceptance of such evidences of training became even more widespread.

By 1938 acceptance of evidences of professional training for certification had developed to the extent that in every commonwealth most of the high school requirements were given in terms of academic degrees and courses in institutions of higher learning. Certificates in the usual academic subjects, English, science, mathematics, and history, for instance, could be obtained in all states on the basis of professional training.[37]

As the state systems developed and as professional training became acceptable for licensing of teachers, the state shifted the responsibility for evaluating the training received by the teacher to the institutions of higher learning. Instead of examining teachers, the state depended upon the college for the training given the teachers and then accepted evidences of that training. The state, therefore, became the unit to evaluate records and to certificate teachers, and the status of the training institution became increasingly important.

Even though the changes in the bases of certification reduced the *former* restrictions in the examinations, there appeared a new and separate problem of restrictions. *With each commonwealth requiring a number of professional and academic courses for certification, and with forty-eight states having separate and somewhat different required subjects, interstate variations appeared to produce a welter of limitations and restrictions.* One of the purposes of the survey of the present study is to ferret out those that existed in 1938 and in 1941.

3. *The recognition by states of diplomas issued by institutions in other commonwealths has increased greatly since 1906.*

States began generally to accept evidences of professional training from *in-state institutions* shortly after the change from examinations as the sole basis on which to issue certificates. It was but a step, although sometimes a long one, to the acceptance of evidences of such training in *institutions of higher learning in other commonwealths.*

In 1906 the recognition given by states to evidences of professional training in out-of-state institutions was not widespread. Commenting on this condition, Cubberley said:

> In nineteen states absolutely no recognition is given to any form of credential from another state. Only eleven states recognize normal-school diplomas from other states; seventeen recognize college or uni-

[37] In Massachusetts, the decentralized certification system leaves the responsibility of certification standards to the local community, except for state-aided high schools and superintendency unions.

versity diplomas from outside the state; and eighteen recognize a life-diploma or state professional certificate from elsewhere. In a number of our states there is no recognition of certificates from one county to another within the state. . . .[38]

There was generally not widespread acceptance of diplomas or courses taken in out-of-state institutions. In 1911 Updegraff said that diplomas from certain educational institutions within many states were generally recognized by their own respective states either as valid teachers' certificates in themselves or as partial or complete fulfillment of the state certification requirements.[39] However, recognition of diplomas from institutions not located in the state was not nearly so general. In fact, eleven states gave no recognition whatsoever to such diplomas: Alabama, Arkansas, Connecticut, Florida, Georgia, Iowa, Kentucky, Louisiana, Mississippi, North Carolina, Tennessee.[40] In addition, Colorado, Ohio, and Oklahoma accepted the grades that an applicant had made in subjects covered by the certificates and required examinations in the remaining subjects. Maine gave consideration only to the diplomas from institutions of higher learning in determining the duration of the certificates, requiring examinations in all subjects. There remained thirty-three states in which recognition of out-of-state institutional credits was established only upon the agreements which any two or more of the commonwealths made with each other.[41]

By 1921 recognition of diplomas from institutions of higher learning in other states had continued to develop as a dominant trend. By that year, forty-two states recognized for certification purposes graduation from "approved," "acceptable," "accredited," "reputable," or "equivalent" institutions.[42] Of the remaining six states, Kentucky, Oklahoma, and Washington specified "state institutions" in the scholarship requirements for certificates. The regulations for Alabama did not specify whether or not institutions outside the state were recog-

[38] Cubberley, *op. cit.,* p. 74.

[39] Harlan Updegraff, *Teachers' Certificates Issued Under General State Laws and Regulations,* p. 244. U. S. Bureau of Education, Bulletin No. 18. Government Printing Office, Washington, D. C., 1911.

[40] Updegraff, *op. cit.,* p. 244.

[41] *Ibid.,* p. 244.

[42] Katherine M. Cook, *State Laws and Regulations Governing Teachers' Certificates,* p. 31. U. S. Bureau of Education, Bulletin No. 22. Government Printing Office, Washington, D. C., 1921.

nized. Connecticut was the only state issuing certificates on the sole basis of examinations, not accepting credits from institutions either within or outside the state.[43]

Generally, state laws required that institutions whose credits are recognized toward certification shall exact entrance requirements and maintain standards equivalent to those within the particular state. Nearly all states which recognized out-of-state institutions kept lists of the ones "accredited" or "approved."[44]

In 1928, when this trend of the acceptance of credits from out-of-state institutions was continuing, the rise and development of state and regional accrediting associations was a pertinent factor in this widespread acceptance. State acceptance of courses and degrees usually depended upon the accrediting status of the particular institutions.[45] Because commonwealths issued certificates often without seeing the applicant, the responsibility of the training institution and the accrediting association became greater in maintaining entrance requirements and other institutional standards. It became increasingly difficult for persons from non-accredited institutions to obtain certification in other states.

By accepting for certification evidences of professional training in out-of-state institutions, the commonwealths began to move away from the restrictive, and often expensive and unreliable, examinations formerly used as a basis for certification. Applicants for certificates no longer were required to go to the state merely for certification.

Although some states would not accept certificates on a reciprocal basis, they would in most instances accept evidences of training in approved teacher-training institutions, making the latter the basis for certification of out-of-state applicants as well as for those within the respective commonwealth.

Greater faith in the status of institutions of higher learning in other commonwealths was indicated in the acceptance of credits from out-of-state institutions. Geographical distance could become greater than formerly between the certificating body and the training institution.

A person could attend an approved college or university and then

[43] *Ibid.*, p. 30.

[44] *Ibid.*, p. 30.

[45] This study could not include an investigation of the development of the accrediting associations.

submit the courses taken or the diploma in more than one state for certification, provided the *same* courses were acceptable in several states as a basis for certification. Greater interstate freedom of mobility was made possible by this interstate acceptance of institutional credits and diplomas. Then too, the training institution became the basic factor in certification rather than the state certificate formerly used. This shift in attention tended to break down interstate restriction and provided greater interstate freedom. The present survey of restrictions in certification in 1938, beginning with the next chapter, will indicate the extent to which state education departments accept courses and degrees from training institutions in other commonwealths as well as from their own.

4. *The recognition by states of certificates issued by other commonwealths increased up to 1921, but since that time has decreased markedly.*

Any discussion of reciprocal relations is complicated by the fact that seldom is it clearly agreed just what reciprocity is. A variety of practices and policies exist under the name of "reciprocity," and it is difficult at any one time to obtain a clear and accurate analysis of such interstate relationships. To illustrate, some states have established reciprocal relations in practice without legal authority; others have the legal authority without having developed actual reciprocal relationships; still others have the legal authority for reciprocity and have also established such relationships with other states. Some such relations are clear-cut; others are hedged about by various conditions or reservations.

After consideration of the researches by Jackson,[46] Updegraff,[47] and Cook[48, 49] and a study by McMullen,[50] it was found that a discussion of the early activities of New York State in regard to reciprocity would give a picture of early interstate conditions. This is true be-

[46] William Roberts Jackson, *The Present Status of the Certification of Teachers in the United States,* p. 468. U. S. Bureau of Education, Report of the Commissioner, 1903, Chapter 10. Government Printing Office, Washington, D. C., 1904.

[47] Harlan Updegraff, *op. cit.,* pp. 254–266.

[48] Katherine M. Cook, *State Laws and Regulations Governing Teachers' Certificates,* pp. 30–31. U. S. Bureau of Education, Bulletin, No. 22. Government Printing Office, Washington, D. C., 1921. Pp. 244.

[49] *Ibid.,* pp. 27–28.

[50] Raymond F. McMullen, "Reciprocity Among the States in the Certification of Teachers." Unpublished Master's thesis, Ohio State University, 1932. Pp. 162.

cause New York was a pioneer leader in the development of reciprocal relations and because through its letters to other states and its studies of the problem, this state gives an excellent picture of early conditions.[51] A brief discussion of events in New York prior to 1900 will clarify the later development of reciprocity of certificates. This factor of reciprocal relations is opposite to that of restrictions, and therefore will be considered in this study.

In 1887 New York State Superintendent Draper said that the New York life certificate was "being accepted by many school authorities in other states as ample proof of the qualifications of the holder."[52] The following year the state legislature conferred upon the state superintendent the power to endorse certificates issued by state superintendents and normal schools in other states and thereby make them equal in value to New York certificates and diplomas.[53] Superintendent Draper in 1888 sent a circular letter to all state superintendents in the nation, explaining this action, expressing a desire to reciprocate, and asking for their opinion on the matter. The responses were not general or satisfactory, but by 1890 Superintendent Draper reported that twelve normal diplomas from five states, Connecticut, Pennsylvania, Massachusetts, New Jersey, and Ohio, had been endorsed.[54] Two years later he complained because little effort was being put forth by other states in enacting legislation permitting reciprocal relationships to be established. New Jersey had in the meantime obtained this authority to endorse other states' certificates.[55]

In 1895 State Superintendent Crooker of New York reported the results of an inquiry he had made of the state superintendents in other commonwealths concerning their power and practice of endorsing New York certificates and diplomas.[56] Four of the states replying had both the legal authority and the inclination to establish reciprocal relations: New Jersey, Oregon, Tennessee, and Vermont.

[51] For more complete details one can refer to the studies mentioned in the text.

[52] A. S. Draper, "Life Certificates," in Thirty-third Annual Report of the State Superintendent of Public Instruction, State of New York, 1887, p. 14.

[53] A. S. Draper, in Thirty-fifth Annual Report of the State Superintendent of Public Instruction, State of New York, 1889, pp. 30–32.

[54] A. S. Draper, in Thirty-sixth Annual Report of the State Superintendent of Public Instruction, State of New York, 1890, p. 832.

[55] A. S. Draper, in Thirty-eighth Annual Report of the State Superintendent of Public Instruction, State of New York, 1892, p. 35.

[56] James F. Crooker, in Forty-first Annual Report of the State Superintendent of Public Instruction, State of New York, 1895, Vol. II, pp. 915–918.

Eight other states accorded limited recognition to out-of-state certificates. Several other states expressed approval of the principle of reciprocity but professed lack of power. In the same report, Superintendent Crooker stated that New York would accept other states' certificates *only if the courtesy were returned.*[57]

Apparently, little progress was made prior to 1900 in the development of interstate reciprocal relationships, although the problem was widely discussed.

The National Education Association has from time to time devoted sectional meetings to discussions of reciprocal relations among states. In 1896, at Buffalo, the State Superintendents' Round Table group agreed that the state should be authorized by appropriate legislation to endorse such certificates and credentials as met its approval.[58] In 1897 the Normal School Section at Milwaukee discussed reciprocity, with a significant proposal made that centralized control of all normal schools within a state would advance interstate reciprocity.[59] In 1898 at Washington, D. C., and also in 1904 the matter of reciprocity was again discussed. In the latter meeting the idea was broached regarding selective admission of students by teacher-training schools.[60] At this meeting State Superintendent G. W. Nash of South Dakota made a plea for the establishment of national standards to which all sections might measure up and thus secure suitable recognition.[61]

Since 1900 several studies have been made by the United States Office of Education regarding certification, including the development of interstate acceptance of certificates.[62] A complete study of the reciprocal relationships in the nation would require a treatment of each state. For purposes of this study the total number of states recog-

[57] *Ibid.*

[58] State Superintendents' Round Table, "Interstate Recognition of State Certificates and Exchange of Official Documents," *National Education Association Journal of Proceedings and Addresses,* 1896, pp. 391–392.

[59] Edward T. Pierce, "Recognition of Diplomas of Other State Normal Schools in Other than the State in Which Issued," *National Education Association Journal of Proceedings and Addresses,* 1897, pp. 715–716.

[60] Z. X. Snyder, "Reciprocal Recognition of State and Normal School Diplomas by the States," *National Education Association Journal of Proceedings and Addresses,* 1898, pp. 451–454.

[61] L. E. Wolfe, "The Recognition of Certificates and Diplomas Granted (a) By State and County Authorities, (b) By Schools of Education," *National Education Association Journal of Proceedings and Addresses,* 1904, pp. 306–307.

[62] Jackson, *op. cit.;* Updegraff, *op. cit.;* Cook, *State Laws and Regulations Governing Teachers' Certificates* (1921), pp. 30–31; and McMullen, *op. cit.*

nizing out-of-state certificates at various periods between 1900 and 1938 will suffice to indicate a trend. The following table (Table III) gives the number of states recognizing out-of-state certificates since 1903. It also gives the number of states recognizing out-of-state training school credits.

TABLE III

Development of Interstate Reciprocity in the Certification of Teachers, as Shown by Investigations Made by the United States Bureau of Education from 1903 to 1937 (From Frazier's Study) *

Date of Study and Name of Investigator	Number of States Recognizing Out-of-State Certificates	Number of States Recognizing Out-of-State Training School Credits
1903 Jackson [a]	14	25
1911 Updegraff [b]	29	37
1921 Cook [c]	38	42
1927 Cook [d]	28	42 **
1937 Frazier [e]	7	48

[a] William R. Jackson, *op. cit.*, p. 468.
[b] Harlan Updegraff, *op. cit.*, pp. 244–245.
[c] Katherine M. Cook, *op. cit.*, pp. 30–31.
[d] Katherine M. Cook, *op. cit.*, pp. 10–11, 27–28.
[e] Benjamin W. Frazier, *op. cit.*, p. 35.
* Benjamin W. Frazier, *op. cit.*, p. 35.
** Certain checks show that this number may have been larger. Some states reported the recognition of credits from standard or approved institutions but did not make clear whether this recognition was limited to standard institutions within the state or extended to similar institutions outside the state.

The outstanding factor in Table III is the decided drop in the number of states extending reciprocity on the basis of out-of-state certificates. Frazier, in 1938, listed seven states extending reciprocity, yet even some of these had certain conditions or reservations. These states included Delaware (conditional), Kentucky (provided Kentucky requirements are met in detail), Iowa, Maine (provided requirements of other states meet Maine's minimum rquirements), Mississippi, Vermont (provided standards of other states are as high as those of Vermont), and Virginia. Frazier states that out-of-state certificates usually are endorsed under conditions that make it as easy to qualify for a new certificate as to obtain endorsement of an out-of-state certificate.[63] The drop in number of states with reciprocal relations is contrasted in Table III with the increase in the acceptance

[63] Frazier, *op. cit.*, p. 35.

of evidences of training in out-of-state institutions of higher learning. Figure 2 illustrates these opposing trends.

Although interstate reciprocity has been thought of in terms of the states' acceptance of certificates issued by other commonwealths, actually a more direct method is the acceptance of evidence of professional training and diplomas and degrees from approved institutions. Collegiate transcripts of credits or primary evidences of training are generally considered more acceptable materials on which to base certification than state certificates.

The decline in the acceptance of certificates from other states brought to a conclusion the acceptance of a "blanket" certificate. If a state accepts the certificate issued by another commonwealth, *it thereby partially ignores its own detailed certification requirements unless the standards of the two states are identical.* In accepting other states' certificates in reciprocal manner there is implied a blanket acceptance regardless of the academic, professional, or specific courses required for its own certificate.

Where the interstate acceptance of certificates tended to cover up differences in requirements among the commonwealths, the increase in the acceptance of evidence of professional training in other states tends to accentuate such differences because the basis of certification becomes detailed courses and degrees.

Fulfilling both the institutional requirements for a degree and the state requirements for certification in one or more commonwealths poses a difficult problem for the student and for the institution training him. Professional guidance, therefore, for students attempting to meet the college standards and the state certification requirements becomes of increasing importance, especially when the student is attempting to meet the certification standards of *two* or *more* states.

The growth in the acceptance of evidences of professional training from out-of-state institutions by commonwealths offers the possibility for wide interstate mobility. Whether such a possibility will ever be wholly realized is a question. The last chapter of this study indicates some possible alternatives to obtain wide interstate mobility.

The problem of obtaining an accredited status in one or more accrediting associations or groups becomes of great importance to a teacher-training institution. The accrediting status of institutions is an important factor also to applicants for certificates, for if they pre-

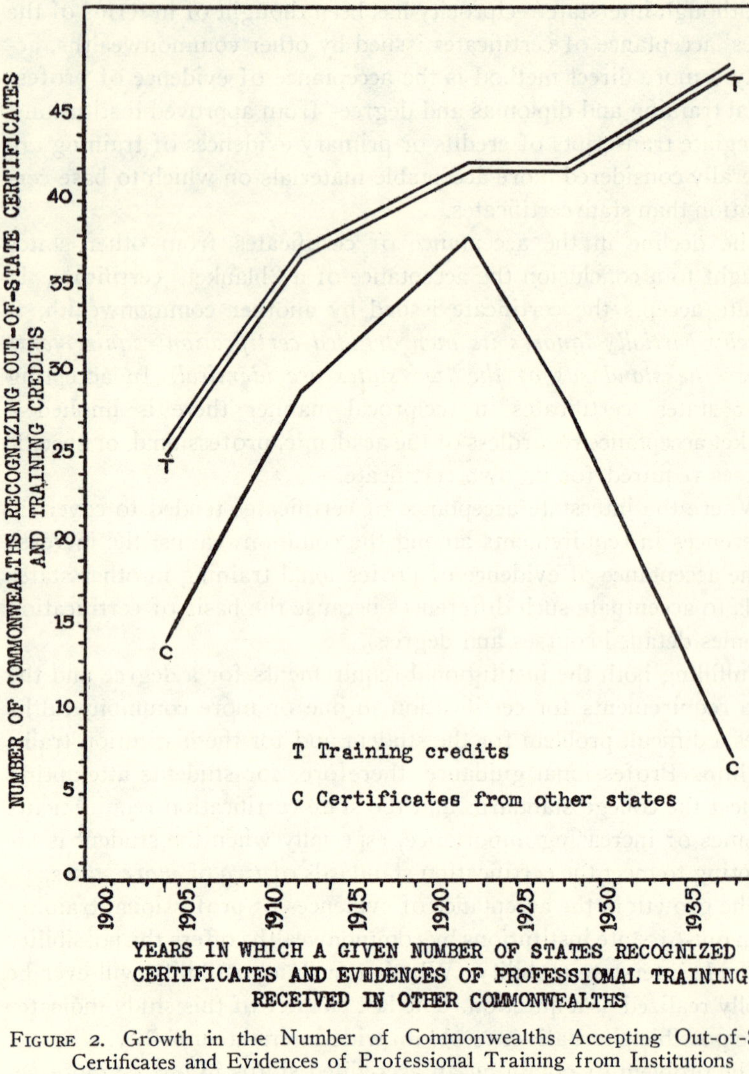

FIGURE 2. Growth in the Number of Commonwealths Accepting Out-of-State Certificates and Evidences of Professional Training from Institutions in Other States for Certification Purposes, 1903 to 1938

sent credits from a non-accredited institution they may not be eligible for certification. It would seem that a state's accrediting of its own institutions is becoming an alternative to the extra-legal interstate accrediting by regional associations.

Certification requirements, such as detailed professional courses, pose a problem for liberal arts colleges because of the increasing use of institutional credits, and the decline in the acceptance of state's certificates. When commonwealths accepted the certificates of other states, a student from a liberal arts college could obtain a certificate in his own state, and on that basis apply for other states' certificates. This application for out-of-state certificates was based only *indirectly on attendance at a liberal arts college.* Now, however, attendance at such a college means that for each state in which a student applies he must meet different professional courses which perhaps were not obtainable in his own college.

Teachers colleges have the problem of attempting to carry appropriate courses in both academic and professional subjects so that their students can meet the detailed certification requirements of one or more states.

5. *Specific state requirements have grown numerically from one in 1889 to forty-three in 1938.*

It was but a step from the states' *accepting* evidences of professional training as a basis for certification to their *requiring* courses from institutions of higher learning. Instead of merely offering collegiate courses in lieu of examinations, a teacher began to find it necessary to ascertain what the state's course requirements were and then to take those courses in an accredited college approved by the state. All of the commonwealths differed in most of their requirements. Obviously, where two states differed in course requirements, to obtain certification in both it was necessary to take each different course required for certification in each of the two states. If two states differed entirely in their course requirements, meeting the requirements of one did not even partially meet those of the other.

The interstate freedom provided by the states' acceptance of collegiate courses was a far cry from the restrictions spoken of by Cubberley in the earlier days of the twentieth century.[64] Certain common-

[64] Cubberley, *op. cit.*

wealths, however, began to require courses that could be met only by attendance at a college within their respective borders, thus making the courses restrictive for out-of-state persons. *Within a trend, therefore, that provided opportunities for greater interstate freedom for teachers, appeared a secondary trend that was restrictive in character.* Such restrictive requirements as specific state courses began to appear in the late 1880's. Their growth, however, was slow at first, and by 1906, when Cubberley made his study, not many of these courses existed. They continued to increase in number, however, and by 1938 they constituted an integral part of the restrictions discussed in this study. The development of these courses, historically, is noted here briefly.

For purposes of this investigation, these particular course requirements are called *specific state requirements.* They include a group of subjects whose promotion may be assumed to have been initiated chiefly by a desire to increase a knowledge of and devotion to our country and its institutions. Most of the closely related subjects are state rather than national in viewpoint, such as the history and the government of a particular commonwealth. Residence within a state, resident study in an in-state institution of higher learning, and courses of unusual nature are among these restrictions. In most instances, each course is unique for the state requiring it, and only colleges within the state including the course in its requirements offer such subjects.

Growth of Specific State Requirements

In 1889, the year that the state of Washington was admitted to the Union, the school laws of that commonwealth included the following provision:

> All applicants for certification . . . shall be examined in . . . school law, and constitution of the State of Washington. . . .[65]

Similar references in the re-enactment of this original law were found in the statutes of 1897,[66] 1899,[67] and 1903.[68] In the law of 1911 [69] the

[65] Session Laws, State of Washington, Chapter XII, Educational, (Title III, Board of Education), 1889–1890, Section 12, p. 359.

[66] Session Laws, State of Washington, Chapter CXVIII, (Title II), Chapter 9, Article 1, Section 141, Olympia, Washington, 1897. (Officers, Their Powers and Duties.) [See page 39 for footnotes 67, 68, and 69.]

subject of Washington State Manual was added as a requirement.

In the adjoining state of Idaho, a requirement for certification passed in 1911 included the following:

> applicants . . . in addition shall pass an examination in Idaho School Law, Idaho State Constitution, and Idaho Manual of the Course of Study.[70, 71]

The genesis of these two requirements in Washington and Idaho can be found in the traditional examination subjects required for certification in earlier years. There was one important difference, however, in that while earlier these subjects had been included among the *examination subjects,* now they were being offered by institutions of higher learning and were being required as *courses* by the state certification groups. *Thus it is seen that the older examination subjects were re-appearing as collegiate course requirements.*

State Law

The certification requirements in the state of Washington included *school law,* but the Idaho requirements twelve years later referred particularly to *Idaho school law.*[72] In 1917 the Rhode Island requirements included a similar requirement, expressly mentioning *state school law.*[73] Oklahoma followed shortly thereafter with its own state law,[74] as did Nevada in 1921,[75] Texas in 1924,[76] Kansas in 1930,

---

67 Session Laws, 1899, State of Washington, Chapter CXLII, Section 21.

68 Session Laws, State of Washington, (Eighth Session), 1903, Chapter 104 (House bill Number 65, Amending the Code of Public Instruction).

69 Session Laws, State of Washington, 1911, Chapter 16, Section 4, Relating to Uniform School System.

70 The School Laws of the State of Idaho, Certification of Teachers, pp. 47–48, Article X. As amended by the Twelfth Session of the Legislature.

71 "At that time we did not have a high school course of study, but along in 1915 we had one published, and thereafter those who were going to teach in high school were expected to take the high school course of study." Letter to the author from Miss Douglas Hilts, Certification Clerk, Department of Education, State of Idaho, October 24, 1938.

72 School Laws, State of Idaho, Article X, Certification of Teachers, pp. 47–48, 1911.

73 Minutes, Rhode Island State Board of Education, December 5, 1917. Also letter to the author from George H. Baldwin, Assistant Director of Education, Department of Education, State House, Providence, Rhode Island, May 3, 1939.

74 On November 8, 1938, a letter was sent by the author to Mr. L. Norman Duncan, Executive Secretary, State Board of Education, Oklahoma City, Oklahoma,

Montana in 1931,[77] New Hampshire in 1933,[78] and Oregon in 1934.[79]

Thus ten commonwealths had instituted a requirement in state law by 1938. Similar wording was found in most of the requirements, except that in Texas the school law was to relate to teachers and pupils. Montana required a "working knowledge" of Montana law. Often the state law was offered in a combination course in which other phases of law adapted to the individual state were included. Although the school law requirements varied from state to state, they usually included legal enactments in the commonwealth that pertained to educational affairs, together with some of the usual practical legal details of importance to the professional workers.

State Constitution

The requirements of Washington and Idaho, previously noted, included courses and examinations in the respective state constitutions. Four additional states have since passed such requirements. Nevada in 1921 had such a requirement. In 1925 Arizona passed the following law:

> That on and after the beginning of the 1925 fall terms, all public schools in this state which are sustained or in any manner supported by public funds shall give instruction in the essentials, sources and history of . . . the Constitution of the State of Arizona, including the study of and devotion to American institutions and ideals. . . .[80]

---

to find the date of the passing of the requirement of Oklahoma history and school law. After some correspondence, on May 8, 1939, he said: "We regret that it is not possible for us to give you the information requested in your letter of May 1."

[75] Nevada School Code, Section 25, Elementary Certificates, 1935, p. 24. (Assembly Bill 284, approved March 21, 1921.)

[76] Public School Laws of the State of Texas, Bulletin, State Department of Education, 1938, Vol. XIV, No. 2, Austin, Texas, February, 1938. Also Acts 1924, 39th legislature, Chapter 124, Article 2886, Certification by Examination, Chapter 17, Teachers Certificates.

[77] Minutes of the Montana State Board of Education (extract), December 14, 1931.

[78] Regulations Governing the Approval of Superintendents, Headmasters, Principals, and Teachers in the Public Schools of New Hampshire, New Hampshire State Board of Education, 1933, p. 4.

[79] Oregon Laws, 1937, Chapter 249, p. 126. Also Chapter XXV, School Laws, 1937.

[80] School Laws of Arizona, Chapter 40, Section 1–5, pp. 85–86, arranged and annotated by Margaret B. Martin, Statistical Clerk for State Department of Education, Phoenix, Arizona. Effective June 11, 1925.

This law reveals that certain groups in Arizona are placing into the certification requirements some subjects with the apparent objective of preventing any losses of American idealism and to build up devotion to American institutions and ideals. This objective in itself is a good one, except that loyalty cannot be legislated or forced, that teachers are specifically singled out for suspicion, and that these requirements are often restrictive. In 1925 the same type of requirement was made a law in Wyoming, with almost the identical statements of the Arizona requirements.[81] One of several things may have caused this duplication: through circumstances both laws had the same wording; one state was duplicating the requirements of another—a perfectly justifiable procedure; or the same social "pressure" groups were placing similar requirements in both states. A similar law requiring the study of the state constitution was passed in Texas in 1930, making a total of five commonwealths that had instituted such a requirement.[82]

United States Constitution

In 1923 California passed a statutory enactment which required the applicant

> . . . to pass a satisfactory examination upon the provisions and principles of the constitution of the United States or complete a course therein in a teachers training institution in the State of California; provided, that a limited certificate, not exceeding one year in term, may be granted without the passing of such an examination or the completion of such a course.[83]

In 1929 this general law was removed and the text thereof was incorporated in the School Code.[84]

[81] School Laws of the State of Wyoming, 1925, Chapter 94, Sections 1–6, pp. 6–7, Bulletin No. 1, Series B. Supplement. Compiled by the State Department of Education, Cheyenne, Wyoming. Approved, February 25, 1925.

[82] School Laws of the State of Texas, Section 346, 2663b, Section 4, Teachers' Certificates.

[83] Statutes of the State of California, Forty-fifth Session of the Legislature, 1923, Chapter 176, Section 3 of a General Law, Statutes 1923, p. 418. Approved May 13, 1923.

[84] Letter to the author from Alfred E. Lentz, Administrative Advisor, State of California Department of Education, November 3, 1938. Also, Part II, Teachers Certificates, Chapter II, Article I, Qualifications, 5.152, School code of the State of

Nevada had earlier, in 1921, passed a similar requirement. In Florida, in 1925, an examination in the Constitution of the United States was initiated as a requirement.[85] In lieu of this examination an opportunity was given to offer a course of six semester hours in American History and Government, including the Constitution of the United States. Arizona passed a similar requirement in 1925,[86] as did the state of Wyoming in the same year.[87] Texas followed in 1930 but included a statement that credit in a course would be acceptable or an examination in the United States Constitution.[88] Six commonwealths, therefore, had passed a requirement in the United States Constitution between 1923 and 1930.

It is apparent that the commonwealths want to retain the authority to give the required examinations in the United States Constitution. Florida has a requirement that includes a revealing phrase:

> The candidate . . . shall also satisfy the examining power of his or her loyalty thereto . . . [the constitution]

Apparently at a time when there are many mixtures of ideologies and loyalties, some consider it important, and perhaps wisely so, to ascertain precisely where the loyalties of the teachers who instruct the younger members of society are located. In Florida and elsewhere has appeared this tendency to incorporate such precautions in the certification or employment standards for teachers. Flanders earlier had studied such precautionary tendencies in relation to the legislative control of the elementary school curriculum.[89] On such a requirement as this in Florida, those who are not loyal to this government can misrepresent their case. Such a requirement will later not prevent their disloyalty. Then, too, this requirement singles out teachers for a loyalty proof, among all others.

California, 1929. Sacramento. Office of Superintendent of Public Instruction, California State Printing Office. (Section 3 of the General Law became School Code, Section 5.152.)

[85] State of Florida, Chapter 10256, Acts 1925, Section 3; Chapter 11908, Acts 1927, Section 1.

[86] School Laws of Arizona, *op. cit.*

[87] School Laws of Wyoming, *op. cit.*

[88] Statutes, Section 346, 2663b, Section 4, Teachers Certificates, State of Texas.

[89] Jesse K. Flanders, *Legislative Control of the Elementary School Curriculum.* Bureau of Publications, Teachers College, Columbia University, New York, 1925. Pp. 242.

State History

In 1898 the State Board of Education of Rhode Island was given the power to certificate teachers and to establish and enforce the requirements for certification. At a meeting on December 5, 1917, the State Board of Education took the following action as a result of the recommendation of the committee on certification:

> All applicants for first, second, and third grade certificates (will) be required hereafter to pass an examination in Rhode Island Education, including . . . History of Education in Rhode Island. . . .[90]

In June, 1932, by vote of the Board, the practice of allowing the applicants to meet the requirements by examination was abolished, and it became necessary to take the course.[91] In 1939 a state regulation made it possible for applicants to wait one year to take this particular subject.[92] Washington had such a requirement in 1889. Oklahoma passed a similar one in 1919. Texas in 1924 required Texas state history.[93] Seven years later Montana passed a similar requirement,[94] with Oregon following in 1934.[95] Six commonwealths altogether have passed the requirement of state history.

Residence Requirements

An entirely different type of requirement was passed by Montana in 1931. An extract from the minutes of the State Board of Education follows:

> No teacher's certificate by endorsement of training from any institution outside the State of Montana shall be granted to any candidate until

[90] Letter to the author from George H. Baldwin, Assistant Director of Education, Department of Education, State House, Providence, Rhode Island, May 3, 1939.

[91] *Ibid.*

[92] In 1939 the state regulations included the following: "The course in Rhode Island Education is required of all applicants for certification, the requirement to be complied with within one year after certification is issued." Department of Education, State of Rhode Island and Providence Plantations, *Certification of Teachers,* Rules and Regulations Revised and in Effect January 1, 1938. P. 15.

[93] Public School Laws of the State of Texas, *op. cit.*

[94] Minutes of the Montana State Board of Education, *op. cit.*

[95] Oregon Laws, 1937, Chapter 249, p. 126. Also Chapter XXV, School Laws, 1937.

the *candidate shall have attended one of the divisions of the Greater University of Montana, for a session of at least nine weeks,* carrying a reasonable load of work in the field or fields appropriate to the certificate sought. . . .[96]

One year later, on November 23, 1932, the State Board of Education of Idaho passed the following resolution. An excerpt from the State Board minutes of that date follows:

Resolution

WHEREAS, during these times of economic stress, surrounding States have devised *means of reserving educational positions for teachers who are residents of their respective states,* and *trained in the educational institutions of said respective states,* and *

WHEREAS, Idaho has adopted *no such protective measures* * for Idaho teachers,

THEREFORE, BE IT RESOLVED That beginning with January 1, 1933, all teachers who present credentials from educational institutions outside the boundaries of Idaho shall be required to:

1. Meet all the requirements set forth in the law and rules governing certification in Idaho, and
2. Shall meet all requirements for certification in the state in which the teacher preparation has been made, and
3. Shall attend one term of one summer session of ten weeks in the case of elementary certificates, or six weeks in the case of high school certificates, in an IDAHO educational institution, before an Idaho certificate shall be granted.

4–7 . . .

8. That all applicants for the state high school life certificate shall, in addition to the other requirements, after January 1, 1933, attend an Idaho educational institutional institution for a term of no less than six weeks, receiving credit for a full term's work before said certificate may be issued.[97]

This excerpt indicates several important factors: First, that other states surrounding Idaho have been restricting or limiting teachers

[96] Extract from the minutes of the Montana State Board of Education, December 14, 1931. Clarification in letter to the author from Ruth Reardon, State Superintendent of Public Instruction, Department of Public Instruction, Helena, Montana, October 26, 1938.

* Italics are the author's.

[97] Excerpt from the Minutes of the State Board of Education, November 23, 1932. Mimeographed Report.

from outside their respective states and have been giving preference to their own residents or graduates of their own institutions. Second, that a period of economic stress was probably fundamental in the conditions leading to this enactment, although there may have been several contributory factors. Third, Idaho, therefore, looked upon this residence study requirement as a protective device. No reference was made to any particular state or states. Of the commonwealths bounding Idaho, including Montana, Wyoming, Utah, Nevada, Oregon, and Washington, five had previously erected specific state requirements. It is not known which of these are referred to in the Idaho enactment.

On March 4, 1933, the legislature in the state of New Mexico enacted legislation which included the following statement:

> . . . no certificate shall be issued . . . to teach in the public schools of this State, to any applicant, unless such applicant shall, in addition to meeting all other requirements . . . *have been an actual resident in good faith of the State of New Mexico for at least one year prior to the issuance of such certificate,* and such applicant shall have had at least six semester hours . . . in an institution of higher learning in the State of New Mexico, of college or university rank.[98]

In 1935, the Session Laws repealed the residence requirement and provided a one-year leeway in meeting the resident study requirements, provided all other requirements had been met. It is now necessary, however, that 6 semester hours be earned in residence, this being a requirement as of September 1, 1938.[99]

The State Legislature of Florida, in 1933, passed a requirement more drastic than any that had previously appeared in any state. This enactment was not a requirement for teacher certification, but referred to all people working for the state in any capacity. The requirement follows:

> An ACT Fixing Residential Qualifications of Persons Employed to Work for the State and Counties, and Making Punishable a Violation Thereof.

[98] House Bill No. 81, Approved March 14, 1933, Chapter 77, Section 1, 1933, Session Laws, State of New Mexico, Santa Fe, Department of Education.

[99] House Bill No. 210, Approved February 25, 1935, Section 1, Chapter 108, 1935, Session Laws, State of New Mexico.

Also letter to the author from Miss Katherine M. Jennings, Director of Certification, Department of Education, State of New Mexico, May 4, 1939.

BE IT ENACTED BY THE LEGISLATURE OF THE STATE OF FLORIDA:

Section 1. From and after the passage of this Act all persons employed to work for the State of Florida or any county of the State, shall be *bona fide residents of the State for two years* next prior to such employment, except only *where after due diligence no person can be found in the State possessing the required qualifications necessary to the particular employment.**

Section 2. It shall be unlawful for any officer or board, either State or County, to employ any person to work for the State or for any County in the State, who has not been a bona fide resident of the State for the last past two years at the time of such employment, except only when after due diligence no such resident of the State can be found possessing the required qualifications necessary to fill the particular employment.

Section 3. Any officer or board of members of any official board, either State or County violating the provisions of this ACT shall be deemed guilty of a misdemeanor, and upon conviction punished accordingly. Any officer violating this ACT shall be subject to removal by the Governor.

Section 4. All laws and parts of laws in conflict herewith are hereby repealed.

Section 5. This Act shall take effect upon becoming a law.

Approved June 7, 1933.[100]

The part of this law which is in italics prevented it from exerting a great deal of influence on the teaching field.[101] No estimate can be made, however, as to the restrictive results of such a requirement upon people desiring to enter Florida to teach. It must be noted that both Florida and California have a special problem. Persons often travel to these two states to take advantage of the climate, for health or vacation purposes. They may teach during the school season, and then become vacationists or "drifters" without becoming permanent residents. This seasonal or periodic factor, coupled with the "drifting inclination," creates a unique situation. The requirement in the state of Florida may have been due to this cause, to economic causes only, or to others.

* Italics are the author's.

[100] Letter to the author from Joe Hall, Supervisor of Certification, Department of Public Instruction, Tallahassee, Florida, January 20, 1938.

[101] *Ibid.*

Other Specific Requirements

Several other commonwealths have, since 1924, passed unique certification requirements. Utah, for example, in 1924 included the following requirement:

> . . . organization and administration of secondary education, four quarter hours. . . .[102]

This requirement, which became effective July 1, 1925, included details unique to that state. A course of this general title, taken in a college outside the state, would not be strictly applicable in meeting this requirement.

In 1933 New Hampshire passed a state board regulation which included the New Hampshire Secondary Program in addition to other subjects included elsewhere.[103]

Florida, in 1935, followed with a requirement of a scope and subject content greatly different from any specific requirement previously passed. It follows.

Subjects Required to Be Taught

Conservation

WHEREAS, Natural resources are the foundation of all social and industrial prosperity, the very existence of our youth being dependent upon them; and

WHEREAS, The conservation of our natural resources is so intimately connected with the welfare of our people and should, therefore, be considered as proper subject matter for fundamental education; Now THEREFORE: Be it enacted by the Legislature of the State of Florida:

INSTRUCTIONS IN CONSERVATION OF NATURAL RESOURCES. That on and after September 1, 1936, all of the higher State Educational Institutions shall give instruction in nature study and the conservation of natural resources, including the study of fish and game, soil fertility and erosion, forests and minerals, and all students in said institutions pre-

[102] State of Utah, Department of Public Instruction, *Requirements for Certification of Teachers, Supervisors, and Superintendents,* p. 6, Salt Lake City, Utah, 1925. State Board of Education, Minutes, February 6, 1924. Also letter to the author from A. C. Matheson, Chairman, Certification Committee, Department of Public Instruction, State of Utah, Salt Lake City, May 10, 1939.

[103] *Regulations Governing the Approval of Superintendents, Headmasters, Principals, and Teachers in the Public Schools of New Hampshire,* New Hampshire State Board of Education, 1933, p. 4.

paring to be teachers shall be required to take such course of instruction.[104]

This requirement pertains only to certification in general science, the broad field of science, and the social studies.[105] *It is unique in that a state problem needing solution, other than strictly educational, and pertaining to conservation of resources, is added to the state certification requirements of teachers in the public schools.* The materials on this subject are also required to be taught in higher institutions and secondary schools, with nature study required for promotion for two years in the elementary schools.

In 1936 a course entitled "Problems of Education in New Mexico" had become a requirement for the Master Teachers Elementary Certificate in that state. This same course became necessary for the new applicants for the Five Year High School Certificate effective September 1, 1938.[106] The requirement follows:

> Professional credits or the equivalent shall be distributed as follows: . . . Problems of Education in New Mexico . . . two semester hours.

Following, in 1934, Oregon included as a new requirement the topic "Oregon System of Education," another subject requirement of unique importance to that commonwealth.[107]

In the state of Louisiana still a different type of requirement appeared in April, 1938.[108] Any teacher, coming into the state to teach in any subject, was required to have nine semester hours of health and physical education, with a distribution definitely assigned. The administrative policies governing this requirement follow:

> . . . the nine semester hours instruction in Health and Physical Education for each teacher . . . becomes effective for every teacher by September 1, 1940. . . . All new teachers will be required to meet this requirement for two reasons: First, for training of self; and second, to lend every possible cooperation toward working out satisfactory health

[104] Laws of the State of Florida, Chapter 17030, Acts of 1935, Section 1.

[105] Letter to the author from Ben J. Perloff, Graduate State Certification Clerk, State of Florida, Department of Public Instruction, Tallahassee, Florida, May 4, 1939.

[106] Letter to the author from Katherine M. Jennings, Director of Certification, State Department of Education, New Mexico, May 4, 1939.

[107] Oregon Laws, Chapter 249, 1937, p. 126.

[108] Bulletin 370, State Department of Education of Louisiana, *Certification of Teachers,* p. 13, April, 1938.

TABLE IV

Development of Specific State Requirements for Certification of High School Teachers of Academic Subjects in the United States, 1889 to February, 1938 [1]

	Subject or Requirement									
Year	School Law	State Constitution	U. S. Constitution	State History	State Manual	Residence in State	Sec. Ed.	Prob. Sys. Ed.	Others	Total
1889...	Wash.	Wash.		Wash.						3
1911...	Idaho	Idaho			Wash.					3
1917...	R. I.[2]			R. I.[2]				R. I.[2]		3
1919...	Okla.[4]			Okla.						2
1921...	Nev.	Nev.	Nev.		Idaho [3]					4
1923...			Calif.							1
1924...	Texas			Texas			Utah [5]			3
1925...		Ariz. Wyo.	Ariz., Fla. Wyo.							5
1930...	Kans.[6]	Texas	Texas							3
1931...	Mont.[7]			Mont.[7]	Mont.[7]	Mont.[7]				4
1932...						Idaho [8]				1
1933...	N. H.[9]				N. H.[9]	N. M.[10] Fla.[11]	N. H.[9]			5
1934...	Ore.[13]			Ore.[13]				Ore.[13]		3
1935...									Fla.[12]	1
1938...								N. M.[15]	La.[14]	2
Total	10	6	6	6	4	4	2	3 [17]	2	43

[1] Chapter VI gives the details of the operation and administration of these requirements in actual practice.

[2] Rhode Island education, including school law, school administration, and history of education in Rhode Island.

[3] Idaho course of study was originally included in the 1911 law, but no course of study was available at that time. One was written, however, by 1921 and adopted.

[4] Approximate date. State Board of Education unable to state definitely the year this was enacted.

[5] Utah State organization and administration of secondary education. Includes school law for Utah.

[6] School organization and administration and Kansas school law.

[7] Resident study for nine weeks, Montana law, Montana history, Montana government, and Montana course of study.

[8] Resident study for six weeks—Idaho.

[9] New Hampshire—secondary program and school law.

[10] Residence for one year within state and six semester hours of resident study.

[11] Florida—residence for two years prior to employment. Not an educational measure but a statewide requirement for all public employees.

[12] Florida—conservation of natural resources.

[13] Oregon—history, school law, system of education.

[14] Louisiana—health and physical education.

[15] Problems of education in New Mexico.

[16] State Manual or State Program of Studies.

[17] Organization and Program of Study of the West Virginia School System as a suggested elective for first High School Certificate.

programs in every school, making it possible for each teacher to contribute her share in the development of the program.[109]

[109] Letter to the author from Jess W. Hair, State Supervisor of Health and Physical Education, October 20, 1938.

A new teacher who came into the system that had a full-time teacher in physical education and who was not required to handle this physical education instruction we would make an exception and we would certify her. However, as far as our Louisiana trained teachers are concerned, we are not giving them certification unless they have had at least nine semester hours in physical education with practically the subjects that we recommend. . . .[110]

A chronological list of enactments of specific course requirements is given in Table IV. Figure 3 indicates in graphic form the rise of these courses among the forty-eight states. This table and the figure present a complete portrayal of specific courses since 1889.

Forty-three specific state requirements have been enacted since 1889 by the several states. The peak years for these requirements were 1925 and 1933, with 1921 and 1931 closely following. State school law is most often represented in the requirements, followed by state constitution, the United States Constitution, and state history.

In three cases, different commonwealths passed the same requirement during the same year. In no instance, however, were these adjoining states. In twelve instances the same state passed two or more requirements in the same year, these often being different phases of a subject group. Idaho followed Montana by a year in passing a residence requirement. This close succession is especially notable because forty-two years elapsed between the enactment of the first specific course requirement studied and the time when Montana passed its specific residence requirement. The year after Idaho's requirement was made a law, two widely separated states passed residence requirements, only one being in the same part of the United States as Idaho and Montana. In a three-year span, therefore, all the residence requirements were passed, with 1933 the peak year for this type of requirement. Since that time six years have elapsed without the appearance of any other residence requirement. The periods 1889–1911 and 1923–1930 were peak years for the enactment of state and national constitutions.

It is noticeable how the specific course requirements are grouped sectionally throughout the United States, most of them being in the Far West, the Pacific Coast region, the Northwest, the New England,

[110] Letter to the author from Jess W. Hair, November 14, 1939.

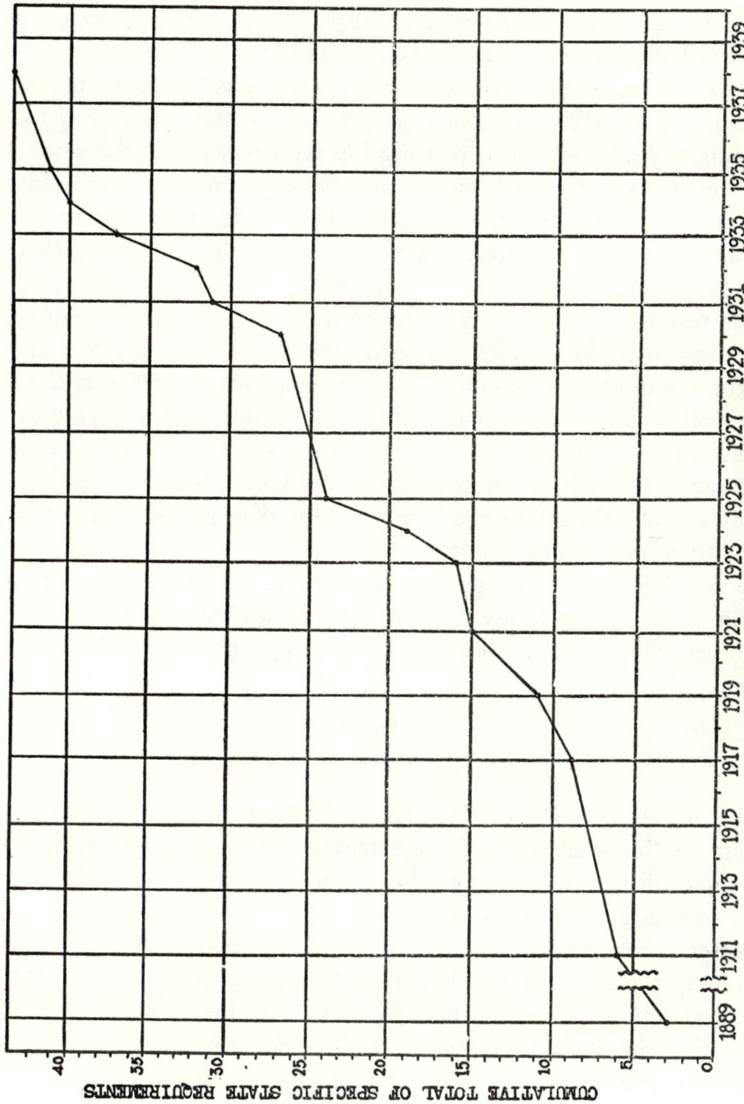

FIGURE 3. Growth of Specific State Requirements in the Forty-Eight States, 1898–1938

the Deep South, and the Southwest States. The Midwest is represented by the state of Kansas. Figure 3 indicates the numerical growth of these specific state requirements.

The certification requirement in Florida listed as "Conservation of Natural Resources" is only one example of many state-wide problems that might yet be placed in certification requirements in the several commonwealths. Each of many states has its own unique problems to meet. However, that the certification standards for teachers is a desirable place for required courses dealing with such problems is open to question.

The restrictive or limiting effect of these specific course requirements lies partly in the fact that such courses cannot be taken in any institutions in other commonwealths. The applicant for a certificate must, rather, attend a particular institution in the state requiring the course. In other instances he must live for a specified period of time within the geographical limits of the state. Expenditure of time and money becomes the restrictive factor and the criterion of certification rather than professional ability.

In meeting any of the specific course requirements in one state a person is not aiding himself to satisfy certification requirements in any other commonwealth because of the unique character of each of these requirements.

Extent of Interstate Teacher Mobility

The preceding pages of this chapter have presented documentary evidence with respect to trends in restrictions in certification practices. The topics discussed were considered important by Cubberley in his study of this general problem in 1906. The present investigation reveals trends between the two studies in a thirty-two-year span. Before examining the study of restrictions in 1938, as described in the following chapters, it is important from an orientation standpoint to know what the present situation is with respect to the interstate mobility of teachers. Have the latter been moving freely across state boundary lines or have they been restricted? Specifically, then, the following question is of importance: To what extent do secondary school teachers of academic subjects cross state lines to obtain certification and employment in other commonwealths? Unfortunately, the answer is not available. After a study of teacher personnel activities and records of the forty-eight state education departments, Emens concluded that "complete data concerning the supply of and demand for teachers are not, at present, available in many states."[111] After studying this general problem at the Midwest Regional Conference on Certification in November, 1939, the conference group concluded that it was extremely difficult to secure information on this problem.[112]

No nation-wide study of the interstate mobility of teachers has been made since Evenden, Gamble, and Blue's study in 1930–1931, published as the National Survey of the Education of Teachers.[113] Although the figures were assembled to give a picture of the demand for and supply of senior high school teachers in the United States, the data are revealing for this study. Table V indicates that of the 84,882 teachers responding to the questionnaire, a total of 17,367 teachers had not been employed in the then-present school system the previous year of 1929–1930. This is a ratio of one new teacher to 4.88 high school teachers. The ratio of these teachers coming from colleges and school systems in other states varies widely, as is indicated in columns 8, 9, and 10 of this table.

By adding the percentages in these columns, one can obtain the *percentage* of the responding senior high school teachers who entered the respective states the previous year. By referring to column 2, one can easily find the *number* of the responding teachers who came into the respective commonwealths from other states. In Idaho, which is third among the forty-eight states in number of restrictions and limitations, 36.3 per cent of the responding teachers had come from other states. In Montana, which is second in number of restrictions among the commonwealths, 43.5 per cent of the responding teachers had come from other states.

These rather large percentages make it appear that there are no restrictions operating to keep persons from entering these states. The

[111] John R. Emens, "A Study of State Administration of Teacher Personnel." Unpublished doctoral dissertation, University of Michigan, 1938. P. 249.

[112] Progress Reports, Midwest Regional Conference on Certification, Russell E. Jones, Chairman. Des Moines, Iowa, November, 1929. (Foreword, p. 1.)

[113] E. S. Evenden, Guy C. Gamble, and Harold G. Blue, *Teacher Personnel in the United States.* In National Survey of the Education of Teachers, U. S. Office of Education, Bulletin No. 10, Vol. 11. Government Printing Office, Washington, D. C., 1935. P. 258.

TABLE V

A Picture of the Supply of Senior High School Teachers in the United States, 1930–31 (From Evenden's Study) [1]

State	Total number senior high school teachers involved	Total number new senior high school teachers	Ratio of mobility—entry in column 3 divided by entry in column 2 ratio of new teachers to total	College or university in same State	Normal school or teachers college in same State	Another school system in the same State	College or university in another State	Normal school or teachers college in another State	A school system in another State	A position other than in educational work	Leave of absence	Return to teaching after having other work the preceding year	Miscellaneous sources
1	2	3	4	5	6	7	8	9	10	11	12	13	14
Alabama	972	239	1–4.07	31.8	1.3	38.1	7.1	1.6	8.4	4.6	0.8	2.5	3.8
Arizona	328	71	1–4.62	19.7	4.2	17	18.3	2.8	22.5	5.7	1.4	4.2	4.2
Arkansas	508	161	1–3.16	24.2	10.6	34.8	5.6	1.9	11.2	3.7	.....	6.2	1.8
California	4,978	672	1–7.41	34.2	4	29.6	3.4	.5	7.8	6.5	3	5.2	5.8
Colorado	789	235	1–3.74	26	11.9	25.5	8.9	1.7	14.9	2.6	1.7	4.7	2.1
Connecticut	1,216	211	1–5.76	4.7	.9	15.7	25.6	4.7	31.3	7.6	.5	4.3	4.7
Delaware	175	28	1–6.25	21.4	.....	10.7	35.8	.....	21.4	7.1	.....	.....	3.6
District of Columbia	257	16	1–16.06	.....	.....	19	19	.....	31	12.4	.....	12.4	6.2
Florida	649	180	1–3.60	15	2.2	40.6	10	1.7	11.7	7.8	.5	5.5	5
Georgia	567	142	1–3.99	27.5	6.3	33.8	8.5	.7	11.3	2.8	1.4	2.8	4.9
Idaho	439	171	1–2.57	19.9	.6	27.5	20.5	.6	15.2	6.4	.6	3.5	5.2
Illinois	4,754	880	1–5.40	27	7	26.4	8.1	2	13.3	7.5	.9	3.7	4.1
Indiana	4,124	769	1–5.36	23.8	10.2	44.7	2.6	.3	7	3.6	.8	4.2	2.8
Iowa	2,679	818	1–3.27	34.8	5.9	36	4.5	1.3	7.8	4.1	.6	3.4	1.6
Kansas	1,826	488	1–3.74	35.9	7.8	34.6	5.1	.4	8.2	3.1	.2	2	2.7
Kentucky	1,013	222	1–4.56	30.2	8.1	25.7	9.5	1.3	12.6	6.8	.4	1.8	3.6
Louisiana	1,305	306	1–4.26	29.1	11.1	36.6	4.9	.6	3.9	5.6	.3	5.6	2.3
Maine	797	171	1–4.66	27.5	6.4	28.1	10.5	1.1	10	6.4	.....	5.9	4.1
Maryland	797	169	1–4.71	37.3	.6	11.8	16.6	2.9	16	7.1	.....	2.4	5.3
Massachusetts	3,622	429	1–8.44	19.6	5.8	35.2	6.7	.9	19.4	6.1	.5	1.6	4.2
Michigan	4,060	709	1–5.73	28	20	22.7	7.1	1.5	7.5	5.9	1.5	2.7	3.1
Minnesota	2,484	604	1–4.11	35.8	2.3	31.6	6	1.5	10.9	5.3	.5	3.1	3
Mississippi	492	173	1–2.84	26.6	7	38.7	5.8	1.1	10.4	3.5	1.1	4.1	1.7
Missouri	2,010	485	1–4.14	27.7	9.7	37.2	4.3	.8	7.8	4.5	.8	3.5	3.7
Montana	533	170	1–3.13	20.6	.....	27.7	19.4	.6	23.5	3.5	.....	4.1	.6
Nebraska	1,290	353	1–3.65	38	8.8	31.5	6.5	.5	6.8	3.1	.3	2.8	1.7
Nevada	103	44	1–2.34	22.7	4.5	20.5	11.4	.....	22.7	9.1	.....	6.8	2.3
New Hampshire	429	112	1–3.83	12.5	17.9	19.7	16.1	4.4	20.6	1.8	.9	3.5	2.6
New Jersey	3,358	503	1–6.67	8.9	5	20.9	18.3	3	30	5.1	.2	4.6	4
New Mexico	255	80	1–3.19	17.5	1.2	21.3	12.5	5	28.8	5	1.2	6.3	1.2
New York	8,703	1,227	1–7.09	27.3	10.8	30	5.6	.3	9.7	7.3	.7	3.4	4.9
North Carolina	1,724	512	1–3.37	33.2	4.1	37.9	7.2	1.8	6.1	3.5	.2	2.7	3.3
North Dakota	604	220	1–2.74	24.5	7.7	28.7	13.6	.5	14.1	5	.....	2.7	3.2
Ohio	5,616	987	1–5.69	41.2	3.9	32	4.8	.8	6.4	4.9	.8	2.9	2.3
Oklahoma	1,132	354	1–3.20	26.3	11.6	39.6	5.9	1.1	6.5	2.8	.3	3.7	2.2
Oregon	1,282	303	1–4.23	41	.....	30	8.3	.3	9.2	5.3	.3	4.3	1.3
Pennsylvania	6,752	1,172	1–5.76	34.6	10.5	29.3	7.7	.6	6.4	5.1	.9	2	2.9
Rhode Island	277	21	1–13.19	19	.....	14.3	23.9	.....	33.4	.....	.....	4.7	4.7
South Carolina	515	119	1–4.33	32.8	4.2	28.6	7.5	.8	11.8	4.2	.....	6.7	3.4
South Dakota	431	144	1–2.99	25.7	6.9	28.5	17.4	.7	16	2.7	.....	1.4	.7
Tennessee	916	207	1–4.42	33.3	7.2	31.9	6.8	1	6.3	4.8	.5	3.4	4.8
Texas	3,360	873	1–3.85	28	6.9	47	2.3	.3	4.5	4.5	.5	3.4	2.6
Utah	420	85	1–4.94	33	.....	29.4	3.5	.....	17.7	8.2	1.2	3.5	3.5
Vermont	286	94	1–3.04	25.6	.....	18.1	16	8.5	13.8	7.4	.....	6.3	4.3
Virginia	1,366	312	1–4.38	31.1	9.9	26.2	7.4	1.6	10.6	3.2	.6	5.2	4.2
Washington	1,898	448	1–4.24	38.2	.2	27.5	7.1	.7	12.1	6.4	.9	3.3	3.6
West Virginia	161	32	1–5.03	28	.....	25	9.4	3.1	12.5	6.3	.....	6.3	9.4
Wisconsin	2,276	515	1–4.42	22.1	11.5	31.9	9.3	1.3	11.5	4.5	.8	2.1	5
Wyoming	354	131	1–2.70	15.3	.....	14.5	19.9	3.8	32.9	7.6	.....	3.8	2.2
Total	84,882	17,367	1–4.88	.....	.....	.....	.....	.....	.....	.....	.....	.....	.....

[1] Adapted from Evenden, Gamble, and Blue, *op. cit.*, Table 27, pp. 90–91. Columns 1 to 4 and 15 to 24 were used.

number of out-of-state teachers within a commonwealth, however, is not reliable proof that restrictions and limitations are not present. *The figures do not reveal how many or how strong were the restrictions and limitations which they were forced to overcome.* Financial conditions, lack of other opportunities to teach, and need for a position may have forced these persons to overcome the interstate barriers in sheer desperation. For example, the Idaho State Board minutes reveal a very clear intention and purpose to bar out-of-state teachers by means of certain requirements. Though the purpose is obvious, the numerical results of such restrictive factors are not so clearly discernible.

Since 1930–1931, when these figures were obtained, the restrictions in community employment policies and practices have increased markedly, a study of the National Education Association Research Division reveals. This trend would affect significantly the number of out-of-state teachers in certain commonwealths. Though the number of such teachers reported in the several states may include some of the better teachers, it is reasonable to assume that exceptional talent from elsewhere was also barred, for example, from Idaho and Montana, by restrictive requirements and practices.

Column 4 of Table V gives the ratio of new teachers to all high school teachers responding. Montana and Idaho, two states which rank high among the states having the greatest restrictions, have also high ratios of new teachers to all high school teachers. Idaho is exceeded only by Nevada in this ratio, while Montana is exceeded only by Mississippi, Nevada, North Dakota, South Dakota, and Wyoming. Idaho and Montana "pull in" a large percentage of teachers from other states, thus escaping the financing of their education, require these teachers to take from six to eight weeks of resident study, and specify definite, restrictive requirements in in-state institutions. These states then reveal some of the highest teacher mobility ratios in the nation. The causes of this situation can be only conjectured.[114]

[114] It may be that the requirement by cities in the state that teachers have one year or more of teaching experience forces teachers into these states for a short time. These persons may then leave Idaho, Montana, and other states to return to their home states and communities to teach. Or, persons may teach in Idaho and Montana for a short time, and then leave to attempt to find better paying positions elsewhere in the Northwest and the Pacific Coast states. Finding teacher mobility high, Idaho and Montana may have required specific state courses and resident study to acquaint a mobile teacher population with some of the history and details regarding education

Some States Training Grounds for Others

Some commonwealths, however, bring in their teachers from neighboring states without restricting them by specific courses, residence requirements, or other devices. This type of activity runs counter to restrictive factors present elsewhere because these states attract out-of-state teachers. As a matter of fact, certain commonwealths are actual training grounds for teachers in neighboring states. For example, according to the Midwest Regional Conference report:

1. Kansas secures teachers from Missouri, Oklahoma, Nebraska, and Colorado. Kansas trains teachers for Missouri.
2. North Dakota secures teachers from Minnesota, South Dakota, and Wisconsin.
3. South Dakota secures many teachers from Minnesota, Iowa, and Nebraska.
4. Wisconsin secures teachers from Minnesota and Illinois and trains teachers for Michigan, Minnesota, and Illinois.
5. Iowa secures teachers from Nebraska, Missouri, Illinois, and Minnesota. Iowa trains teachers for Illinois.[115]

This report adds further that it is believed that availability of teacher-training institutions in adjoining states is a major factor in determining the interchange of teachers. For example, Iowa has no training institutions in the southwest and therefore draws heavily from Missouri and Nebraska institutions. Similarly, the several Iowa colleges located on the Mississippi River furnish teachers for Illinois.

This problem of supply of and demand for teachers cannot be treated in this study in detail. It is referred to, nevertheless, as a factor in the total situation. It is obvious that where certain commonwealths depend upon training institutions in other states for their teachers, factors contrary to restrictions are operating.

---

in Idaho and Montana. Without reference to any particular commonwealth, it would seem better to eliminate restrictions to out-of-state persons, and improve the financial situation of the schools of the state and thus the salaries so as to attract the best possible teaching talent. Once having obtained this talent, efforts should be made to retain it as long as possible. Some commonwealths, finding their teacher turnover high, hastily throw up restrictive state requirements. At the same time these commonwealths are adding to their difficulties rather than helping to solve them because of the restrictive aspects of the requirements they enact. Efforts should be made to solve the basic problems rather than to restrict out-of-state teachers.

[115] Progress Report, Midwest Regional Conference on Certification, Des Moines, Iowa, November, 1939, Foreword, pp. 1–2.

Mobility of the Lay Population

Of further value in finding what numbers of teachers from other commonwealths are teaching in each of the states is the extent of interstate mobility of the lay population. If figures could be accurately determined as to the immigration and emigration of a particular commonwealth, they would shed some light on this general problem. It may be that enough "new blood" and "new ideas" are entering each of the commonwealths to offset any professional restrictive factors that may be operating. However, the only nation-wide, reliable figures available are those of the Fifteenth Census, taken eight years prior to the present study. These data were not recent enough to be used.

Then, too, important population changes have occurred since that time,[116] as, for example, a definite slowing down of population growth, a widening difference between the rates of natural increase for certain groups, a steady rise in the average age of the population, new geographical concentrations of the population through a redistribution of people in relation to natural resources and social institutions, and a shift in emphasis from the productive and extractive occupations to the mechanical, managerial, professional, and service occupations. Also, changes can be traced through these census data only by decades, so trends within a decade or for any one year cannot be indicated. The figures given by the census each decade do not indicate whether the persons counted ten years apart are the same persons; ninety per cent may be, or twenty per cent. Nor is it known from these data how many teachers or persons planning to enter the teaching profession are included in this internal migration, though the number can be estimated. Appendix F contains the census figures.

Interstate Mobility Through Exchange Teachers

A possible factor in this study is the exchange of teachers, a procedure by which a teacher of one community or state is exchanged for another elsewhere for a period of one year or more. This study can merely allude to this problem as a phase of the entire matter of

[116] National Education Association Research Bulletin, *"Population Trends and Their Implications,"* Vol. XVI, No. 1, January, 1938.

restrictions. The extent of the use of exchange teachers is not accurately known. However, these teachers often receive a provisional certificate regardless of whether or not they meet the exact certification requirements of the states into which they go. This exchange of teachers of course overcomes interstate restrictions, *but this very fact indicates that it is considered desirable for the better teachers to move into other cities and states regardless of whether they meet the detailed certification requirements.* That certification requirements are often waived for such exchange teachers is an inherent admission that the better teachers are wanted or deemed desirable regardless of the courses taken to meet certification. The arrangement of exchange teachers is created partly because of such interstate restrictions and limitations. In and of itself, the problem of teacher exchange is a revealing factor. Few arguments could be better advanced for the elimination of state and community restrictions than this matter of teacher exchange.

Interstate Mobility Lessened by Desire to Teach Near Homes

That more teachers are not teaching in other than their own states may not be due entirely to restrictions, but to the fact that many persons choose to teach in or near their homes. Again this study cannot do more than merely refer to this problem. It is a factor that tends to retain teachers in their own communities and states rather than restrict them from entering others.

Interstate Mobility Lessened by Out-of-State Tuition Fees in College

Students are often restricted from entering colleges in other commonwealths by non-resident or out-of-state tuition fees markedly higher than resident tuition fees. Such fees are a factor in this study of restrictions. A nation-wide survey[117] revealed a wide disposition on the part of state institutions to exact extra fees from those living outside the commonwealth. These extra charges are usually based on the fact that it often costs more to educate a student than he pays

[117] Study made by the author.

in tuition fees. To educate the residents of the commonwealth is one responsibility of such institutions of higher learning; a non-resident obtaining the benefits of such training must pay an extra differential. Other types of institutions besides state-supported colleges also charge such fees. The survey of non-resident fees showed an increase in amounts, over and above the resident fees, from ten dollars to three hundred dollars. Students finding they cannot pay the extra tuition fees in out-of-state institutions try to enroll in an in-state institution. These non-resident fees enter the picture of restrictions rather early in the career of teachers, operating to restrict them long before they are ready for certification and employment.

Conclusions

Administrative units of certification. Numerous and heterogeneous administrative units of certification in the early 1900's caused restrictions which Cubberley described. Centralization of certification has since tended to eliminate many of these restrictive factors. The state, in taking over the function of certificating, has separated it from employment responsibilities, the latter being assumed by communities.

Examination and training courses as bases of certification. Examinations, widely used as bases for certification in 1906, protected the teachers in any given locality from outside competition, but a person legally qualified to teach in one locality was restricted from teaching elsewhere. Distrust of the examination method and the rise of the normal schools brought an increase in the use of evidences of professional training and a decrease in the use of examinations. By 1938 every state gave a certificate on the basis of evidences of training received, listing its requirements in courses and degrees. Thus the training and examining of teachers were shifted to teacher-training institutions, but the state retained its evaluating and certificating responsibilities.

State recognition of diplomas issued by institutions of learning in other states. In 1906 the acceptance by states of diplomas from teacher-training institutions in other commonwealths was not widespread, nineteen states not giving such recognition. By 1921 this acceptance was the usual practice in forty-two states. By 1938 a person could attend an approved institution of higher learning in any commonwealth, and then on the basis of that training could apply for certification in any of the forty-eight states soon after receiving the training or years later. Many of the earlier restrictions were eliminated by this state acceptance of institutional diplomas from other states.

State recognition of certificates issued by other commonwealths. The commonwealths were slow in recognizing certificates issued by other states. The peak of interstate acceptance of such certificates was reached in 1921, when thirty-eight states had some kind of reciprocal agreements with at least one other state. By 1937, however, only seven states had such reciprocal arrangements, and even in these it was as difficult to obtain a reciprocal certificate as it was to obtain a new one. Evidences of training in out-of-state institutions of learning became increasingly acceptable for certification purposes, whereas acceptance of other states' certificates declined and was almost nonexistent by 1938.

Specific state requirements and courses. Beginning in 1889 certain specific state courses which had been examination subjects began to appear as certification course requirements. By 1938 a total of forty-three specific state requirements appeared in the several states. Most of these courses appeared in the Pacific Northwest, the Pacific Coast region, the Far West, the Southwest, and the New England States, with scattered instances in the Deep South.

Cubberley wrote of the restrictions inherent in the examinations used for certification purposes. Although such licensing has come to be based on evidences of professional training, specific state requirements are assuming certain restrictive characteristics of the older examination subjects. The problem of protection of the "home product teacher" continues, with the restrictive factors appearing in different forms from those described by Cubberley. At least one state wrote in its regulations that its specific course requirements were definitely for the purpose of restricting out-of-state teachers and were enacted in retaliation for similar laws in other commonwealths. Similar requirements exist in thirty-nine instances, and although the purposes are not always discernible, the restrictive effects seem to be comparable.

Most of the states require that all certification requirements be fully satisfied before an applicant is eligible for certification or employment. The specific requirements therefore restrict out-of-state persons even from applying for a certificate, let alone employment. Such specific requirements tend to "screen out" some persons among whom may be many superior teachers who could be of professional value to the state. Employers in many instances do not see teachers who are unable to clear the hurdle provided by these specific state requirements.

Some factors of interstate teacher mobility. The extent of interstate teacher mobility can be ascertained only for 1930–1931, and the numerous limitations of such data prevent a clear understanding of the present situation. The figures show the number of out-of-state teachers but do not reveal the restrictions which they had to hurdle. Idaho and Montana, which have the most restrictions, have also the highest ratio of new teachers from other states.

The extent of interstate mobility of either the lay or the professional population cannot be clearly ascertained because of lack of data. The extent of teacher interstate mobility is made greater by some states "pulling in" teachers trained by other commonwealths and by the practice of exchanging teachers. Interstate mobility is lessened by the tendency of teachers to want to teach in or near their home towns and by the charge of non-resident fees by teacher-training institutions.

From the materials presented in this chapter it seems imperative that these topics be considered: certification requirements of degrees, academic and professional courses, practice teaching standards, specific state requirements, and community employment policies and practices. These problems will be considered in the chapters following.

CHAPTER III

RESTRICTIONS AND LIMITATIONS IN THE CERTIFICATION REQUIREMENTS OF DEGREES, ACADEMIC AND PROFESSIONAL COURSES

To meet the second objective of this study, namely, to reveal the restrictions and limitations in certification in 1938 and 1941, this chapter and the two following present an analysis of certification requirements and practices.[1] These questions will be considered:

1. In what certification requirements and practices do restrictions and limitations exist?
2. In what states are these restrictions and limitations present?
3. On what groups of teachers in particular do these restrictions and limitations fall?

The analysis of the certification laws of the forty-eight states revealed comparable factors in most of the state requirements so far as broad categories are concerned. The certification requirements for the state of Oregon will serve as an illustration.

Requirements for High School Teachers of Academic Subjects for the State of Oregon[2, 3]

(a) *Graduation from a standard college, university or teachers college* which has been accredited as a college or university.[4] The applicant must also complete twenty semester hours of work beyond graduation from a four-year college course.[3]

[1] As of February, 1938 and 1941.

[2] *Circular of Certification for the State of Oregon,* May, 1939. Issued by Rex Putnam, Superintendent of Public Instruction, p. 7.

[3] From February 10, 1941, to February 10, 1943, thirty term hours of work beyond graduation will be required, of which not less than 15 term hours shall be professional training. After February 10, 1943, a full year's work or 45 term hours beyond graduation from a standard college or university will be required. *Ibid.,* p. 8.

[4] A standard college or university is one which is on the accredited list of some standardizing association that has adopted the standards of the American Council on Education. *Ibid.,* p. 7. Also, letter to the author from Rex Putnam, Superintendent

(b) *Academic requirements*[5]

(c) *Professional requirements,* semester hours in Education . 25

Principles of Secondary Education

(General Techniques) 2

Secondary Education 2

Educational Psychology . . . . 2[6]

Electives 17

(d) *Supervised teaching*

(Under essentially secondary school conditions) . . 2[7]

(e) *Specific state requirements* 2⅔

A minimum of four term hours (2⅔ semester hours) covering Oregon history, Oregon school law, and the Oregon system of education, taken at a standard college, university, or normal school. This may be included in the twenty five hours required above.

The divisions represented by these requirements are fairly typical of those found in the remaining forty-seven states. This chapter discusses the first three categories—graduation from standard institution, academic requirements, and professional requirements—with the following two chapters taking up the two remaining topics—supervised teaching and specific state requirements—in order.

Degree Requirements, Restrictions and Limitations

In the analysis of the degree requirements for certification these factors were studied:

---

of Public Instruction, State of Oregon, February 21, 1941. In addition, *High School Standards, State Department of Education,* Rex Putnam, Superintendent, Salem, Oregon; Revised and adopted by the State Board of Education, January 8, 1941. Pp. 11. Mimeo.

[5] No academic requirements are specifically stated; however, if an institution is fully accredited according to Oregon requirements, the academic standards are accounted for indirectly through accrediting, not direct certification, mandate. Beginning with the year 1943–44, however, specific academic standards will be recommended. See *High School Standards, op. cit.,* pp. 3–5.

[6] General Psychology in the amount of two semester hours is required as a prerequisite to Educational Psychology. *Circular of Certification,* p. 8.

[7] A teacher otherwise qualified by law for a high school certificate may substitute five years of successful teaching experience acceptable to the superintendent of public instruction in lieu of the Supervised Teaching, provided the last year of said teaching experience has been within the three years immediately preceding application for such certificate. *Circular of Certification,* p. 8.

1. Variations in degree requirements.

2. Administrative policies and practices relative to the degree standards.

1. *The degree requirements in the forty-eight states are practically uniform except for nomenclature.*

The analysis of degree requirements of all the commonwealths reveals that in forty-four states a minimum of a baccalaureate degree is necessary for high school certification. Four states require the equivalent of a master's degree. Only slight variation in the nomenclature of these requirements occurs, as Table VI clearly shows.

Seven categories are listed, six specifying a bachelor's degree and one a master's degree or the equivalent. Maryland asks for four years of college work, while New York requires for its provisional certificate an approved four-year curriculum. Other states disregard the time spent in obtaining the degree, and merely require evidence that the degree has been obtained. In these instances a person could qualify in certain universities by examination without reference to time consumed.

Four states, Arizona, California, New York, and Washington, require a year of graduate work or a master's degree. Of these, California requires that one half of the graduate work be completed in the institution recommending the candidate. The qualifying statements vary from a mere statement of a bachelor's degree, as in Colorado, to a carefully formulated requirement of graduation from an institution that requires four years of work for graduation and that was standard at time of graduation, as in Florida. A definition of the word "standard" is given in the latter specifications, with accrediting groups listed. Michigan goes even further by requiring a bachelor's degree in a curriculum for secondary teachers approved by the State Board of Education and from an institution approved by this board for teacher-training purposes. New Hampshire mentions *post-secondary* education, which could be in several types of collegiate institutions; other commonwealths refer to particular types of colleges. These illustrations are typical of the variations in the degree requirements among the states. Four years of undergraduate work, usually concluded by a baccalaureate degree, constitute the common element in most of these particular requirements.

TABLE VI

Nomenclature of Degree Requirements for General, Academic, Secondary School Certification in the Forty-Eight States, February, 1941 [a]

Degree Requirement	Number of States
Bachelor's degree from a standard college or university	18 [b]
Bachelor's degree from an approved institution	11 [c]
Bachelor's degree from an accredited college	9 [d]
Bachelor's degree	3 [e]
Four years of college work	2 [f]
Degree from a recognized college	1 [g]
Master's degree or equivalent	4 [h*]

[a] Data taken from state certification pamphlets or mimeographed materials.

[b] Standard. Alabama—Class C secondary professional certificate; Delaware; Florida—graduation from institution that requires four years' work for graduation and that was standard at time applicant graduated; Indiana—graduation with a baccalaureate degree from a standard or approved college with a minimum of 120 semester hours of credit; Kansas—a college requiring the completion of four-year courses of 120 semester hours in advance of a standard four-year high school course; Kentucky; Massachusetts—or from a four-year course in a teachers college or normal school for certification of teachers in *state-aided* high schools—other schools employ teachers certificated by decentralized plan by communities; Nevada; New Hampshire—post-secondary education in standard institutions; North Carolina; Oklahoma—standard, accredited colleges; Oregon—standard college that has been accredited as a college or university; Rhode Island—four years of attendance for graduation after graduation from a standard secondary school; Texas; Virginia; West Virginia—graduation and recommendation from a standard college; Wyoming.

[c] Approved. Arkansas—an approved four-year college; Connecticut—graduate of a four-year, secondary teacher-preparation curriculum of an approved college; Georgia; Louisiana—for four years of work above high school level; Michigan—by State Board of Education for teaching-training purposes; Mississippi; New Mexico—with a minimum of 120 semester hours of credit; New York—an approved four-year curriculum leading to baccalaureate degree or approved equivalent preparation—for provisional certificate; Ohio—graduation from a four-year college course of an approved teacher-training institution; South Dakota—approved as a teacher-training institution; Tennessee—approved by the State Commissioner and State Board of Education; Vermont—approved by the Vermont State Department of Education.

[d] Bachelor's degree from an accredited college. Idaho—A.B. or B.S. from such; Iowa—accredited by the Board of Educational Examiners; Maine—four-year course; Minnesota; Montana—four-year normal or university; North Dakota—bachelor's degree from such—approved as a teacher-training institution; Pennsylvania—approved four-year education curriculum; South Carolina; Wisconsin—approved four-year course.

[e] Bachelor's degree. Colorado—A.B. or equivalent degree; Nebraska; New Jersey.

[f] Four years of college work. Maryland—applicant must have ranked in the upper four-fifths of his class; Utah—completed a standard college course of four years.

[g] Degree from a recognized college. Illinois.

[h] Master's degree or equivalent. Arizona—evidence of satisfactory completion of not less than thirty semester hours of graduate work acceptable toward an advanced degree at the University of Arizona or similar accredited institutions and also acceptable to State Board of Education for certification purposes; California—in addition to bachelor's degree, one full year of graduate work of not less than twenty semester hours offered by institution approved for graduate work by the State Board of Education, one-half of which must be completed in the recommending institution; New York—candidate shall have completed an approved four-year curriculum leading to the baccalaureate degree or approved equivalent preparation and in addition 30 semester hours in approved advanced work (This requirement is effective, however, on and after January 1, 1943. Until then only a baccalaureate degree is necessary.); Washington—applicants for secondary certification must have completed, in a fully accredited college or university, a five-year course designed for the training of secondary teachers and including at least thirty semester hours in addition to the number of hours regularly required by the institution for a bachelor's degree.

* New York requires a full year of graduate work in addition to baccalaureate degree for a *permanent* certificate.

In spite of the variations in the degree nomenclature, an institution of higher learning need not lie *within the particular state boundaries* to meet that state's degree requirements in each of forty-seven states.[8] In Mississippi a situation exists in which only in-state colleges are recognized for certification purposes, but a certificate to teach is issued on the basis of equivalent certificates and training from other states. In forty-seven commonwealths, therefore, if a college is "recognized" by one state, it is also a "first class" institution for another state. If a college is "standard" for one state, it is usually "approved" by another.

Accrediting associations aid in providing for interstate acceptance of degrees by state certification officials.

Whether or not a college is "accredited," "approved," "accepted," or "recognized" by a state for certification purposes usually depends on the accrediting status obtained by that college. A number of accrediting groups and regional associations[9] have become established, receiving widely varied acceptance by the several commonwealths. Table VII shows the number of states accepting the accrediting standards of certain of these groups. A graduate of a college that is accredited by the North Central Association, for example, can apply for a teaching certificate in any of forty-four states with the understanding that the degree will be accepted by that commonwealth toward a certificate. Several facts in Table VII stand out:

Many states accept the standards of more than one accrediting association, with most of the commonwealths accepting the standards of all five regional associations, which, collectively, cover forty-eight states.[10] Though membership in an accrediting group is voluntary for an institution, the maintenance of professional status often requires that an institution retain its accredited status in more than one association or group.

Considerable overlapping is apparent. Especially noticeable is the fact that such widely varied types of groups accredit institutions and use such varying criteria for this accrediting. However, *the states tend to overlook this basic lack of comparability in their general acceptance of the standards of more than one group.* Viewed from the

[8] Data from question 1, State Certification Data Sheet. See Appendix A.
[9] Regional associations are not all accrediting bodies. See Appendix C.
[10] One state is a member of two regional accrediting associations.

TABLE VII

Groups Whose Accrediting of Colleges and Universities, or Whose Standards, Are Accepted by State Certification Officials in the Forty-Eight States, February, 1938 *

Name of Accrediting Group	Number of States Accepting the Accrediting of These Groups
North Central Association	44
Northwest Association	42
Middle States and Maryland Association	40
Southern Association	40
New England Association	38
Association of American Universities	22
American Association of Teachers Colleges	22
State departments of education in the state in which the institution is located	20
State department of education in own state	11
State teachers colleges in own state	8
National University Extension Association	5
State teachers colleges in other states	4
Association of Colleges for Negro Youth	2

* Data from question 2, State Certification Data Sheet; see Appendix A. This question was formulated after a preliminary investigation of all forty-eight states.

Regional associations are not all accrediting bodies. See Appendix C.

standpoint of states' rights and responsibilities, nine of these accrediting associations are, in a way, extra-legal in character because they spread over more than one state's boundaries.

It should be noted that there is a difference between a state's inclusion within a regional accrediting association and a state's accepting the standards of that same group. Although forty-four states accept the accrediting of the North Central Association, only twenty are included in this association, as is indicated by Figure 4.

Only about half as many commonwealths accept the accrediting of institutions by state education departments as accept the accrediting of regional associations. However, some institutional leaders are looking more to the state departments for accrediting purposes than to the regional associations. Should the state departments do more accrediting of institutions for certification purposes in the future, at least two paths would be open: the states could require similar stand-

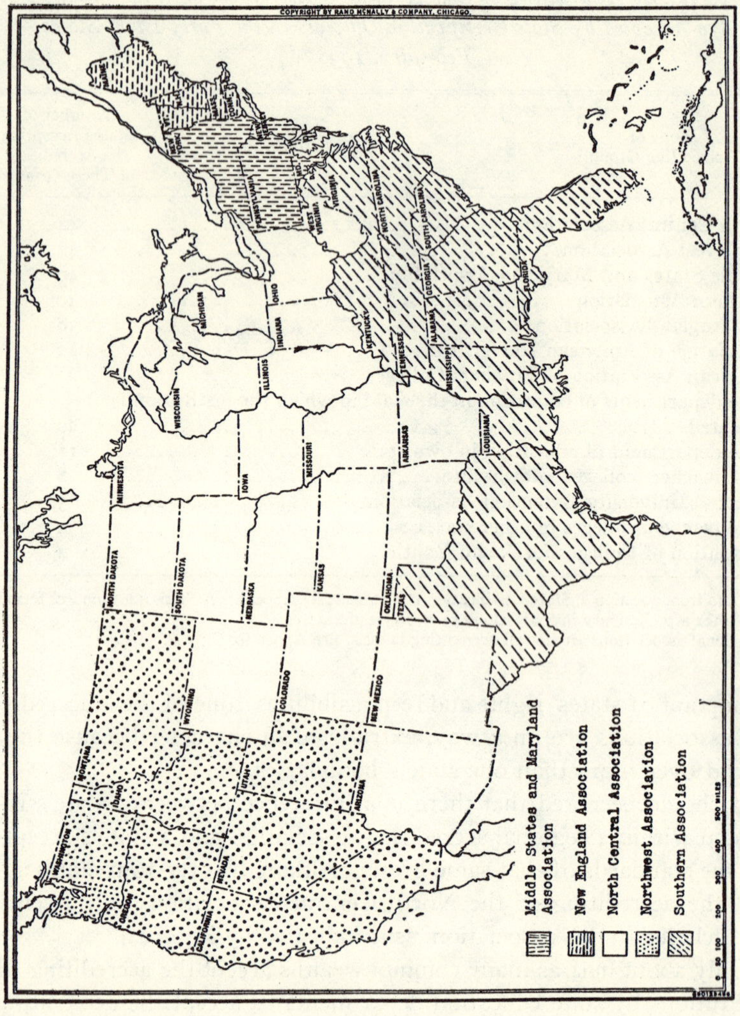

FIGURE 4. The Regional Accrediting Associations and the Included States

ards and thus develop nation-wide comparability; or the states could proceed individually to require different standards and thus bring into existence from one to forty-eight accrediting associations or groups with inherent limitations and restrictions for teachers.

2. *The administration of degree requirements provides for interstate freedom.*

In administering the degree requirements for certification, forty-seven states certificate applicants from within and outside the state on similar terms, provided the applicants have attended accredited institutions.[11] Mississippi is the sole variant.

Few commonwealths accept courses or degrees from non-accredited institutions of higher learning. Only three states accept degrees or courses from non-accredited institutions outside their respective states,[12] and only six accept courses or degrees from non-accredited in-state colleges or universities. Various types of penalties are imposed upon applicants for certification who have been graduated from these non-approved schools. These penalties range from complete refusal of a certificate to an extra assignment of a few make-up courses in deficiency subjects.[13] It may be said that the student and not the institution training him should be the deciding factor in this problem. If the student were the deciding factor and not the training school, an alternative basis for certification would be an evaluation by the state, such as individual examinations which, in the form then used, were so restrictive in 1906. As long as the certification procedure is administered on the basis of recognition of college credentials, the state must give some weight to the selective processes in the training institutions, even though it is uncertain what these selective processes are.

Few states waive their academic requirements for certification, adhering rather closely to the listed requirements. This applies to both out-of-state and in-state teachers.[14] Three states waive their degree requirements for graduates of in-state institutions;[15] two waive theirs for out-of-state graduates. Apparently, exceptions to certification requirements are rarely made.

[11] Data from question 3, State Certification Data Sheet. Appendix A.
[12] Data from question 4, State Certification Data Sheet. Appendix A.
[13] Data from question 5, State Certification Data Sheet. Appendix A.
[14] Data from question 6, State Certification Data Sheet. Appendix A.
[15] Data from question 6, State Certification Data Sheet. Appendix A.

Conclusions

Variations in degree requirements. Forty-four states require a bachelor's and four a master's degree for high school certification in the academic subjects. The nomenclature and details of the requirements vary but slightly.

Administrative policies and practices. Widespread acceptance of degrees for certification purposes is evident in forty-seven states. Regardless of the qualifying statements in the nomenclature of the degree requirements, an "accredited" college is also an "approved" or "accepted" institution.

There is widespread refusal by states to accept courses or degrees from non-accredited institutions of higher learning. Experienced teachers without degrees, coming from other states, find it as difficult in most states to obtain a certificate as inexperienced trained persons.

Rarely do states waive their degree requirements for any applicant.

No restrictions occur in the degree requirements, as far as the research methods of this study distinguish. Some limitations exist for certain groups.

Persons without a master's degree or at least thirty semester hours of graduate work are, of course, limited from entering California, Arizona, New York, and Washington. In these instances it is considered that the professional standards are being raised to a satisfactory level at this time and that whatever limitations exist are counteracted by the higher standards made available. These higher standards do not differentiate on the basis of residence but only in training received, and the training can be obtained in any state in the Union.

Persons who take baccalaureate degrees other than Bachelor of Arts or Bachelor of Science may encounter some slight difficulty in a few states. Apparently, however, the type and accrediting status of the institution mean more than the kind of baccalaureate degree for certification purposes.

Some states accept the accrediting standards of five or more accrediting associations which have somewhat different standards. In thus accepting their accrediting, the commonwealths overlook these differences in standards.

In the administration of degree requirements, the state certification officials apparently evaluate credentials without conscious differentiation, whether they are from in-state applicants or out-of-state applicants, and whether or not the degrees are from in-state institutions.

Although these data may tend to reveal the better phases of the situation, it is evident that to find restrictions and many limitations to graduates of accredited colleges and universities, one must look elsewhere than in the degree requirements. It may be that in the *total* requirements of degrees there is great interstate freedom, yet *within* that total may be the limitations and restrictions.

Academic Course Requirements, Restrictions and Limitations

In analyzing the academic or subject matter requirements for certification, the following factors were studied:

1. The presence of academic subject requirements.
2. The amount required in semester hours for an academic teaching field.
3. The presence and amount of a *core curriculum*.[16]
4. The administrative policies and practices relative to these academic requirements.

The investigation of these phases of the academic requirements revealed no evidences of restrictions but did indicate several types of limitations, some of which were rather severe in actual practice.

The basis for most of the limitations found lies principally in the fact that the academic requirements *vary greatly in amount and pattern*. To illustrate: Maine stipulates directly no academic requirements whatsoever, relying upon the institutions themselves to give an adequate amount. Kentucky requires a 24 semester-hour major and two 18 semester-hour minor subjects, making 60 hours altogether, while Louisiana has only a 12 semester-hour major requirement. All of the other forty-five commonwealths have requirements between these extremes.

[16] Certain subjects in given amounts are required by some states of all applicants for certificates, regardless of their major fields. For purposes of this study such a group of subjects is called a core curriculum.

1. *Some degree of interstate comparability is attained by direct specifications of academic requirements in thirty-seven states and by indirect requirements in eleven states.*

All but twelve of the states mention directly their requirements in academic subjects of one kind or another. In the group of widely scattered states that do not directly specify academic requirements in the certification pamphlet or bulletin are Colorado, Idaho, Kansas, Maine, Minnesota, Montana, Nevada, North Dakota, Oregon, Rhode Island, South Carolina, and Vermont. One of the few statements of academic requirements made by any of this group is the requirement by Minnesota that the training course must be "balanced as to academic and professional content and designated for the training of high school teachers."

The absence of specified academic standards in the certification pamphlet in this group of states does not mean that the requirements are lower than those of other commonwealths or that academic subjects are ignored. It merely means that these states obtain their academic requirements in some other way. To illustrate: These states accept degrees from institutions of higher learning that are accredited by certain groups or associations. The standards maintained by these accrediting groups include academic specifications. Even though academic requirements are not actually stated in the certification requirements, the assumption is that if the institution giving the degree is properly accredited, the academic training has been taken into consideration.* This may be a wise and liberal policy.

* Academic requirements for teachers as prescribed by regional accrediting associations and others, February, 1938 (see Appendix C):

Accrediting Group	Statement of Academic Requirement
Middle States and Maryland Association	No academic requirements stated.
New England Association	No academic requirements stated.
North Central Association	15 semester hours in the academic subject taught.
Northwest Association	All teachers in new schools and all new teachers in major and minor specialization in college preparation. A minor shall be interpreted to mean not less than 12 semester hours.
Southern Association	Teachers should not teach outside the fields of their college specialization.
American Association of Teachers Colleges	24 semester hours of undergraduate work or graduate work in the field taught and also professional courses in that field.

The remaining thirty-seven states mention in some manner an academic subject, group, or total requirement.

2. *Wide differences occur in the amount of the academic requirements.*

The variability of the academic requirements can perhaps best be illustrated by the data in Table VIII. With thirty-seven states specifying some form of academic training for a certificate, it is not possible to include a complete listing of all requirements for every academic subject; the very detail required would detract from its contribution to the study. Table VIII shows the different requirements for one academic subject—English. If a *general* academic requirement is given by the states without any definite amounts for *particular* subjects, the requirement is listed merely as a "major," with the subject of English as an example. If, however, separate requirements are listed for each of the teaching academic fields, the particular requirement chosen is that for English. More than one number listed for the semester hours required indicates a double or a triple subject requirement.

Fourteen of the states mentioned the amount of academic content or subject matter in a particular area, such as English, while eleven states left the amounts required to the accrediting groups. Fifteen states mentioned both major and minor subjects, a combination which tends to increase materially the prescription of total academic material. Eight mentioned a major subject and gave no detailed requirements for individual subjects.

The wide range and the variations of the academic requirements are especially noticeable: New Jersey has a 30 hour major and an 18 hour minor, while New York requires only 18 hours for an English major. Michigan asks altogether for 54 semester hours, while Ohio has a total of 45 hours required in the academic field. Illinois asks for three majors of 16 hours each; Louisiana requires only 12 hours for academic major. Massachusetts requests two majors of 18 hours each; Connecticut requires 15 hours in English to teach this subject. Nebraska requests 15 hours, yet Iowa requires 35 altogether in major subjects. For only one major subject, a person in the state of Virginia would need to take only 12 hours of English to meet the academic requirements of a teaching certificate in that state. If he wanted

TABLE VIII

Academic Certification Requirements of the Forty-Eight States for a Major Subject, or a Minor, or for Preparation to Teach an Academic Subject, in a General or a Particular Area, February, 1941

State	Number of Semester Hours Major	Minor	Particular Subject	Total
Alabama	24	18		42
Arizona	24	15		39
Arkansas			18	18
California	24	12		36
Colorado [a]				
Connecticut [b]	15	6		21
Delaware			18	18
Florida			24	24
Georgia			24	24
Idaho [c]				
Illinois [d]	16, 16, 16			48
Indiana			25	25
Iowa	15, 10, 10			35
Kansas [e]			15	15
Kentucky	24	18, 18	(30)	60
Louisiana	12			12
Maine [f]				
Maryland			24	24
Massachusetts [g]	18, 18			36
Michigan	24	15, 15		54
Minnesota [h]				
Mississippi			30	30
Missouri			24	24
Montana [i]				
Nebraska	15	15		30
Nevada [j]				
New Hampshire	18	12, 6		36
New Jersey	30	18 (or 12, 12)		48
New Mexico	24	15		39
New York			18	18
North Carolina			24	24
North Dakota [k]				
Ohio	15, 15, 15			45
Oklahoma [l]			30	30
Oregon				
Pennsylvania	18			18
Rhode Island [m]				
South Carolina [n]				
South Dakota	24	15		39
Tennessee			24	24

TABLE VIII (*Continued*)

State	Number of Semester Hours Major	Minor	Particular Subject	Total
Texas	24	12		36
Utah	20	12		32
Vermont [o]				
Virginia	12			12
Washington	24	12, 12		48
West Virginia			24	24
Wisconsin	24	15, 15		54
Wyoming	15			15

States mentioning major amount alone	8
States mentioning major and minor amounts	15
States mentioning particular subject amounts	14
States not directly requiring academic standards but indirectly requiring them through accrediting groups	11
	48

	Hours
Mean average of major alone	27.6
Mean average of major and minor together	40.9
Mean average of particular subjects alone	23.
Mean average of total academic major, minor, and particular requirement	31.27
Mode of total academic major, minor, and particular requirement	24

Range of requirement totals	12–60 hours
States with lowest total amount of academic requirement	Louisiana, Vermont
State with highest total amount of academic requirement	Kentucky

Top states in amount of academic requirement: Kentucky, Michigan, New Jersey
Lowest states in amount of academic requirement: Louisiana, Vermont, Kansas

[a] COLORADO—Only 6⅔ semester hours of academic work are mentioned and this in an elective group.
[b] CONNECTICUT—In field to be taught. Teachers should be masters of the content area they are to teach.
[c] IDAHO—No academic requirements stated.
[d] ILLINOIS—Or one major of 32 semester hours and a minor of 16 hours.
[e] KANSAS—For class A.
[f] MAINE—No academic requirements listed for English.
[g] MASSACHUSETTS—Requirement only for state-aided high schools. May be one major and one minor.
[h] MINNESOTA—No academic requirements listed.
[i] MONTANA—No academic requirements listed. Major and two minors mentioned but no amounts.
[j] NEVADA—No academic requirements listed.
[k] NORTH DAKOTA—No academic requirements listed.
[l] OKLAHOMA—For life certificate; 16 for 1-year certificate.
[m] RHODE ISLAND—No academic requirements listed.
[n] SOUTH CAROLINA—No academic requirements listed.
[o] VERMONT—No academic requirements listed.

a certificate in Maryland, he would need 24 semester hours; in Pennsylvania, 18; and in West Virginia, 24. A teacher in Nebraska would need 30 hours in a major and minor for a Nebraska certificate but would need a major of 24 hours in South Dakota, a triple major of 15, 10, and 10 hours in Iowa, and 24 hours in Missouri. A teacher in Delaware needs 18 hours, but for New Jersey certification he would need 30 hours in one academic subject and 18 in another. A teacher in Louisiana needs only 12 hours of an academic subject for a teaching certificate major, yet would need 30 hours in Mississippi on the one side, 24 hours in Texas on the other, 18 in Arkansas, and 30 in Oklahoma. (See Figure 5.)

Some of these total academic requirements are based upon a certain number of high school units. Florida, for example, bases an eighteen-hour requirement on four units. Then too, within the total amounts required is a certain amount of prescription, as in West Virginia and Mississippi.

From a professional standpoint, many of these academic requirements are very low, demanding as little as one-tenth of the work for a bachelor's degree in a subject for a teaching major. Such requirements are hardly adequate. It is doubtful if much information can be gained in a field in which a person takes only twelve hours of training, let alone mastery of a subject he needs to teach. However, some teachers must go into schools where they will teach more than one subject, often as many as four or even more. With the requirement for any one subject low, say, 12 hours, training can be had in each of several areas, whereas if the requirement for any one subject is large, training in others must necessarily be less. A high requirement tends to lead to specialization and professional competency; a low requirement may lead away from specialization toward training in more subjects, with less competency in any one. It is not surprising with the low standards in several states that there exists at times an estimated over-supply of teachers in certain teaching fields. A general raising of academic requirements on the part of many of the states would tend to even the disparities among the commonwealths.

In some states with low academic requirements for certification the major subject requirements for graduation from some institutions of higher learning are high. One reason for low requirements is that certification standards must be enacted by legislative bodies

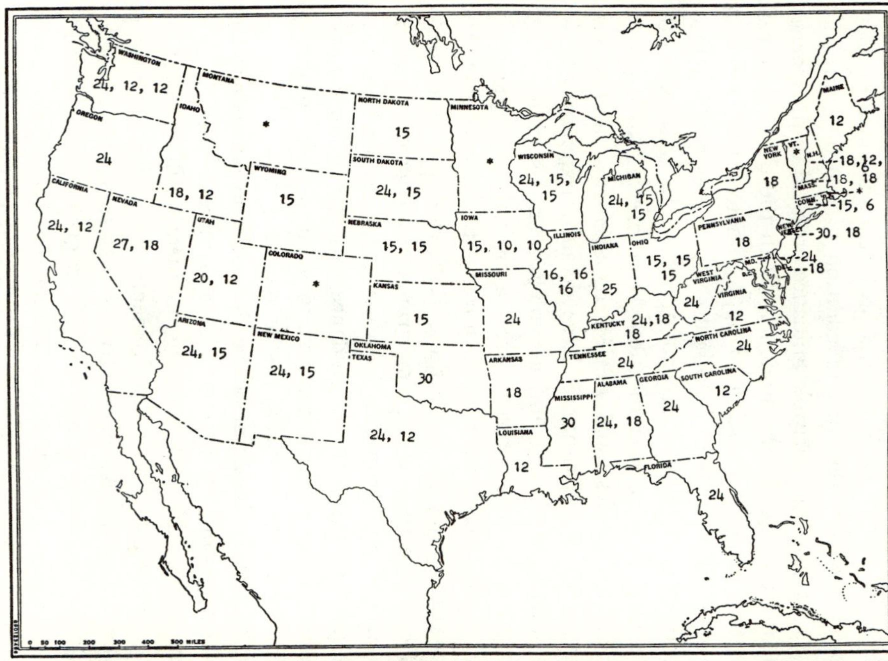

FIGURE 5. The Amount of Academic Training Required by the Forty-Eight States in Major, Minor, or General Training Fields for High School Certification, February, 1941

* Academic requirements not stated in semester hours. Results are obtained indirectly through the acceptance of credits and degrees from accredited colleges. To be accredited, standards are implied and some guaranteed. Majors and minors are often included together. Lone numbers may be major subject requirements or standards for a particular field, such as English.

that move slowly. Flexibility in certification administration is rare, and requirements tend to lag far behind what is generally accepted to be a need for high standards.

Institutional and state requirements present a guidance problem. Heavy certification requirements, in addition to institutional graduation standards, present a sizeable guidance problem to the teacher-training institutions and to the students. With the usual four-year undergraduate program consisting of approximately 120 hours, an academic subject requirement of 30 hours constitutes one-fourth of the total, and is equal to one full year of study. In addition to the academic requirements for certification, there are allocated certain core requirements, professional subject requirements, and specific state requirements. If institutions have detailed requirements for graduation, such as prescribed subjects and groups, designated major field or program, definite prerequisites, a prescribed sequence of studies, and a total semester hour requirement, students may find difficulty in attempting to meet these certification requirements. Those who can plan their college programs in advance to meet all such requirements are fortunate. In some instances the burden on the student and the institutional guidance program is very heavy, especially when the student is not sure in what state he wishes to teach or how many state requirements he may need to satisfy.

Whether the present disparities in academic requirements grow or become less depends in part upon which states increase their requirements. Commonwealths with high requirements will increase the disparities if they enact higher requirements, yet such increases are professionally desirable. An alternative is that states with low requirements raise their standards to achieve greater comparability with other states. As the variations among the states become less, teachers will find fewer limitations with regard to these academic requirements. It happens, however, that the states with high requirements are often the very ones to see the need for further requirements. Oregon, after January 1, 1939, increased its requirements 10 semester hours, with 3⅓ of these being in *professional* courses. The maximum increase in *academic* requirements here is 6⅔ hours.

In some commonwealths the brunt of the burden of preparing teachers lies with the teachers colleges, in other states with the liberal arts colleges. Some teachers colleges do not offer elaborate programs of academic courses, giving over a large part of their work to professional courses. On the other hand, many liberal arts colleges do not offer the necessary professional courses.

A disparity often exists between certification requirements and the curriculum offerings of dominant institutions of higher learning in a given state. For example, academic requirements, even in states where the liberal arts colleges have traditionally been firmly entrenched, are low. In the New England States, the home of the older liberal arts colleges, the academic requirements are usually not high. Connecticut, which has the lowest professional requirement in the nation, presumably to assist the graduates of liberal arts colleges in obtaining certificates, has an academic requirement of only 15 hours.

3. *Core curriculum subjects are often required in addition to the academic standards.*

Some commonwealths have, in addition to their academic requirements, certain groups of academic subjects that are considered the "core" or basic content materials for all teachers regardless of their major fields. Fundamentally, such core requirements may be an attempt to prevent too much specialization, or they may be considered too valuable a group to be omitted from any teacher's training. Table IX lists these core curriculum requirements for fifteen states.

Viewed superficially, these core requirements do not appear to be very limiting to teachers. Some of them, such as those specified in Colorado, Illinois, Utah, and Washington, are subjects usually included in an undergraduate program. The course "Principles of American Government" in Iowa may not be available in many colleges and would be limiting in this respect. On the other hand, nine commonwealths have rather heavy core curriculum standards. Kentucky requires more than 40 per cent of the entire four-year program in its core curriculum, while Alabama, Arkansas, Mississippi, Missouri, New Jersey, and West Virginia definitely allocate almost an entire year's work to this basic group.

The total amount of prescription in such requirements is made less by the fact that in some instances the courses within the core curriculum are also in the student's major subject field. To illustrate, Alabama has a 24 semester-hour requirement in a major subject, for example, English. The core curriculum requirement of 12 hours in

TABLE IX

Core Curriculum Requirements for High School Academic Teaching Certificates, February, 1941

State	Details of Requirements	Amount of Academic Prescription		
		Core	Academic Subject Preparation	Total
Alabama	English, 12; History, 6; Political Science, Sociology or Economics, 6; Science, 6; General Psychology, 3	33	42 [a]	75
Arkansas	English, 12; Social Studies, 12; Science, 6; Physical Education, 6; Conservation of Natural Resources, one course, 2	38 [b]	18	56
Colorado	Two of the following groups: Psychology, Principles of Education, History of Education, Administration and Supervision, Special Methods, Philosophy (or Sociology, Anthropology, Biology, Political Science)	16 [c]		16
Florida	Science, Social Science, English, 6 hours each; Health Education, 1; Physical Education, 1	20	24	44
Illinois	English, 6 hours. Construction and use of good English	6	48	54
Iowa	Principles of American Government	2	35	37
Kentucky	English, 12; Science, 12; Health, 2; Social Sciences, 12; Mathematics, 6 or foreign language, 6–12; Physical Education, 1	45–51	60	105–111
Mississippi	English, 12; Social Studies, 12; Science, 12; Physical Education and Health, 4	40	30	70
Missouri	English Composition, Literature, Mathematics, Physical or Biological Science, Social Studies, Foreign Language, Physical Education and Health,[d] 2 yrs.	25	25	50
Nebraska	Physiology and Hygiene	2	30	32
New Jersey	English Language and Literature, 12; Social Studies, 12; Science, 6	30	48	78

TABLE IX (*Continued*)

State	Details of Requirements	Amount of Academic Prescription		
		Core	Academic Subject Preparation	Total
Oklahoma	English, 8 if English is not major; American History and Government, 6; Oklahoma History, 2 [e]; Agriculture, 2	10–16 [f]	30	40–46
Utah	Health Education, 2; Ethics or Sociology, 6⅔; Physical Education, 2	10⅔ [g]	32	42⅔
Washington	Contempory Social Problems (Current History, Political Science, Economics and Sociology), at least 10 hours	10	48	58
West Virginia	English, 8; Public Speaking, 2; Social Sciences, 12; Science or Mathematics, 6	28	24	52

Range . . . 16–105 semester hours
Mean . . . 54 semester hours

[a] Class B certificate.
[b] Reasonable deviation permitted until September 1, 1943. Must include a course in Conservation of Natural Resources, Act 312 of the Acts of 1939.
[c] Of 20 semester hours required, 4 must be in Practice Teaching, leaving 16 in this group.
[d] Twenty-five hours in any three fields. (Missouri.)
[e] See chapter on Specific State Requirements, No. 5.
[f] Ten if major is English, 16 in this group if otherwise. (Oklahoma.)
[g] Or 3.2 semester hours in one of these fields and 3.2 semester hours in Political Science and Economics. (Utah.)

English would not constitute a separate requirement at all for a student majoring in English and so would not be limiting in any sense of the term. This same situation would be true for a student majoring in English, science, or social science in Kentucky. The limitations of these core requirements would affect most of all students majoring in fields other than those included in the core requirements.

The purposes behind the state adoption of these core curriculum standards are not known. The entire series of such requirements may be an attempt on the part of those interested in liberal arts college curricula to insure a given amount of training in the academic fields.

Such requirements may have been included without any regard to a dichotomy between liberal arts and teachers colleges, yet a comparison of these core and academic requirements and the professional standards reveals a conflict among types of training institutions.

Viewed practically, severe limitations exist in the allocation of large and specific amounts of subject matter by the state for certification purposes. The student has not only the state certification requirements to meet, but also the institutional requirements for graduation in many different types of colleges throughout the nation. He must also meet the detailed certification requirements of not only one but also two or more commonwealths. Where the requirements in both the college and the state can be fitted together, no difficulty exists; but where they differ, limitations are numerous for the student preparing to be a teacher.

4. *Administrative policies and practices provide interstate freedom.*

In examining the various administrative practices, it seemed essential for the purposes of this study to find out whether any academic courses had to be taken in certain institutions of higher learning in any particular state, whether any practices restricted out-of-state applicants, and whether any academic courses were required to have exact or definitely worded titles for purposes of certification.

In the thirty-eight states reporting on this question, there was unanimity on the general policy that no academic course needed to be taken in any particular institution within any given state.[17] In other words, academic courses are accepted from any recognized institution in any state if the courses meet the requirements.

Persons meeting the academic requirements of any commonwealth in out-of-state institutions are certificated on an equal basis with those applying from within the commonwealth. This is true of thirty-seven states answering this question.[18]

That academic requirements are seldom waived is indicated by the fact that only four states reported that they sometimes waive even partially the academic requirements for applicants from within the state. Only one state reported it sometimes waived partially the state

[17] Data from question 7, State Certification Data Sheet. See Appendix A.
[18] Data from question 8, State Certification Data Sheet. See Appendix A.

requirements for an out-of-state person.[19] The better phase of the situation may be indicated here in that individual exceptions may be made more often than reported. From the information obtained, however, it is apparent that the requirements are strictly adhered to.

In thirty-three responding states no academic course need have an exact title for purposes of certification.[20] This is significant in that institutions throughout the nation are not definitely "tied down" to any specific course nomenclature. If the content of a course is such that the registrar or a comparable official in the college offering the course certifies it to meet a state requirement, that is all that is necessary. Often the state certification officials make the decisions as to the equivalency of courses to meet requirements. In this case, the descriptions of the courses are often taken from the respective college announcement or bulletin.

Close adherence to the requirements is revealed by this analysis. For example, teachers who have had five years' experience in another commonwealth and who meet all other requirements in a given state with the exception of three, four, or five semester hours in academic work are not given certificates, except in two states which will partially waive their academic standards.[21] For inexperienced teachers who meet all other requirements but who are deficient three, four, or five semester hours in academic work, only seven states issue temporary certificates good for one year.[22]

Conclusions

No restrictions are present in the academic course requirements or in the administration of them. Several types of limitations, however, exist, and are fairly widespread.

Although only thirty-six states mention directly an academic requirement, the remaining twelve states achieve the same ends indirectly in accepting degrees only from accredited institutions, thus insuring that the academic standards have been maintained.

The academic requirements vary from a 12 semester hour requirement to 60 hours in a major subject or academic teaching field. Ken-

[19] Data from question 9, State Certification Data Sheet. See Appendix A.
[20] Data from question 10, State Certification Data Sheet. See Appendix A.
[21] Data from question 11, State Certification Data Sheet. See Appendix A.
[22] Data from question 12, State Certification Data Sheet. See Appendix A.

tucky has the highest total academic prescription in requiring a 24 hour major and two 18 hour minor subjects. Michigan asks for a 24 hour major and two 15 hour minors. Illinois and New Jersey both require 48 semester hours in academic work. Louisiana in 1941 had the lowest requirements of 12 hours.

The academic requirements, taken for any group of states, vary widely and thus provide limiting factors for teachers in crossing the state lines.

Some of the given requirements are based upon a certain number of high school units. Academic requirements are greater where the specific high school preparation has not been obtained.

A controversial problem exists in the amount of academic training that constitutes an "adequate" preparation to teach. Teachers are often required to teach several subjects other than their major field. Low academic requirements are then "convenient" for the teacher in this situation. On the other hand, high academic requirements provide for greater competency. Some commonwealths provide examples of highly specialized requirements and others broad yet rather low standards.

Fifteen states have a core curriculum requirement in addition to the academic requirements. These core requirements range from 2 semester hours to 51 hours. Five states have a core requirement of 30 semester hours or more.

These core curriculum requirements, added to the academic course requirements, make rather large prescriptions, ranging from a minimum of 37 hours to a total of 111 hours. Seven states prescribe requirements totaling more than 50 semester hours each. Kentucky prescribes 87 per cent of a full four-year program. Of the states having core curriculum courses in addition to a specified academic requirement, Colorado has the smallest prescription, 16 hours in all.

Combined with the professional and specific course prescriptions, the total academic requirements make up a large proportion of the four-year undergraduate program.

No academic course requires a specific title nor need it be taken in any institution within a given state. Applicants from within and from outside the state are treated on an equal basis by certification officials.

The academic course requirements are seldom waived. They are not waived even for experienced teachers who lack only three, four, or five semester hours of academic work. Teachers with considerable teaching experience are therefore held as strictly to the listed requirements as inexperienced teachers. Only seven states issue one-year temporary certificates for those who just miss the total academic requirements by three, four, or five hours and who meet all other requirements.

One of the factors making the core curriculum group less limiting is the possibility that a person may be majoring in one of the very subject areas required in the core group. This factor also lessens the prescription total in some instances.

Professional Course Requirements, Restrictions and Limitations

To reveal the restrictions and limitations in the professional course requirements for certification, a study was made of the following:

1. The total *amount* of the professional course requirements without reference to included courses or other details.
2. The *extent of allocation* of courses or semester hours.
3. The amount of elective courses permitted.
4. The administrative policies and practices relative to these professional requirements.

1. *The investigation reveals wide variability in the amount of professional course requirements.*

The differences in professional requirements for certification range from 6 semester hours in Connecticut * to 24 hours in Alabama and 400 clock hours in Rhode Island, the latter being the equivalent of eight to thirteen courses. Maine asks for only 18 hours in *approved courses* with no specification, while Arkansas lists eight integrated courses and nine more specific single subjects that might be used instead. For its provisional certificate, New York gives a leeway of 2 to 6 semester hours for two subjects and 2 to 9 hours for two other courses, while Iowa completely allocates its requirements Georgia lists 9 hours in broad fields like "The School and Society" or "High School Curriculum and Methods" and 9 additional hours

* Six hours for September 1, 1940; 12 hours for September 1, 1941; and 18 hours for September 1, 1943.

TABLE X

Professional Requirements for Certification of High School Teachers of Academic Subjects, February, 1941

State	Professional Requirements in Semester Hours	State	Professional Requirements in Semester Hours
Alabama	24 [a]	Nebraska	18
Arizona	24 [b]	Nevada	18
Arkansas	16 [c]	New Hampshire	12 [j]
California	24 [d]	New Jersey	18
Colorado	20 [e]	New Mexico	18
Connecticut	6 [f]	New York	18 [k]
Delaware	18	North Carolina	18
Florida	18	North Dakota	16
Georgia	18 [g]	Ohio	17
Idaho	15	Oklahoma	10–20 [l]
Illinois	15	Oregon	28 ⅔ [m]
Indiana	19 [h]	Pennsylvania	18
Iowa	15	Rhode Island	*400 [n]
Kansas	18 [i]	South Carolina	18
Kentucky	18	South Dakota	15
Louisiana	18	Tennessee	18
Maine	18	Texas	24 [o]
Maryland	16	Utah	18
Massachusetts	12	Vermont	12
Michigan	20	Virginia	18
Minnesota	15	Washington	16
Mississippi	18	West Virginia	20
Missouri	18	Wisconsin	18
Montana	15	Wyoming	16

Range 6–28.66 semester hours
Mean 17.4 semester hours
Mode 18 semester hours

* Clock hours.

[a] Alabama—For class B secondary professional certificate. Includes 9 semester hours of electives in Secondary Education. See state pamphlet *Certification of Alabama Teachers*, Bulletin 1939, No. 5, p. 17.

[b] Arizona—Not less than 6 semester hours of graduate courses in education nor less than 5 in practice teaching. Six courses or areas named in requirements.

[c] Arkansas—Six to 8 hours in junior year and 10–12 in senior year, latter to include directed teaching. Eight integrated courses listed, with possibility of acceptance of suggested individual courses.

[d] California—Includes 18 hours plus at least 6 hours of graduate work in education.

[e] Colorado—Of 20 required semester hours, 4 must be in practice teaching and 6⅔ hours may be in a group of five named academic subjects, leaving 9⅓ semester hours in education courses required.

[f] Connecticut—Six semester hours of practice teaching required beginning September 1, 1940. One year later, September 1, 1941, 12 hours required, including the laboratory course, and 18 hours will be by September 1, 1943.

[g] GEORGIA—Nine semester hours required in each of two groups. One includes Orientation in Education, Educational Psychology, The School and Society, and High School Curriculum and Methods. The second includes materials and methods on the high school level, directed observation and practice teaching, and vocational guidance.

[h] INDIANA—A total of 15 hours required plus professional academic credit consisting of a two-semester hour course in methods of teaching each of the two subject groups elected.

[i] KANSAS—Three-year renewable for life certificate. If master's degree, 6 hours in education, including 2 in practice teaching will be required.

[j] NEW HAMPSHIRE—See *Regulations governing the approval of superintendents, headmasters, principals and teachers in the public schools of New Hampshire*, Reprint, 1941, p. 8.

[k] NEW YORK—For provisional certificate, 8 semester hours of professional courses are required as a minimum with the upper end of the range 30 hours. This requirement applies also to permanent certificate except that 30 additional advanced hours in approved equivalent preparation are required, but not necessarily in professional subject matter.

[l] OKLAHOMA—Ten semester hours of professional work for a one-year certificate and 20 hours for the life certificate.

[m] OREGON—The applicant must also complete 20 semester hours beyond baccalaureate work in addition to specific state requirements listed in another chapter. These include 10 semester hours in professional work. On February 10, 1943, these requirements will increase to a full year's work beyond undergraduate degree.

[n] RHODE ISLAND—*Certification of Teachers* pamphlet states that no credit is permitted for a course less than 30 clock hours or more than 50 clock hours. From 8 to 13 courses would thus be permitted to meet this professional requirement. No basis for credit-semester-hour requirement is given in the pamphlet or by correspondence with the State Department. Possible range with each course at two semester hours is from 16 to 26 semester hours. Mean is 21 semester hours. Four hundred additional hours are required in practice teaching.

[o] TEXAS—Unfortunately, the latest requirements sent by the State Department of Education in Texas do not give explicitly the requirements needed. The figure used is from 1938.

in functional courses like "Vocational Guidance," while Idaho gives no allocation but recommends practice teaching. Florida insists that 12 of 18 hours be taken in residence; other states seldom mention how the work may be taken. New Jersey allocates 15 of 18 semester hours, whereas North Dakota states only what may *not* be taken, such as general psychology, logic, or ethics. Oklahoma differentiates sharply between a one-year certificate and a life certificate, requiring only 10 semester hours of education for the former and just double that for the latter. Connecticut carefully describes the courses required; South Carolina gives no details except that 18 hours are required. In short, the professional requirements of these states vary widely in detail but not so much in amount as the academic standards. Table X gives the professional requirements of each of the forty-eight states.

The range among the states in total requirements is from 6 to 28.6 hours—not a wide span. The arithmetic mean of the total is 17 hours, and not many states deviate greatly from this mean. Nevertheless, variations are present and may be limiting factors for many teachers.

A person within any state who desires a certificate in another commonwealth, probably one adjoining, must meet the different standards revealed in Figure 6, which gives the requirements by states geographically distributed. Wide differences in total course requirements exist in certain parts of the country. To illustrate: a graduate of Yale University, the Teachers College in New Britain, the Danbury State Teachers College, or any other institution in Connecticut would meet the following situation if he wanted one or more state certificates to teach. For his own state he would find that he had a very small professional requirement of 6 semester hours. For a certificate in New York, New Jersey, or Pennsylvania he would need 18 hours of professional work. In Massachusetts, Vermont, or New Hampshire he would need 12 semester hours. An additional difficulty for this applicant lies in the fact that the courses required within each total requirement in these states vary in content. Unless he had planned ahead to meet the requirements of specific states, he would need to attend from one to three summer sessions to fulfill just the professional requirements for a certificate.

In Oklahoma, 10 hours of professional work are needed for a one-year certificate. Near-by Texas, however, requires more than double that total, Louisiana 18 hours, Arkansas 16, Mississippi 18, and Alabama 24. If a prospective teacher had taken just enough courses to meet his own state's requirements in Louisiana, he would encounter these several limiting factors in the interstate variations of requirements.

In some groups of states, however, the differences are not very great. Eight southern states require 18 semester hours each: Virginia, North Carolina, South Carolina, Georgia, Florida, Mississippi, Tennessee, and Kentucky. In the Northwest the states vary only slightly in their professional standards.

Just as some teachers colleges would not be able to meet the academic requirements previously discussed, because of the amount of subject matter required, so many liberal arts colleges could not meet some of these professional requirements. The students in these liberal arts colleges would therefore find many of these requirements to be limiting to some degree in their obtaining of a certificate in one or more states. The offerings in professional courses in some liberal arts college programs are so meagre that a graduate cannot possibly meet the requirements of any state except his own. Typical of such

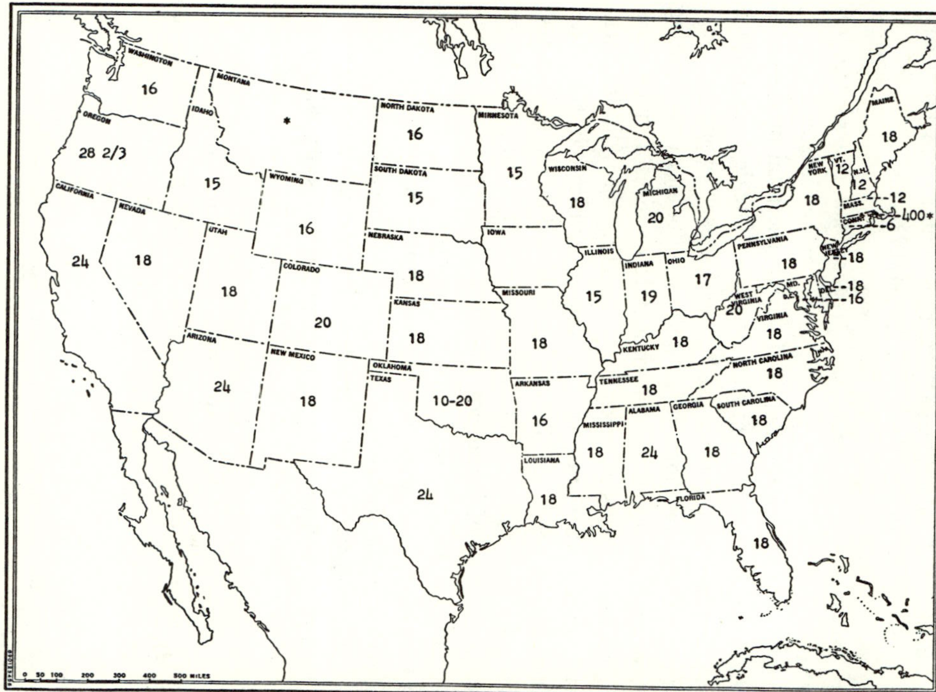

FIGURE 6. The Amount of Professional Training Required by the Forty-Eight States for Secondary School Academic Certification, February, 1941

* Not required. Rhode Island requires its professional training in terms of clock hours rather than in units of semester hours. All others are in semester-hour units.

difficulties are those experienced by students in the liberal arts colleges in the New England States in trying to obtain teachers' certificates. The same is true of students in such colleges in the Eastern States. Kendall[23] and Gildersleeve[24] are representative of those who have pointed out these difficulties in no uncertain terms.

2. *Few states allocate entirely the professional course requirements, yet considerable prescription of such courses exists.*

The content of the courses required within the total professional requirements varies greatly from state to state. The degree to which states allocate particular courses to be met by each applicant for a certificate is considered important from the standpoint of the limiting factors involved. The extent to which a state requires a given number of courses and permits no flexibility in meeting them, limits teachers in nearly every other state in obtaining a certificate in this state.

The entire professional requirement is allocated in but four states: Connecticut, Indiana, Iowa, and Oklahoma. This type of prescription means that regardless of institution attended, training, or experience, certain definitely stated courses in given amounts are ear-marked with variation from them depending upon their administration.

In still other commonwealths, the amount of allocation of courses and semester hours varies considerably. In some, the prescribing is done by means of subject fields, for example, "History of Education." In other states, the ear-marking is done by naming broad fields in which freedom in courses is permitted.

As an example of a state having total prescription, Iowa requires 15 semester hours in professional education. This must include the following:

	Hours
a. Introduction to, History of, or Principles of Education . .	3
b. Psychology and its Application to Education, including Measurements	6
c. Methods of Teaching	3
d. Directed Observation and Supervised Practice Teaching .	3

[23] Raymond L. Kendall, "The Closing Door," *Journal of Higher Education,* IX, No. 5 (May, 1938), 258–259.

[24] Virginia C. Gildersleeve, "And Sadly Teach. State Requirements That Discourage Educated Persons from Teaching," *The American Scholar,* Vol. 5, No. 4 (September, 1936), 426.

Educational measurements must be included under psychology or methods of teaching. These courses seem to be pertinent, insofar as preparation for teaching is concerned. A slight amount of election is allowed in the first-named requirement, but the courses and amounts, however, are definitely prescribed. Whether a teacher is from a liberal arts college, a teachers college, a normal school, or any other type of school, he must "match" these course requirements.

In the Southwest, Oklahoma also typifies the extreme amount of prescription in professional requirements (for the life certificate):

		Hours
Professional requirements in semester hours		20
a. Educational Psychology	2	
b. Psychology of Adolescence	2	
c. Philosophy of Education or History of Education	4	
d. General Methods and Management including Oklahoma School Law	2	
e. Educational Measurements	2	
f. Principles of Secondary Education	2	
g. Apprentice Teaching in Secondary Schools	6	

There is much to be said for the state that knows what it wants, names the desired courses, and administers these definite prescriptions. There is also much to be said for allowing some leeway in meeting a state's requirements. The different types and kinds of teacher-training institutions and departments in this nation vary greatly in their offerings of courses. Every teacher, regardless of his training or experience, and irrespective of the institution from which he comes, must match every single requirement in Oklahoma, item for item. This type of allocation provides a "bottleneck" of requirements that virtually disregards every other professional course. The limitations in this type of prescription are numerous. It is conceivable that many institutions offer courses to meet at least half the requirements; it is beyond credulity that every institution can meet all of the requirements or that even a good fraction of teachers have taken enough courses to meet these requirements without extra summer sessions or more than a full semester's work.

Table XI shows the extent of this prescription among the states. The allocation, whether slight or large, is given in terms of subject fields and in some instances in terms of broad fields which cover large areas of information.

TABLE XI

Amount of Professional Requirements Allocated by the States, February, 1941

State	Amount of Allocation	Type of Allocation	State	Amount of Allocation	Type of Allocation
Alabama	15 [a]	SF-5, BF-1 *	Nebraska	3	SF-1
			Nevada	4	SF-1
Arizona	15 [b]	SF-6	New Hampshire	0	
Arkansas	12 [c]	SF-4	New Jersey	15	SF-9
California	6 [d]	SF-2	New Mexico	12	SF-5
Colorado	8 [e]	SF-3	New York	8–30 [p]	SF-6, BF-2
Connecticut	6 [f]	BF-5	North Carolina	9	SF-5
Delaware	18 [g]	BF-1, SF-4	North Dakota	0	
Florida	3 [h]	SF-1	Ohio	11–17	SF-5
Georgia	18 [i]	SF-5, BF-2	Oklahoma	10, 20 [q]	SF, 4–8
Idaho	18 [j]		Oregon	8	SF-4
Illinois	5 [k]	SF-2	Pennsylvania	12	SF-3
Indiana	19 [l]	SF-6	Rhode Island	0	
Iowa	15	SF-6	South Carolina	0	
Kansas	11 [m]	SF-5	South Dakota	3	SF-1
Kentucky	9	SF-2, BF-1	Tennessee	10	SF-5
Louisiana	4 [n]	SF-1	Texas	12	SF-2
Maine	0		Utah	14⅔	SF-5, BF-1
Maryland	10	SF-3	Vermont	3 [r]	SF-1
Massachusetts	6 [o]	BF-1	Virginia	8	SF-2
Michigan	13	SF-4, BF-3	Washington	10⅔	SF-3, BF-1
Minnesota	12	SF-4	West Virginia	14	SF-3
Mississippi	6	SF-2	Wisconsin	10	SF-3
Missouri	9	SF-7	Wyoming	8	SF-4
Montana	8	BF-1			

Total number of hours of professional courses required	42⅔ semester hours.
Total number of professional courses allocated	413⅓ hours.
Percentage of courses given that are prescribed	49%
Mean of prescription	8.61 semester hours.
Mode of prescription	8 semester hours.
Range of allocation, not including all courses totally allocated or totally elective	3–19 hours.

* SF = Subject field prescribed.
BF = Broad field or area of information prescribed.

[a] ALABAMA—For class B professional certificate. Broad field is secondary education.

[b] ARIZONA—In addition, requires 6 semester hours in graduate work in education. No specification, however, is made for this work.

[c] ARKANSAS—Names eight integrated courses, and then lists nine subjects acceptable in lieu of these courses.

[d] CALIFORNIA—Four semester hours of directed teaching definitely required. State credential specifies: a course dealing with the aims, scope and desirable outcomes of the secondary school; no number of semester hours mentioned. Minimum is here taken as 2.

[e] COLORADO—Only practice teaching required. Seven groups mentioned, of which three must be represented, including practice teaching. One group includes only academic work.

[f] CONNECTICUT—This is to represent a basic introduction to the field of American education, the organization, administration of the school system, including the secondary school, the history and principles and the philosophy of American education.

[g] DELAWARE—Eighteen hours required, but the rules and regulations are largely permissive, not mandatory, on what shall be taken. The rules say the total *may* include such-and-such, with no direct specification.

[h] FLORIDA—Three options given for practice teaching. See state regulations.

[i] GEORGIA—For a professional four-year certificate.

[j] IDAHO—No education course specified, but practice teaching recommended.

[k] ILLINOIS—Five hours of practice teaching are recommended only. Five hours of electives.

[l] INDIANA—Includes psychology, secondary education, principles of teaching, supervised teaching, and professional academic credit consisting of a two-semester-hour course in methods of teaching each of two subject groups elected.

[m] KANSAS—Three-year Renewable for Life Certificate.

[n] LOUISIANA—For a Class 1-A Professional certificate.

[o] MASSACHUSETTS—For state-aided high schools only. Two of nine given fields should be filled with at least 12 semester hours. Secondary education is broad field.

[p] NEW YORK—A broad leeway is given from 2 to 6 hours and from 2 to 9 hours in two areas, respectively.

[q] OKLAHOMA—Ten hours specified for the one-year certificate and 20 hours for the life certificate. All are allocated in each instance.

[r] VERMONT—For a high school professional probationary certificate. At least three of twelve hours must be in Observation and Practice Teaching. Not more than six of the twelve credits may be in Psychology and only three of the six credits may be in General Psychology.

In addition to the states which prescribe their entire professional requirements, a number of commonwealths allocate from none to a large fraction of their total requirements. This is shown in Table XI. Georgia prescribes 18 hours; Indiana 19 hours. Alabama, Arizona, Iowa, Nebraska, and New Jersey each prescribe 15 hours of the total professional standards. Exclusive of the entirely elective requirements, the lowest prescribed total is 3 hours in Florida, South Dakota, and Vermont. Of 842⅔ semester hours (total amount of professional courses required) 413⅓ semester hours are prescribed, or a total of 49 per cent. Though no one knows how much prescription is superfluous, the amount of such allocation is considerable. In some instances a teacher can have one and even two or more years of training beyond the total requirements for certification and yet not be able to qualify because of the amount and the number of prescribed courses.

Some of the prescribed courses are in specifically designated subjects. To illustrate: Alabama designates four subject fields as required—Educational Psychology, Principles of High School Teaching, Materials and Methods of High School Teaching (with 3 hours in the major subject or 3 hours in the minor subject), and Directed Teaching in the major or minor subject in high school. These are all definite courses. By far the majority of prescriptions are in subject fields, most of them with definitely named titles. These can be met by courses with different titles but fairly equivalent content, if certified as such by the registrars of the training institutions.

A few of the prescribed requirements are in broad fields, in which any one of many courses might be offered. To illustrate: Montana requires that 8 semester hours must be specifically in "secondary education." While this is a definite, broad field, it still is not necessarily a subject or course title. Not many of the states have these broad field requirements, as Table XI clearly shows.

It is apparent that although only a few states prescribe the *total* professional requirements, a great many states prescribe or allocate a *large fraction* of their requirements. Limitations arise in the variability of the requirements and in the prescriptions. Many teachers of superb qualifications may not have taken a single course required by a number of these states and yet may have fulfilled more than the total requirement of professional education. The limitations lie in the matching process wherein teachers try to match the courses they have taken with the prescribed and total requirements. Considering the number and variety of teacher-training institutions, departments, and schools, the number of different subjects taught in them, and the number of individual variations in courses taken by students, it can be seen that the number of limitations is far greater than the total requirements indicate. None of these courses are restrictive, but the limitations are numerous.

3. *Very few states permit entire freedom in electing professional courses; in a few others a small number of elective courses are permitted.*

Seldom do the commonwealths allow entire freedom in the selection of professional courses. The assumptions behind complete freedom in electing courses are that the institution in which the courses were taken is accredited, that the calibre of work done in the courses is entirely acceptable, and that the person offering the courses used reasonable judgment in selecting courses of pertinent value in teaching. No limitations are present in the content or pattern of these professional requirements where complete freedom of selection is allowed. The states permitting entire freedom of electives in professional courses are Idaho, Maine, New Hampshire, North Dakota, and South Carolina. The absence of limitations in professional requirements is more than made up, however, in the case of Idaho, by specific state requirements of heavy restrictive calibre, as will be pointed out in Chapter V. Idaho asks for 15 hours of education work; it recommends that practice teaching be included but does not require it. Maine also asks for 18 hours in education, with no qualifying statements regarding the kind of courses required. In this commonwealth a person has complete freedom of selection.

The amount of semester hours and the number of courses in which free election may be taken vary widely. The number of hours for any commonwealth can be found by subtracting the prescribed hours, as given in Table XII, from the total of the professional requirement for the particular state. Another factor enters the picture, however, in that there are two ways of interpreting the word "elective." In one sense, a person may elect any course he wishes from the entire field of education. In another sense, and one in which many of the states concur, an elective course is one that may be taken at the discretion of the teacher but must be confined to a list of courses or subjects specified by the state. In other words, some commonwealths call courses elective when actually they are courses from which the teacher is "permitted" to select the ones needed or wanted. Table XI gives the amounts of electives allowed by each state and the number and types of courses from among which the electives can be chosen.

It can be seen from Table XII that there is considerable variation in the amount of electives permitted in the various states. To illustrate: five states give complete freedom of elective courses in the professional area: Idaho, Maine, New Hampshire, North Dakota, and South Carolina. On the other hand, six states give no electives, but require that all professional courses be in either broad subject fields or more narrow course titles. These states include Connecticut, Delaware, Georgia, Indiana, Iowa, and Oklahoma.

West Virginia gives 6 hours of electives, and lists thirteen subject fields from which an applicant might choose. Pennsylvania lists fourteen subject fields from which to select 6 hours of work. Mis-

TABLE XII

The Amounts of Elective Courses Allowed in Professional Education and the Number of Courses or Fields Allocated for These Electives by the Forty-Eight States, February, 1941

State	Amount Electives Allowed	Number of Courses Named	State	Amount Electives Allowed	Number of Courses Named
Alabama	9	1BF *	Nebraska	15	
Arizona	9		Nevada	14	
Arkansas	4 [a]	5SF	New Hampshire	12 [l]	11SF
California	12 [b]		New Jersey	3	
Colorado	12 [c]	12SF	New Mexico	6	
Connecticut	0		New York	0–10 [m]	
Delaware	0 [d]	3SF, 1BF	North Carolina	9	
Florida	15 [e]		North Dakota	16	
Georgia	0		Ohio	0–6	6SF
Idaho	15 [f]		Oklahoma	0	
Illinois	10 [g]		Oregon	20 [n]	
Indiana	0 [h]		Pennsylvania	6	14SF
Iowa	0		Rhode Island	20 [o]	
Kansas	7		South Carolina	18	
Kentucky	9	1BF	South Dakota	12	
Louisiana	14 [i]		Tennessee	8	1BF
Maine	18		Texas	12	
Maryland	6	1BF	Utah	3⅓ [p]	8SF
Massachusetts	10**	9SF	Vermont	9	
Michigan	7 [j]		Virginia	10	11SF
Minnesota	3		Washington	2–8 [q]	
Mississippi	12		West Virginia	6	13SF
Missouri	9		Wisconsin	8	
Montana	7		Wyoming	10	

Total amount in semester hours of electives allowed . . . . 414 ⅔ hours.
Total number of courses named from which electives might be chosen . . . . 98 courses.
Number of states with complete freedom in total professional requirement . . . . 6 states.
Mean of electives allowed . . . . 9.87 hours.
Mode . . . . 12 hours.
Range . . . . 0–18 hours.

* BF = Broad field of information prescribed.
SF = Subject field prescribed.
SFR = Subject field recommended.
[a] ARKANSAS—Lists 16 semester hours of integrated courses in eight areas. Gives individual courses acceptable in lieu of such. Three of these courses are listed by the same titles as the integrated

courses. Canceling out the three duplicates, this figure is obtained by using a two-semester-hour value for each individual course except directed teaching and principles which are 5–6 each.

[b] CALIFORNIA—Listing the course dealing with aims, scope, and desirable outcomes of the secondary school as 2 semester hours. Other courses as approved and recommended by the school of education.

[c] COLORADO—Four of 20 semester hours must be in practice teaching. Other 16 elective in six named areas, including one academic group.

[d] DELAWARE—The requirements demand 18 hours of work in the aims and methods of secondary education, which *may* be in a number of courses listed. This is permissive, apparently, not mandatory.

[e] FLORIDA—Of 18 hours required, option b gives 3 semester hours to practice teaching, leaving 15 elective. Two other options.

[f] IDAHO—Fifteen hours required, but practice teaching is recommended, not required. Neither is any other course required.

[g] ILLINOIS—With 5 hours of practice teaching recommended but not required, and 5 hours elective work permitted.

[h] INDIANA—All courses named with no electives, yet requirements say *approximately* such courses are required as are listed.

[i] LOUISIANA—For class 1-A Professional Certificate. Of 18 semester hours, 4 are in practice teaching.

** MASSACHUSETTS—For state-aided high schools only.

[j] MICHIGAN—Besides practice teaching for 5 hours, four subjects or their equivalents listed. If these are taken at 2 semester hours each, the elective balance is 7 hours as given here.

[l] NEW HAMPSHIRE—The candidate must also pass certain examinations or take certain courses. See state certification requirements.

[m] NEW YORK—This span occurs because the four areas required are given from 2 to 6 hours and from 2 to 9 hours. Subtracting the totals from the 18 hours required gives this figure used.

[n] OREGON—This considers the courses required as of 2 semester hours each where they could be 3 just as well. This considers the 10 hours of graduate work required as of February 10, 1941.

[o] RHODE ISLAND—Because of the requirement stated in terms of clock hours, comparable figures cannot be given here with exactness. No credit for less than 30 or for more than 50 clock hours will be permitted for any subject. 400 clock hours required.

[p] UTAH—Two hours each for four courses and 6⅔ semester hours for training all subtracted from 18 hours.

[q] WASHINGTON—A span of semester hour requirements is given for this commonwealth, leaving a span of electives.

souri, on the other hand, lists from 3 to 9 hours of elective work, but gives three broad fields in which to take the courses.*

So it develops that even where electives, so-called, are permitted, there is still prescription. The size and type of such allocation vary greatly but amount to not an inconsiderable total of prescribed courses, when the other prescribed courses are taken into account. Even so, some freedom is permitted in a number of the states in the selection of types and contents of courses. Wherever freedom is permitted, limitations are diminished. Where prescription plays an active role, limitations increase numerically and in strength, which cannot be measured because of the variable factors involved.

* Some of the electives in certain states include courses that are required in other commonwealths. In the past two years several of these courses have changed from the elective category to required status, presumably to give institutions an opportunity to meet the requirement.

4. *Administrative policies and practices relative to professional requirements reveal considerable interstate freedom but also numerous limitations.* Despite the many professional courses required among the states, only six states require courses that have specific titles.[25] Colleges throughout the nation, therefore, do not have to offer sharply delineated course titles, provided the content of the courses can be certified by registrars[26] as meeting the professional requirements. To illustrate, the course "Principles of Secondary Education" may be titled by several other names, but if the content is satisfactory, the course can be used to meet the requirement. Equivalency of content and not of title is the criterion. In obtaining evidence to support this statement, eighty professional courses were taken at random among the states, and their titles were altered. The question was then asked whether or not the state officials would accept these courses to meet their particular requirements.

Equivalents, however, are not accepted by most states in lieu of the written certification requirements.[27] A course in "Principles of Education" may not be offered for a course in "History of Education," for example. The problem of specific versus general training comes into the picture because some professional courses give an awareness to certain problems but do not give technical information. In requiring one subject a state thereby ignores other courses, perhaps just as important.

As certification requirements are now administered, a teacher who has a master's degree with one year's experience beyond that required by forty-five states and who does not meet a particular four-hour requirement in a certain course, may not be able to obtain certification. Cubberley, in 1906, declared that differences in requirements and refusal to accept equivalents were two of the greatest certification problems of that time. *These two difficulties are still unsolved and persistent problems.*

Further investigation reveals that only two states require attendance at in-state institutions of higher learning to meet professional requirements.[28] Teachers may therefore meet most professional course requirements by attendance at any approved institution offer-

[25] Data from question 13, State Certification Data Sheet. See Appendix A.
[26] Data from question 20, State Certification Data Sheet. See Appendix A.
[27] Data from question 19, State Certification Data Sheet. See Appendix A.
[28] Data from question 14, State Certification Data Sheet. See Appendix A.

ing such courses. The certification officials in forty-seven states revealed that they make no conscious differentiation among persons from inside and from outside the state.[29] The state officials certificate persons on equal terms regardless of residence.

Apparently there is strict adherence to the certification requirements, for only three states even partially waive their professional requirements for in-state applicants or for those from other commonwealths.[30]

Conclusions

Professional requirements vary from 6 semester hours in Connecticut to 28⅔ semester hours in Oregon and 24 in Alabama, Arizona, California, and Texas. Adjoining states often differ widely in the required amounts of professional training. The total professional requirements in most states are low, amounting to something less than one-eighth of a four-year collegiate program. Numerically, these professional requirements do not burden the liberal arts colleges that are training teachers as much as the academic requirements burden the teachers colleges.

The professional requirements are allocated completely in but six states. The amount of such allocation in the remaining forty-two states is considerable, 49 per cent of the total amount of professional work being prescribed. On the other hand, five states permit absolute freedom in the selection of courses to meet the professional requirements. One of these commonwealths restricts out-of-state teachers in other ways. The amounts of electives permitted in the other states range from 18 hours to none at all. Even where elective freedom is supposedly permitted, investigation reveals suggested, listed, or circumscribed fields.

Few states definitely require exactly titled courses, depending upon equivalency of content instead. Courses of different content are not accepted in most states to meet professional requirements. Regardless of experience or previous training, a teacher must meet all requirements in every state. In thirty-seven states an inexperienced, trained teacher must meet all requirements in detail before he is permitted to teach. Nine commonwealths give one one-year temporary

[29] Data from question 15, State Certification Data Sheet. See Appendix A.
[30] Data from question 16, State Certification Data Sheet. See Appendix A.

certificate to inexperienced, trained teachers not meeting every detail of the requirements. Ten states give such to experienced, trained teachers.

Chapter Summary

Limitations and restrictions are almost entirely absent from the degree requirements and practices. In the academic standards are found numerous limitations, particularly in the varying amounts of subject matter required. The total allocation and prescription of both the academic and the professional requirements, amounting to as much as 95 per cent of the college program, constitute a considerable group of limitations for out-of-state teachers. The statement regarding interstate freedom, so apparent in the survey of degree requirements, must now be modified in terms of the findings with reference to academic and professional courses.

The wide variety of *limitations* in the forty-eight commonwealths was indicated by the materials of this chapter. It is evident, however, that if there are many *restrictions* as established by the definition originally given, they must be sought in practice teaching requirements, in specific state requirements, or in community employment policies. These topics are treated in this order in the following chapters.

CHAPTER IV

PRACTICE TEACHING REQUIREMENTS, RESTRICTIONS AND LIMITATIONS

This chapter presents an analysis of various phases of the practice teaching requirements to indicate the restrictions and limitations in them.

Practice teaching, student teaching, or cadet work is a distinct type of certification requirement, differing from other courses in its content, method, and purpose. It usually includes actual classroom instructing by the cadet under supervision, and observation by and conferences with the supervising teacher. This cadet work has become firmly established in other occupations and professions, a notable example being medicine, where more time and responsibility are usually given the "intern" than in education. Valentine says in this regard:

> Advocates of compulsory practice teaching use medical interneships as an argument. The parallel between interneships in medicine and practice teaching for schools is not a sound one. No medical student enters upon interneship until after he has really mastered his subject of medicine—for reasons obvious to those who go to hospitals as patients. But most teaching candidates have not mastered their subjects of instruction, as the American Council report clearly states. In time spent in intensive content education, those who begin practice teaching are from three to four years behind the medical student beginning his interneship. We are far more cautious about turning a hospital patient over to an interne than we are about turning thirty defenceless school children over to a far less qualified practice teacher.[1]

The professional importance of practice teaching has been indicated by several writers, among them Whitney[2] and Ullman,[3] who

[1] Alan Valentine, "Teacher Training versus Teacher Education," *The Educational Record,* XIX (July, 1938), 342.

[2] E. L. Whitney, *The Prediction of Teaching Success.* Public School Publishing Company, Bloomington, Ill., 1924. Pp. 85.

[3] R. R. Ullman, *The Prognostic Value of Certain Factors Related to Teaching Success.* Ashland College, Ashland, Ohio, 1931. Pp. 133.

rank such a course as first among the criteria of later teaching success. On the other hand, criticisms have been made of the practice teaching requirements as at present constituted. For example, Valentine makes the following searching comment:

> There is also need for a detached and scientific inquiry into the necessity of the present practice teaching requirements. Should so many hours of practice teaching be an absolute requirement for all? Are there not cases in which a broader and deeper understanding of the subjects to be taught would be in the long run more valuable than a running start into the technique of instructing a class? Colleges and universities select young men for instructorships largely on the basis of their scholarship and promise. They often give three-year appointments to young men who have not had any teaching experience. They estimate a candidate's chances of becoming a good teacher, but they do not take a poor scholar even if he thinks he teaches well. If such young instructors have been wisely chosen, they usually prove satisfactory teachers, sometimes even brilliant ones, under conditions no less exacting than those in the schools. Some of the best teachers in college now, and in school in my time, never read a book on educational psychology, or underwent formal instruction in teaching. Their methods of instruction differ widely; each has worked out his own method consistent with his own personality. Formalized instruction in teaching methods might have robbed them of the originality that makes them effective.[4]

Notwithstanding these arguments, there seems to be need of a well-considered, probationary period for beginning teachers or students just completing their training program. Some would have observation and even participation during the four years of training, including practice teaching later in their program. Others point out that such observation work, though not in every instance the best possible, is of considerable help to the student teacher. It brings the school and the training institution closer together, with advantages to both. The fact that practice teaching is not yet ideal does not detract from the need and usefulness of such training; rather, it indicates that considerable revision and improvement are needed.

Despite the controversy, thirty-nine commonwealths require practice teaching for certification of all high school teachers of academic subjects.

With regard to limitations and restrictions, the questions which this chapter will discuss are as follows:

[4] Valentine, *op. cit.*, pp. 341–342.

1. What are the various amounts of the practice teaching requirements among the states?
2. How many *clock* hours of practice teaching are asked for each *semester* hour of the college course requirement?
3. Is *teaching* experience accepted in lieu of *practice* teaching? If so, how much experience is accepted?
4. What is the level[5] required for practice teaching?
5. What restrictions and limitations are there present in the practice teaching requirements?

1. *The amount of practice teaching required among the states varies widely.*

In spite of the professional importance of practice teaching, as indicated by writers on the subject, nine states do not have such a requirement for secondary school certification. Of the remaining states, thirty-seven give the requirements in terms of semester hours and two in terms of clock hours of teaching. Table XIII shows the amounts of the various requirements for the forty-eight states.

The states not requiring practice teaching are Maine, Massachusetts, and New Hampshire in New England, Delaware on the Atlantic seaboard, South Carolina in the South, Illinois in the Midwest, and Idaho, Montana, and North Dakota in the Rocky Mountain area. Of these, Massachusetts requires 12 semester hours of education in at least two of nine fields specified for state-aided high schools only. A student is free, however, to include two or more of the other subjects specified and to omit practice teaching. New Hampshire includes cadet teaching as an elective only. Idaho and Illinois recommend practice teaching, but it is not mandatory.

A great variety of detailed regulations prevails among the states requiring practice teaching. Some commonwealths, Alabama, for example, require the practice teaching in the major or minor subject; others mention only that such cadet work is required. Others, like New Jersey and Rhode Island, state their requirements in terms of clock hours, with detailed regulations within such. New Jersey, for instance, asks that 90 clock hours be in actual classroom teaching, with the remaining 60 clock hours in observation and conference.

[5] That is, on what school level, elementary, junior high, or high school, can the practice teaching be completed for high school certification?

TABLE XIII

Minimum Requirements in Student Teaching for High School Certificates Issued to Inexperienced Teachers of Academic High School Subjects on a Basis of Four Years of College Preparation, February, 1941 *

State	Number of Semester Hours Required of Student Teaching	State	Number of Semester Hours Required of Student Teaching
Alabama	3 [a]	Nebraska	3 [x]
Arizona	5 [b]	Nevada	4 [y]
Arkansas	5–6 [c]	New Hampshire	0 [z]
California	4 [d]	New Jersey	6 [aa]
Colorado	4 [e]	New Mexico	4 [bb]
Connecticut	6 [f]	New York	2–6 [cc]
Delaware	0 [g]	North Carolina	3 [dd]
Florida	6 [h]	North Dakota	0
Georgia	3 [i]	Ohio	3–5 [ee]
Idaho	0 [j]	Oklahoma	4 [ff]
Illinois	0 [k]	Oregon	2 [gg]
Indiana	3 [l]	Pennsylvania	6 [hh]
Iowa	3 [m]	Rhode Island	400 cl. hrs. [ii]
Kansas	3 [n]	South Carolina	0 [jj]
Kentucky	6 [o]	South Dakota	3 [kk]
Louisiana	4 [p]	Tennessee	2 [ll]
Maine	0	Texas	6 [mm]
Maryland	4 [q]	Utah	5⅓ [nn]
Massachusetts	0 [r]	Vermont	3 [oo]
Michigan	5 [s]	Virginia	6 [pp]
Minnesota	3 [t]	Washington	2⅔ [qq]
Mississippi	9 [u]	West Virginia	5 [rr]
Missouri	5 [v]	Wisconsin	5 [ss]
Montana	0 [w]	Wyoming	2 [tt]

Mean average ** 4.56 semester hours for 39 states having such requirements. Mode 3 hours range 0–21 semester hours. Mean average is 3.7 semester hours for all 48 states.

* State Boards and Departments of Education, Rules and Regulations governing the certification of teachers, February, 1941. See Bibliography. The rules and regulations may be secured upon request of the State Departments of Education or comparable offices. See also data sheets in Appendix A. Some of these data show the requirements for a slightly later period where a transition was then in process in a definite form with full authorization.

** Round number. Figures 4.49 semester hours.

[a] ALABAMA—Directed teaching in major or minor subject. See Table XVI for exceptions for teaching experience.

[b] ARIZONA—Not less than 5 semester hours in practice teaching in grades 7 to 12, inclusive.

[c] ARKANSAS—Directed teaching. Shall be in student's major or minor field. All courses in such on senior college level and only students in upper 75 per cent in scholarship may enroll.

[d] CALIFORNIA—Directed teaching.

[e] COLORADO—4 semester hours practice teaching required.

[f] CONNECTICUT—Laboratory course of 90 clock hours of observation and practice teaching and at least 60 hours in responsible practice teaching under supervision required of all those entering the service September 1, 1941.

[g] DELAWARE—The 18 semester hours required are in the aims and methods of secondary education and *may* include, among others, 6 semester hours of practice teaching. Regulations are permissive, not mandatory.

[h] FLORIDA—Beginning September 1, 1941, this requirement changed from 3 to 6 semester hours, in option 2 of requirements. Others include teaching experience and an interneship program. See rules and regulations of the state education department.

[i] GEORGIA—Directed observation and practice teaching in typical high school situations.

[j] IDAHO—After January 1, 1938, 3 semester hours of practice teaching were recommended but not required.

[k] ILLINOIS—Five semester hours of practice teaching recommended but not required.

[l] INDIANA—Supervised teaching.

[m] IOWA—Directed observation and supervised student teaching.

[n] KANSAS—Supervised practice teaching.

[o] KENTUCKY—Supervised student teaching with at least 3 semester hours in the secondary school.

[p] LOUISIANA—Two session hours in practice teaching in the subject or subjects specialized, for Class 1-A professional certificate. One session hour equals two semester hours.

[q] MARYLAND—Special methods. Observation (at least 10 group observations and 10 additional) and supervised practice teaching (from ten to twenty periods).

[r] MASSACHUSETTS—Practice teaching is only one of several options. This requirement is for only state-aided schools.

[s] MICHIGAN—Directed teaching in secondary grades.

[t] MINNESOTA—Observation and practice teaching.

[u] MISSISSIPPI—Materials, methods, observation and practice teaching in the secondary schools.

[v] MISSOURI—Supervised teaching in the high schools. Student or apprentice teaching.

[w] MONTANA—Nothing said about practice teaching.

[x] NEBRASKA—In supervised teaching in grades 7–12. Initial plan.

[y] NEVADA—Of practice teaching.

[z] NEW HAMPSHIRE—Cadet teaching is one of 11 subjects which may be considered as work in education, however, as an elective.

[aa] NEW JERSEY—The requirement calls for 150 clock hours, 90 of which must be in actual classroom teaching and the remaining 60 clock hours in observation and conference. "The requirement is usually covered by six semester hours of work at Rutgers University, New Brunswick, New Jersey," for example. Letter to the author, from W. A. Ackerman, Secretary, State Board of Examiners, New Jersey, January 5, 1941.

[bb] NEW MEXICO—In supervised teaching.

[cc] NEW YORK—The range is from 2 to 6 semester hours in supervised student practice teaching in secondary schools, including conferences on teaching problems.

[dd] NORTH CAROLINA—Observation and directed teaching.

[ee] OHIO—Student teaching in grades 7–12.

[ff] OKLAHOMA—Four semester hours in apprentice teaching in secondary schools for the one-year certificate; six for the life certificate.

[gg] OREGON—Supervised teaching under essentially secondary school conditions.

[hh] PENNSYLVANIA—Student teaching—based on not less than 180 clock hours of actual teaching under approved supervision, including the necessary observation, participation, and conference.

[ii] RHODE ISLAND—Compliance with the 400-clock hour requirement of practice teaching is proved by certificate naming the school and critic teacher, and the grade or the subject in which the practice teaching was undertaken, identifying the period of time from date to date within which the practice teaching occurred, specifying the actual time of practice teaching in clock hours, and signed by a properly certificated and approved critic teacher. *Practice teaching for credit must be rendered in Rhode Island schools.* Using 40 clock hours for each course, the equivalent is used as 10 courses or 20 semester hours.

[jj] SOUTH CAROLINA—Nothing regarding practice teaching in regulations.

[kk] SOUTH DAKOTA—Of practice teaching in major or minor subjects.

[ll] TENNESSEE—Directed or practice teaching listed as part C of education requirements—*Tennessee Educational Bulletin*, Vol. XVII, No. 4, p. 7. Nashville, Tennessee. Dec. 1939.

[mm] TEXAS—No regulations obtained from department in February, 1941, for unknown reason. This figure taken from 1938 records.

[nn] UTAH—Work must include 8 quarter hours or 5⅓ semester hours in training.

[oo] VERMONT—In observation and practice teaching in the public schools. For high school professional probationary certificate.

[*Continued on page 106*]

[pp] VIRGINIA—Supervised student teaching for 3 session hours, 6 semester hours.

[qq] WASHINGTON—Applicants will be required to file satisfactory evidence of having completed four quarter hours of directed teaching.

[rr] WEST VIRGINIA—Directed teaching of 90 clock hours. This shall be completed on the junior or senior high school level in the fields designated on the certificate. Each semester hour shall require a minimum of 18 clock hours consisting of at least 50 minutes in the classroom. Of the total clock hours submitted for the minimum requirement, a maximum in observation shall not exceed 30 per cent.

[ss] WISCONSIN—Practice teaching.

[tt] WYOMING—Supervised teaching.

Rhode Island requires that the name of the school and the critic teacher be entered on the certificate, together with grade, subject, time span covered, and number of clock hours of actual teaching completed. Furthermore, *the practice teaching for credit must be rendered in the Rhode Island schools.* West Virginia goes into almost as much detail by requiring that the clock hour of practice teaching consist of at least 50 minutes in the classroom. The type of activities in the classroom is tacitly understood to be actual teaching. Table XIV gives a recapitulation of the amounts of practice teaching required in the forty-eight states.

From no practice teaching standards at all in nine commonwealths, the requirements range to two different maximum amounts with different units: *9 semester hours* in one state and *400 clock hours* in another. The limitations involved in the variations in the requirements become more apparent after considering their practical application. For example, not all students take practice teaching courses in their training programs; in fact, a survey of 61,563 teachers in forty-eight states shows that 24 per cent had no credit for practice teaching.[6] Then, too, students in the nine states that do not require practice teaching may not take such a course if it is not required. It follows that teachers without practice teaching experience would find limitations to obtaining certification in even the three states which have two-hour practice teaching requirements. Similarly, teachers in these three commonwealths would encounter limitations in going into the ten states with the three semester hour standard, or into the three states between the two and three hour standard, in addition to all the states with still higher practice teaching requirements. Finally, teachers from every other state in the Union would have difficulty in ob-

[6] E. S. Evenden, Guy C. Gamble, and Harold G. Blue, *Teacher Personnel in the United States.* National Survey of Education of Teachers, U. S. Office of Education, Bulletin No. 10, Vol. 11. Government Printing Office, Washington, D. C., 1935. Pp. 258.

TABLE XIV

Semester Hours of Practice Teaching Required for Academic Secondary Teaching Certificates in the Forty-Eight States, February, 1941

Amount of Requirement in Semester Hours	Number of States
0	9[a]
2	3[b]
2⅔	1[c]
2–6	1[d]
3	10[e]
3–5	1[f]
4	7[g]
5	5[h]
5⅓	1[i]
5–6	1[j]
6	7[k]
9	1[l]
400 clock hours (20 semester hours)	1[m]

[a] Delaware, Idaho, Illinois, Maine, Massachusetts, Montana, New Hampshire, North Dakota, and South Carolina.
[b] Oregon, Tennessee, and Wyoming.
[c] Washington.
[d] New York.
[e] Alabama, Georgia, Indiana, Iowa, Kansas, Minnesota, Nebraska, North Carolina, South Dakota, and Vermont.
[f] Ohio.
[g] California, Colorado, Louisiana, Maryland, Nevada, New Mexico, and Oklahoma.
[h] Arizona, Michigan, Missouri, West Virginia, Wisconsin.
[i] Utah.
[j] Arkansas.
[k] Connecticut, Florida, Kentucky, New Jersey, Pennsylvania, Texas, and Virginia.
[l] Mississippi.
[m] Rhode Island. This amount used arbitrarily.

taining certification in Rhode Island, which has a practice teaching requirement of 400 clock hours that must be fulfilled in the Rhode Island public schools.[7] This last requirement is the only restriction in the United States, but a number of limitations are apparent in merely the *amount* of practice teaching required.

Geographically, teachers seeking certificates in any two or more

[7] The certification officials in this commonwealth obtain the number of clock hours by multiplying the number of times the class meets each week by the number of weeks the class is in session during the semester (Letter to the writer from Dorothy F. Betts, Certification Clerk, Department of Education, State House, Providence, Rhode Island, December 26, 1939). For example, a class meeting three times a week for fifteen weeks is the equivalent of forty-five clock hours.

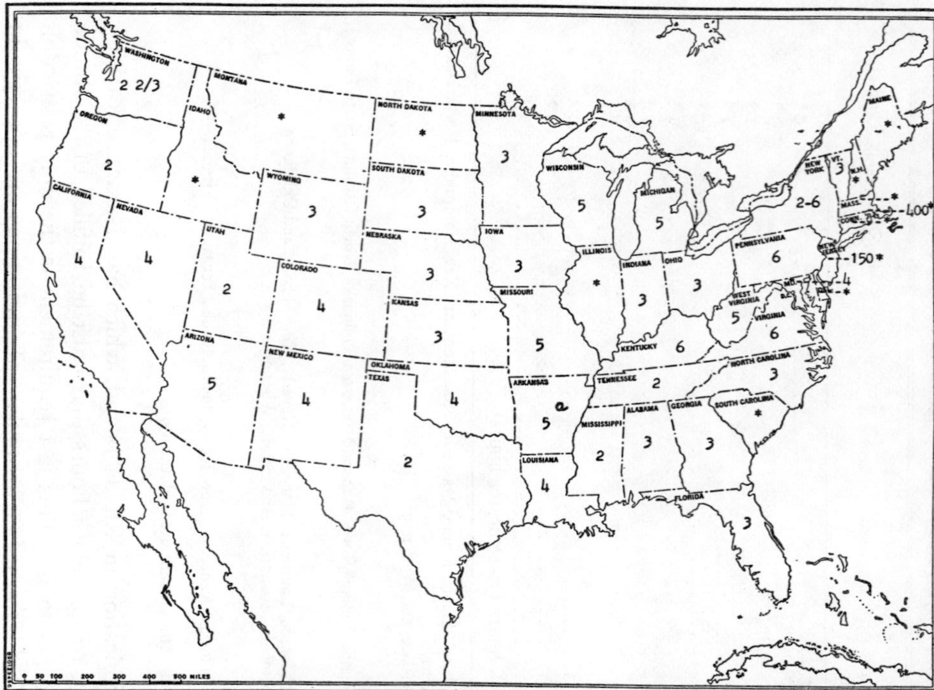

FIGURE 7. The Amount of Practice Teaching Required by the Forty-Eight States, February, 1941

* Practice teaching not required.

In some instances, practice teaching is recommended but not essential for certificate. Clock hours used as units in New Jersey and Rhode Island. The rest are in semester-hour units.

[a] Ninety clock hours or the equivalent. [b] Beginning Sept. 1, 1941, ninety clock hours of observation and practice teaching required.

states would find that the distribution of total practice teaching requirements varies widely, as Figure 7 clearly indicates. In the Pacific Coast and the Northwestern States the variations are particularly noticeable. Washington, Idaho, California, Utah, Oregon, and Arizona all have different amounts of practice teaching requirements. This is true, too, for the New England and Middle Atlantic States—Vermont, Massachusetts, Rhode Island, New Jersey, and Maryland all differ.

In the Northwest and Rocky Mountain areas, if teachers registered for practice teaching courses only in the amount required by their own states, the teachers in Washington, Oregon, Nevada, Idaho, and Wyoming would experience difficulty in obtaining a certificate in California or Utah. On the other hand, teachers in these two states would have no difficulty in meeting the practice teaching requirements in the first five commonwealths, which have lower requirements in this regard.

Similarly, in the Southwest, teachers who had taken only the minimum requirements in Oklahoma would experience some difficulty in meeting the practice teaching requirements of Mississippi and Texas. Those from Louisiana would experience limitations in Arkansas, Texas and Mississippi. On the other hand, teachers meeting the practice teaching requirements in the last-named commonwealths could meet at least the semester-hour practice teaching standards anywhere in the United States, with the exception of Rhode Island. Similar comparisons could be made for any group of states. These differences, with one exception, are not restrictions (inasmuch as a person need not meet the given requirement within any particular state), but they are limitations.

Some Effects of Limitations

The effects of these limitations are especially severe on the inexperienced, trained teacher who concludes his undergraduate courses usually in June, the time when most superintendents have either employed their teachers for the following year or are actively engaged in doing so. If a prospective teacher has two semester hours of practice teaching and needs three or more to teach in a given state, how and where can he obtain this cadet work? Practice teaching courses are not offered by all colleges that are open during the summer because practice teaching means classes to be taught and pupils are not always available during the summer vacation period. Often colleges enroll the children of faculty members and of students attending summer school in demonstration classes, but in this situation classes are visited usually to learn new techniques from skilled teachers, not to watch inexperienced practice teachers. The latter therefore do not have an opportunity to do much actual teaching under supervision or to obtain credit for it. Often applicants find it impossible to take the extra hours required except in their own undergraduate colleges where they first had practice teaching, and again, this is often not possible because of limited student teaching assignments. The financial problem is also limiting for teachers who have just been graduated and who, in addition to expenses for baccalaureate degree, must then attend summer school for a practice teaching course, if such is available, to meet a requirement in some other state.

Administrators tend to employ the applicant who is already certificated or who is assured in writing that he qualifies for such a certificate. In these cases, where other qualifications are fairly similar, the applicant needing another hour or so of practice teaching loses out in competition for the position. More often than not, the loser is an out-of-state person who lacks some details in meeting the requirements. Practice teaching offers numerous detailed requirements that cause such difficulties.

However, sometimes teachers take practice teaching courses for a larger number of semester hours than their own states require for certification. Evenden, Gamble, and Blue, including this problem in a survey of teacher personnel in the United States,[8] showed that of 61,563 persons responding in their study, the first quartile range of credit for practice teaching was from two to six semester hours, the median from four to twelve, and the third quartile from six to nineteen. In some of the states that do not require practice teaching for certification, it was found the median number of hours taken by teachers were: Idaho, Illinois, Maine, and Massachusetts, 6 each; Montana, 5; New Hampshire, 12; and South Carolina, 5. Apparently the institutions request more practice teaching than the states require

[8] Evenden, Gamble, and Blue, *op. cit.*, p. 58. Adapted from Table 17, column 11. See Appendix C.

for certification, or they offer more, with the students enrolling for larger amounts than needed in the particular commonwealth for certification. Professionally this is a good situation because state certification requirements are looked upon as minima above which the individuals and institutions are urged to go.

More serious, on the other hand, is the fact that 24 per cent [8] of the teachers responding to the national survey just indicated had no credit for practice teaching. This group would find many limitations in attempting to obtain certificates to teach in thirty-six states. Then too, a number of commonwealths now *require for certification* a larger amount of practice teaching than the median amount taken by teachers answering the survey in these respective states. In two states, Pennsylvania and Virginia, the state requirements are equal to the median amount of semester hours taken by the responding teachers, but greater than the first quartile amount. Considering the large number of widely different teacher-training institutions, the variation in practice teaching courses, the differences in state practice teaching requirements, the details of these standards, and the variability of student enrollment, the number of limitations is seen to be quite large.

Administrative problems with regard to student teaching courses and requirements are numerous for the teacher-training institutions. If a given state requires more semester hours of practice teaching than an institution offers, how can students in that college meet the particular state requirements? Administratively, for any group at a given time it is difficult for colleges to change the hours given in any certain course. Sometimes it is impossible for some colleges to meet certain state requirements for practice teaching.

Student Problems

Two different types of problems exist for the student in meeting practice teaching standards: First, he may find it impossible to obtain the practice teaching needed at the institution he is attending because the course with the needed amount or detail is not given; second, the course may be available but the student may have taken a different amount of hours in such a course from that required by any given state. It is true that with adequate guidance, a student can plan ahead and with administrative offerings favorable, can meet most of such requirements. Often, however, he is limited by the varied practice teaching requirements, by changing certification standards, or by lack of guidance.

Graduates of liberal arts colleges encounter severe limitations in the practice teaching requirements of some states. For example, the older liberal arts colleges in New England find it difficult to meet the practice teaching requirements of some of the Eastern states, such as New Jersey's 150 clock-hour practice teaching requirement, or that in Rhode Island. Few liberal arts colleges honestly give the required number of hours in such a course. The graduates of liberal arts colleges in New England and on the Eastern seaboard seem to be severely limited by such requirements. Even graduates of teachers colleges often find difficulty in meeting such standards. These requirements tend to "close the door" of teaching to many graduates of the best liberal arts colleges in the country as well as to many graduates of some teachers colleges. A deep-seated conflict between the liberal arts colleges and the teachers colleges is revealed in these practice

TABLE XV

Number of Clock Hours Required by the States for Each Semester Hour of the Practice Teaching Requirements, February, 1941 *

Number of Clock Hours Required for Each Semester Hour	Number of States	Number of Clock Hours Required for Each Sem. Hr.	Number of States	Downward Cumulative Total of States with Less Requirement than Those at Level or Below
Left to standards of		10......	1	9
institutions.........	1	13......	1	10
		15......	4	11
		18......	10	15
Did not answer		20......	2	25
question...........	12	22.5....	2	27
		30......	3	29
		38......	1	132
No practice teaching		150 cl. hrs...	1	33
requirements.......	9	400 cl. hrs...	1	34

* In this table, one state, for example, requires 10 clock hours of teaching for each semester hour of the practice teaching requirement. Persons who had planned only on meeting their own state requirements in the 9 commonwealths requiring no student teaching would meet severe limitations in going to this or any of the other 39 states. Similarly, persons in at least 29 states would encounter limitations in trying to meet the standards in the commonwealth asking for 30 clock hours. Similarly, persons in 34 states would have extreme difficulty in meeting the 400 clock hour requirement in Rhode Island. In every case in the right-hand column, 12 states must be deducted from possible number because 12 states did not answer.

teaching requirements, with the administrative weapon of certification on the side of the latter.

Sometimes these differences in semester hours can be counteracted by the number of clock hours which the student teachers have taught. The variation in semester hours can sometimes be overlooked if the student has taught the required number of hours. This brings up the following problem:

2. *There is no uniformity in the number of clock hours of practice teaching required.*

The total requirement of practice teaching has been discussed but not the details within those standards, such as the number of clock hours of practice teaching required for each semester hour. Table XV reveals a wide range.

3. *Teaching experience is not always accepted in lieu of practice teaching.*

Often a teacher with considerable experience in teaching may have had no practice teaching course in his college program of studies. Whether commonwealths will accept that experience for the practice teaching course is a problem for such a teacher. Table XVI gives an indication of actual practices among the states in February, 1941.

Teaching experience is accepted in lieu of practice teaching in fourteen states. The length of experience accepted, however, varies greatly. Two states will accept eight months of experience, while four states will accept three years. Stress apparently is laid on these requirements of supervised teaching. *Six states will not accept any amount of teaching experience in lieu of practice teaching.* Limitations are present for the experienced teacher as well as the inexperienced one in trying to obtain certificates in some states.

Practice Teaching versus Teaching Experience

In view of the rather low median number of years a person remains in the teaching profession, these limitations are stronger than might at first be thought. Inflexibility in the application of these requirements is also present. Why should a state not accept experience in lieu of practice teaching when in that experience the state has a commonly acceptable criterion of future success? Such a policy does not

TABLE XVI

Amount of Teaching Experience Accepted in Lieu of Practice Teaching Requirements of the General Academic Secondary School Certification Standards of the Forty-Eight States, February, 1941

Policy	Number States Having Policy	Policy	Number States Having Policy
8 months	2 [a]	Experience not accepted in lieu of practice teaching	6 [i]
1 year	1 [b]		
16 months	1 [c]		
21 months	1 [d]		
2 years	3 [e]		
3 years	4 [f]	No answer	22
5 years	1 [g]	No practice teaching required	9
Experience accepted but no amount given	2 [h]		

[a] California and Washington.

[b] New Jersey.

[c] Florida, according to one of three options.

[d] Georgia. This means presumably 21 months of teaching, which is a greater chronological span than two calendar years in category *c*.

[e] Nevada, Vermont, Virginia.

[f] Alabama, Arkansas, Colorado, Kansas and Kentucky.

[g] Virginia.

[h] Oregon, Missouri and Wisconsin.

[i] On the data sheets returned from these states, the statement was made that experience was not acceptable in lieu of cadet teaching.

invite experienced teachers into a state; rather, it restricts them more or less severely. It narrows the potential teaching field of a teacher. What is there so revealing in practice teaching that experience cannot be accepted in lieu of such a course? Even in one year of teaching, a teacher has already accomplished more actual teaching with greater responsibility for his achievement than in most if not all practice teaching courses, yet only three states accept that one year of teaching or a close approximation in place of practice teaching courses.

The grade received by the practice teacher is not of importance to the state education department insofar as certification is concerned. Evidence that the course has been completed satisfactorily usually suffices. Some states ask for *successful teaching* experience, without mentioning the criterion for that success. No information is usually requested as to the responsibilities of the practice teacher or the direct outcomes of his cadet teaching with specific regard to his successes or failures in personnel adjustments with students or teaching staff.

A consideration of the factors pro and con the non-acceptance of teaching experience in lieu of supervised teaching, or the acceptance only of several years of teaching, leads to the conclusion that the certification requirements of many states have not been carefully thought through.

There are several arguments in favor of the acceptance of experience in lieu of cadet teaching: The student teacher, although carrying some responsibilities, does not have the full burden of the classroom teaching and so may avoid some of the best possible learning situations that the employed teacher has. The regular teacher must meet emergencies and the occasional critical situation; on the other hand, the cadet teacher can turn to the supervising teacher for aid, and knowingly or not, escape the best learning opportunities. The classroom teacher starts the class at the beginning of the year, provides the background, takes the students through the year, and concludes the year's learning experiences with a continuity of teaching that the practice teacher seldom receives. Without the background and the experience which the regular teacher obtains, the cadet teacher often participates in a mechanical or a theoretical way with isolated objectives or plans. Sometimes the cadet teacher is allowed to teach once a week for a semester, sometimes less, often more. The arguments seem to be in favor of accepting experience in lieu of practice teaching.

The claim occasionally is made that the specified and rigidly enforced practice teaching requirements are of value, for otherwise the weak teacher might be admitted. This argument is based on the factor of restricting the poorly qualified teacher, but it almost always ignores the fact that the better qualified teacher and the superior teacher are also limited in moving across state boundaries.

4. *Practice teaching is usually required on the level of the desired certificate.*

It is important in this study to find out if states require that practice teaching courses for high school certification, be completed in a secondary school class. Twenty-three states[9] require that the cadet teaching be accomplished on the level of the certificate desired. Four

[9] Alabama, Arizona, Arkansas, Connecticut, Georgia, Kentucky, Louisiana, Maryland, Michigan, Minnesota, Mississippi, Nebraska, New Jersey, New York, Ohio,

commonwealths accept cadet teaching on any level for high school certification, and nine do not require practice teaching. Kentucky requires that the last three of six semester hours be completed on the level of the license, while some accept practice teaching in the elementary grades for secondary certification. Arizona, Nebraska, and Ohio request the practice teaching in grades 7 to 12, inclusive. Georgia asks for such training in typical high school situations. Louisiana, Minnesota, South Dakota, and Tennessee want the practice teaching in the subject specialty or major. Others, like New Jersey, want *approved* training which implies close attention to the level on which practice teaching is carried on. In twenty-three states it is difficult for an elementary teacher to obtain a high school certificate because such a procedure would require his taking another practice teaching course on the high school level. This is true regardless of the number of years the elementary teacher has taught or the success he has achieved. The argument that a good elementary teacher should remain in the elementary grades does not help with the problem. This type of requirement tends to "freeze" the elementary teachers in the lower grades unless they can obtain practice teaching in high school in the evenings, over week ends, during the academic year, or during the summer vacation.

5. *Some administrative factors vary with regard to practice teaching requirements.*

Investigation of administrative practices of the commonwealths indicates that thirty-nine reporting on this problem maintain the identical requirements for practice teaching whether the person is from within the respective state or from outside. Only Rhode Island requires practice teaching to be rendered in its public schools.

Problem of Out-of-State Teachers

It is important to note that prospective teachers in any given commonwealth have probably planned to meet that state's requirements and have been able to do so because the college program and courses are "geared" to satisfy that particular commonwealth's requirements.

Oklahoma, Oregon, Pennsylvania, Rhode Island, South Dakota, Tennessee, Utah, and West Virginia.

Those coming from other states have attended any of a great number of different institutions, with diversified opportunities of meeting or failing to satisfy a requirement. They have not been able to take advantage of a college program integrated with the particular state's requirements; no doubt they have had an entire program of courses different in content or detail from those needed for certification.

The problem for out-of-state prospective teachers is complicated by the fact that the practice teaching requirements in all their details are usually strictly enforced by the states, which usually demand that the details be completely satisfied before certification is given. Few of the practice teaching requirements are waived by the states, so far as this study reveals. Through no fault of their own, therefore, many very capable prospective teachers are restricted from other commonwealths because of the limitations and restrictions in requirements and practices which tend to "screen" out applicants, not on their professional ability but on the chance meeting of detailed requirements which vary from state to state and which do not in the end actually guarantee professional promise. Of all the requirements the practice teaching standard is probably one of the most limiting because of the differences in the amounts required, the clock hours demanded, the acceptance or non-acceptance of experience, the level on which practice teaching is required, and administrative policies of the states.

CONCLUSIONS

Numerous limitations exist in the variations of practice teaching requirements, which range from none at all in nine states to nine semester hours in one commonwealth. The mode lies at three semester hours. New Jersey and Rhode Island present their standards in different categories or measurement, asking 150 and 400 clock hours, respectively. A difference of even one semester hour between the number of hours taken in a course and the number required by any given commonwealth presents a difficult problem for the prospective teacher, and consequently a limitation for him. Of 61,563 teachers responding to a national survey questionnaire, a total of 24 per cent had no credit for practice teaching. By starting with those nine states with no practice teaching requirement and ranging up the scale to the commonwealths with the highest requirements, it is seen that great numbers of teachers find numerous limitations in trying to cross state lines in what should be a national, professional service.

Geographically, the cadet teaching requirements vary widely, even in near-by states. The effects of these variations are severe, especially on the inexperienced, trained person who is looking for a position. How and where a prospective teacher can obtain an extra semester hour or so of practice teaching is a sizeable problem. Often because of variations, an applicant is penalized.

The differences in practice teaching amounts are made less by the fact that in many commonwealths the students enroll for more practice teaching than is required by their respective states. On the other hand, some enroll for less than their own state demands, and 24 per cent of the 61,563 teachers responding to the national survey questionnaire had not taken any such courses.

The wide variations among the commonwealths in practice teaching standards pose a problem for a teacher-training institution, whose courses are difficult to alter for any group at any given time so as to prepare persons to meet certain standards. This problem is especially acute for liberal arts colleges, though many types of institutions must face the issue involved.

The number of clock hours required for each semester hour of the practice teaching standard varies from ten to thirty-eight. The many different types of colleges, the wide variations in requirements, and the college-school relationships established complicate the problem.

Practice teaching is considered so important that six states will not accept any amount of quality of teaching experience in lieu of such standards. The grade received in practice teaching, however, is not of specified importance. No evaluation of actual teaching is accepted by some commonwealths in place of student teaching.

Twenty-three states require that the student teaching be completed in high school classes for high school certification, while four states accept cadet teaching on any level. Kentucky requires that the last three of six hours be completed on the level of the desired certificate.

Only one state, Rhode Island, requires that the practice teaching be completed within the boundaries of the respective commonwealth. No state, apparently, waives the practice teaching requirement wholly or in part for any applicant, whether from within or outside the state, so far as such is revealed by this study.

CHAPTER V

SPECIFIC STATE REQUIREMENTS, RESTRICTIONS AND LIMITATIONS

THIS chapter presents an analysis of the current specific state certification requirements and indicates their restrictions and limitations. As described in Chapter II, the oldest of these particular standards dates back to the year 1889 in Washington, when that state was admitted into the Union. This requirement included an examination in State School Law and the State Constitution for Washington. *It was unique in that it was applicable only to that commonwealth.* Such a specified course was not like a course requirement in history, English, or science, subjects which could be studied in colleges anywhere in the nation and which were fairly similar to many other state requirements. On the contrary, *the requirement was peculiar to the commonwealth of Washington, with no other state having a similar standard.* Through the years, state after state has included this type of certification requirement until in 1938 there were thirty-nine such requirements in sixteen commonwealths. Presumably the subjects included are intended to increase a knowledge of and devotion to the country, the individual commonwealths, and their institutions.[1] Heterogeneous in nature, these specific requirements include five distinct categories, which are listed below, together with the states requiring them.

Specific State Requirements, 1906 to 1938	*State Making Requirement* [2]
A. National	
United States Constitution	Arizona, California,* Florida,* Nevada, Texas,* Wyoming

[1] Jesse Knowlton Flanders, *Legislative Control of the Elementary School Curriculum.* New York: Bureau of Publications, Teachers College, Columbia University, 1925. Pp. 242.

[2] States which in the latter part of this chapter are found to have provisions that

Specific State Requirements, 1906 to 1938	*State Making Requirement*
B. State	
State Constitution	Arizona, Idaho, Nevada, Texas,* Washington, Wyoming
State Law	Idaho, Kansas,* Montana, Nevada,* New Hampshire,* Ohio,* Oklahoma,* Oregon, Rhode Island,* Texas,* Washington
State Government	Montana
State History	Montana, Oklahoma, Oregon, Rhode Island,* Texas, Washington
State Course of Study	Idaho, Montana
State Manual	Idaho, Montana, Washington
State Secondary Program of Studies	New Hampshire *
State Organization and Administration of Secondary Education	Utah
State Problems of Education	New Mexico,* Rhode Island *
State System of Education	Oregon
C. Residence within the State	Florida,* Idaho, Montana, New Mexico
D. Resident Study in an In-State Institution of Higher Learning	Idaho, Montana, New Mexico
E. Unusual Courses Adapted to State's Needs	Florida, Louisiana

These certification standards are called *specific state requirements* because most of them are unique for a particular commonwealth. For example, Idaho has a requirement that every out-of-state candidate for a high school certificate must have had a course including Idaho School Law. No other commonwealth has this identical requirement, and no institution of higher learning in any of the other forty-seven states offers such a course. It is a specific for Idaho.

In attempting to find the causes of these restrictive or limiting measures, several hypotheses can be advanced. One is that the newer

prevent the requirements from being restrictive in their actual application or which now do not have such a requirement but have had some time since 1906 are indicated by asterisks.

states in the Union adopted restrictive requirements in times of heavy internal population migration. In examining the list of commonwealths[3] which have or have had restrictive, specific state requirements, one finds only four states that are included among the first twenty-four to enter the Union. On the other hand, fourteen commonwealths with specific requirements are in the latter half of the states to become a part of the Union. Furthermore, the last eight to enter all have or have had such restrictive measures. It may have been that in the older commonwealths there was enough time between early settlement and later educational legislation to adjust the supply of and demand for teachers to prevent an oversupply; and restrictive measures therefore were not necessary in most of these states. In the newer states, however, large increases in population through immigration, annexation of territory, and a high birth rate, together with the opening of the frontier, caused a heavy influx of teachers. Then, partly in self-defense, these commonwealths may have erected these certification barriers. Persons were attracted to the West because of the opportunities for land, gold, or a new start in life, and then became part of the large "floating" population. Teachers included in this group would teach in a state for a short time, and then move on to other states. In this connection Miss Hilts, Certification Clerk in Idaho, says:

[3] Chronological order of entrance of the states into the Union is given below. States in which restrictive requirements have appeared since 1889 are indicated by an asterisk.

State	Year	State	Year	State	Year
1. Delaware	1787	17. Ohio	1802	33. Oregon *	1859
2. Pennsylvania	1787	18. Louisiana *	1812	34. Kansas *	1861
3. New Jersey	1787	19. Indiana	1816	35. West Virginia	1863
4. Georgia	1788	20. Mississippi	1817	36. Nevada *	1864
5. Connecticut	1788	21. Illinois	1818	37. Nebraska	1867
6. Massachusetts	1788	22. Alabama	1819	38. Colorado	1876
7. Maryland	1788	23. Maine	1820	39. North Dakota	1889
8. New Hampshire *	1788	24. Missouri	1821	40. South Dakota	1889
9. Virginia	1788	25. Arkansas	1836	41. Montana *	1889
10. New York	1788	26. Michigan	1837	42. Washington *	1889
11. South Carolina	1788	27. Texas *	1845	43. Idaho *	1890
12. North Carolina	1789	28. Florida *	1845	44. Wyoming *	1890
13. Rhode Island *	1790	29. Iowa	1846	45. Utah *	1896
14. Vermont	1791	30. Wisconsin	1848	46. Oklahoma *	1907
15. Kentucky	1792	31. California *	1850	47. Arizona *	1912
16. Tennessee	1796	32. Minnesota	1858	48. New Mexico *	1912

> . . . In both 1911 and 1921 the majority of Idaho teachers were from the Middle West. Many of these taught for a year or two and floated on to other western states. Their lack of knowledge of Idaho needs was appalling, and we have felt through the years that the regulation requiring all people to have a little knowledge of our school program before beginning to teach in our schools was one of the highest regulations we have ever had.[4]

The difficulty involved in such a measure has been that, while conditions have changed radically since the time Idaho included restrictive certification requirements, the latter have remained on the statutes to restrict teachers in other commonwealths.

Another possible cause for these restrictive requirements is also mentioned by Miss Hilts. In times of economic recession, persons in the heavily populated centers sometimes attempt to go to less populous sections of the nation to apply for positions. According to Miss Hilts, this was true in Idaho. In speaking of the residence requirement which will later be discussed, she says:

> . . . It was largely a depression measure in that we were being besieged by teachers from many parts of the Union for positions where they would be paid board and room only, and we felt that our Idaho teachers should have an opportunity to our schools.[5]

One difficulty, however, is *that the statute has lingered on under changing conditions.* Many persons now restricted from Idaho by these requirements would be professionally a fine addition to the Idaho schools. In some of the other commonwealths, it was not possible to trace in this manner even the slightest reason or cause for these restrictive statutes.

The origins of these specific state requirements pose still another and entirely different problem: There are groups and agencies entirely apart from the government, and therefore not subject to popular control, which are definitely working to induce legislatures to adopt specific laws affecting the content and procedure of the certification requirements. In reading the laws, one is immediately impressed by the duplication of wording in certain sections and even of entire laws. Statements of good authority from widely scattered

[4] Douglas Hilts, Certification Clerk, State of Idaho. Letter to the author, October 24, 1938.

[5] *Ibid.*

parts of the nation indicate that these similar laws have been placed among the requirements by the same so-called "pressure groups." Of course, this duplication may not be harmful; it may even be desirable where similar conditions warrant the duplication. However, the fact that these laws were placed upon the books by these vocal and often powerful minority groups is significant. Several organizations, national in scope, are interested in promoting definite ideas and programs and have utilized the teaching certification requirements as a focal point of their activities.[6, 7] It is not known accurately how many of these groups there are or what attempts are being made to adopt similar laws in more than one commonwealth. Most of these specific state requirements which have proved to be most restrictive were initiated and passed as certification requirements through the efforts of minority groups *that are known in most instances.* A particular cause may thus be served—but, in any case, the teaching personnel in the respective commonwealth is affected.

Some groups are active in making the Constitution of the United States a legal requirement in some commonwealths; other groups are promoting courses in state law, state history, or the conservation of the state's natural resources. The motives behind this type of propaganda no doubt vary widely. They may be of the highest, yet the effects of some of the requirements may be more complex and far-reaching than first thought would reveal. Efforts to control certification requirements or to affect them are not made solely by groups outside education, however. Groups within education have special interests to serve. For example, some college administrators and other officials wield a heavy hand in certification procedures and requirements.

The politics of these certification, legislative enactments are revealing. The schools have long been a focal point for the operations of more or less organized groups or the so-called "pressure groups," which have impressed their will or opinion on the school program or administration. Each community is a community of communities; each person is a group-joiner; and all the groups, open or closed, constitutional or otherwise, formal or informal, have objectives and

[6] Flanders, *op. cit.*

[7] Bruce Raup, *Education and Organized Interests in America,* Chap. II, III, VII, and VIII. G. P. Putnam's Sons, New York, 1936.

activities more or less individual. Dean James E. Russell of Teachers College in his annual report for 1925 called attention to the importance of such groups and of the problem of legislative enactment affecting the "freedom of teaching." The seriousness of the situation is portrayed in the following paragraph:

> The trend of public opinion in matters educational is part and parcel of the tendency of the times to shape conduct by legal enactment. Whether we like it or not, some school boards will sit in judgment on history texts and some will bar out modern science. The war taught us that German could be eliminated from our schools. Who knows what labor unionists, or chambers of commerce, or Biblical fundamentalists will insist on next? I foresee trouble enough to keep us from stagnation. Once a homogenous group, bent on having its own way, gets the notion that the schools can be used to promote its particular tenets, that group will surely seek to shape educational procedure. As soon as one group succeeds in influencing school affairs, some other group will rise in opposition and demand to be heard. This is no idle speculation: parties and sects and unions are even now contending for preferment in a way embarrassing to those who look to the larger good. The most hopeful sign is that contending groups may neutralize each other, thus giving the teacher a chance to work out his own salvation.[8]

A specific example will indicate the type of pressure and the politics involved in exerting such pressure upon legislators. The example in point is that of the United States Constitution:

In 1922 the American Bar Association organized a citizenship committee, which had as its major purpose the enactment of legislation requiring that the Constitution of the United States be taught in all publicly supported educational institutions. The records disclose that the Association was prompted to take such action by a genuine fear of a radical socialistic uprising. Something of the purpose of the Association may be gathered from the following statement quoted from the report made by the Committee on American Citizenship to the Association in 1923.

> The report of the Committee on the Promotion of American Ideals (1922) . . . showed the anti-American propaganda that was disseminated; the attacks upon our Constitution; the bitter prejudice manifested against the courts in every community; the fact that socialistic

[8] James E. Russell, *Report of the Dean of Teachers College,* 1925. See also Flanders, *op. cit.,* p. iii.

doctrines were being taught in many of our schools and colleges; the gross indifference of our people to the duties of citizenship; and in general the challenge that was being made as to our form of government, not only by "soap box orators," secret societies, and radicals who work both openly and insidiously, but also members of the United States Senate and others high in authority who attack the Supreme Court of the United States and demand a radical change from the government we have developed under a written constitution.

During the past year the conditions above named have not abated, but if anything have grown more pronounced and threatening. It is stated on competent authority that there are 1,500,000 radicals in this country who are clamoring for a change in the nature of our government from its present form to one of various degrees of a communistic state. It is said there are four hundred newspapers and periodicals that represent similar views and that are read regularly by 5,000,000 people. It is also said that $3,000,000 was spent during the past year on behalf of "Red" propaganda.[9]

The report of the Committee on American Citizenship continues with a quotation from an address made by General John J. Pershing:

> Dangerous elements are actually moving toward a revolution in America, both openly and secretly, because national problems have not been thoroughly discussed. There is a disruptive tendency toward radicalism of all sorts. The slump in patriotism and the consequent increase in the dangerous elements among us must be checked.[10]

To check the alleged growth of radicalism, the American Bar Association proposed that all public schools, colleges, and universities be required to offer a separate course in the Constitution of the United States. An attempt was made, seemingly with much success, to organize a citizenship committee in every state and local bar association in the country. Members of the bar associations and members of the legal profession in general were urged to become "Minute Men of the Constitution" and to work vigorously for the enactment of laws requiring the teaching of the Constitution in all public educational institutions.[11]

[9] *Report of the Committee on American Citizenship,* Report of the Forty-sixth Annual Meeting of the American Bar Association (1923), pp. 443–44.

See also John Dale Russell and Charles H. Judd, *The American Educational System,* pp. 67–69. New York: Houghton Mifflin Company, 1940.

[10] *Ibid.,* p. 444.

[11] Russell and Judd, *op. cit.,* pp. 68–69.

The fundamental purpose of the American Bar Association was undoubtedly commendable, but the educational concept on which the Association acted is open to serious criticism. It was evidently the accepted idea of the Association that a formal knowledge of the Constitution is enough to influence the thought and behavior of citizens. The Association made no demand or provision for the cultivation of a critical understanding of American political institutions. The theory seems to have been that the teaching of the Constitution must be carried on with something of religious fervor, and that the mind of the prospective citizen must be molded while it is still plastic. As Weaver pointed out, "The ultimate purpose of the movement is to inspire the emotional culture necessary to give permanency to our democratic institutions."[12] Thus it was said in the report of the Committee on American Citizenship of the American Bar Association in 1922:

> . . . In teaching citizenship, the real essential is "atmosphere." An appeal must be made to the heart, to the spirit and to the emotions, as well as to the intellect.
>
> Gratitude must be developed, pride must be aroused, love must be inspired. We doubt whether pride can be stirred or whether love can find a place, in any heart in which gratitude is not alive.
>
> The college or university which confers a degree upon any student until such person understands and *feels* that under our Constitution this is a government by the people, with self-imposed limitations based upon a recognition of inalienable individual rights, is sowing the seed of destruction of the faith of the fathers. . . .
>
> The schools of America should no more consider graduating a student who lacks faith in our government than a school of theology should consider graduating a minister who lacks faith in God.[13]

Such is the story behind the scenes of much of the legislation leading to certification requirements of the United States Constitution, the state constitutions, and similar types of legislation, such as curriculum subjects in the schools. The intent may be of a high order; the effects sometimes are otherwise for the profession.

[12] Samuel P. Weaver, "Teaching the Constitution," *American Bar Association Journal,* XV, p. 542, September, 1929.

[13] *Report of the Committee on American Citizenship,* Report of the Forty-fifth Annual Meeting of the American Bar Association (1922), p. 421.

See also Russell and Judd, *op. cit.,* p. 69.

A former member of a state education department, who for years had been intimately associated with the legislation behind certification requirements, said in this regard:

> The administration of certification requirements, and the prohibition of such requirements, are political tasks of the highest rank and of the greatest difficulty. It is a matching of pressure groups against other groups; it is a throwing together of votes in a hurry from several members of the legislature to save or stop a bill; it involves dinners and drinks over the fountain of the corner drug store, where votes are pulled out, one by one, for or against a measure; it involves taking members of the legislature from their homes, from beer parlors, from golf links, to stand them in their places to vote for measures; it involves pulling the strings of dozens of puppets that the committee would throw out or keep a measure. I had to know the representatives of each of many pressure groups so I could reach them on a few minutes' notice. I had to know where these groups stood on certain issues and how their votes would be cast, if at all. Such a task takes a strong man who knows the political play of give-and-take. The procedure of passing a certification requirement involves writing the bill as we want it, of getting the support of the majority party or groups of legislators who have been approached by friends of ours who have been "sold" on helping us. It involves being on the job with members of the committee, night and day, by means of dinners, luncheons, parties, and night club routines, until the bill is passed along, to have the same job repeated. The final vote by the two houses of the legislature is often swung by but a few votes over what are absolutely needed—but many times I have brought people by the arm into the floor of the House or the Senate and have watched them while they voted—to be sure certain measures would pass.[14]

In defeating certain legislative enactments of one legislative body or in defeating a bill in committee, this administrator used similar tactics. For example:

> I knew immediately what groups were behind a bill. In a few minutes I would contact representatives of those who I knew stood on the other side of the fence. The farmers would be against big business, one church against another, manufacturers against certain other manufacturers. I have often telephoned priests, ministers, high church men, to influence legislators of their faith. I have threatened, debated, pleaded, and argued. I have had to throw schools against schools, class against class; but I more often than not achieved my goal. The democratic procedure is a mass-play by pressure groups, and that administrator who

[14] Name withheld on request of administrator.

doesn't know his groups had better remain outside the fold. He will not be able to do more than scratch the surface.

For some time the nature of the activities of pressure groups and their effects on the school curriculum have been known. Apparently, the pressure groups have also been active and successful in many instances in passing the *limiting or restrictive enactments in certification.* In *every* instance it is not known who the major pressure groups were that put certain requirements into effect; in other instances they are known. The above statements give additional insight into reasons why certification requirements are similar in two or more states.

After learning what takes place in the legislating of a specific certification requirement, one may decide that the making of certification laws lies in the hands of a trained, administrative official and a board of lay persons who help only on broad principles or policies or who confer with their trained executive on professional issues. Such a state board, with their administrator of certification and staff, would not be immune to the influence of pressure groups—as a matter of fact, they would be the focal point of considerable pressure—but theirs would be a professional task for which they are responsible to the people. Their group is smaller than a legislature; their duties involve more direct responsibilities perhaps than do those of the legislators. The entire problem of social and political relationships is here involved.[15] The implications of the situation presented here go far deeper than the present problem, into the very foundations of democracy. With the great world philosophies challenging the very existence of the liberal nations, such a problem is basic. As Flanders has indicated succinctly:

> Either we must devise a way for men in the mass to profit by experience and by conscious thought processes or the nations of the world are doomed to a mediocre existence, subject only to intermittent progress of the happy-chance variety.

And then again:

> . . . There must be a way by which an organized group, acting as a group, can acquire sufficient skill and wisdom to enable it to choose the

[15] See Flanders, *op. cit.*, Chap. XI, "Conclusions."

means of pursuing a given end which will not defeat the very end pursued.[16]

Each of the following specific state requirements, therefore, has a complex history, as well as a sociological background into which it is often impossible to penetrate very far. Suffice it to say that the purposes which motivated many of these requirements are varied and deep-rooted. In some instances the advancement of education was not a primary reason for their initiation or development. They represent the accretions of the years; rarely has such a law been removed from the statute books, yet others have been added from time to time.

The requirement of the United States Constitution, which follows, is typical of many of these specific state requirements.

NATIONAL *

UNITED STATES CONSTITUTION

In 1923 the state of California passed a statutory enactment requiring an examination on the provisions and principles of the United States Constitution. Six years later this enactment was taken from the statutes and incorporated into the School Code. Florida, Arizona, and Wyoming all included such a requirement in 1925, with Texas following in 1930. The activities of two organizations that are nation-wide in scope seem to have been prominent in each instance in initiating and passing these laws. The theory, as far as can be determined, is that the study of the Federal Constitution brings an appreciation of that document, a knowledge of its contents, and a patriotism that might otherwise not be inculcated. It is conceivable that the spreading of propaganda by other groups may have prompted such activity on the part of these organizations.

Specifically, Arizona requires a "satisfactory examination upon the provisions and principles of the Constitution of the United States." [17] The peculiar restrictive qualities of such a requirement

[16] *Ibid.*, p. 186.

* For historical discussion of the courses discussed in this chapter, refer to Chapter II.

[17] Rules and Regulations Governing the Certification of Teachers in Arizona. Effective October 1, 1936. State of Arizona, Department of Public Instruction, Phoenix, Arizona.

are seen by the administrative details of this course, for credit is not granted for such a subject taken in any out-of-state institution.[18] Furthermore, a person is required to take the examination in this subject within the commonwealth of Arizona. Examinations are not sent outside the state.[19] In practice, this requirement meets fully the established definitions of restrictions.

In California, a similar requirement stipulates, "A course in the principles and provisions of the Constitution of the United States of not less than two semester hours completed in a California teacher-training institution.[20] Because this requirement may be postponed for one year and completed for renewal, or may be satisfied by passing an examination prescribed by the Superintendent of Public Instruction,[21] it is not restrictive. Moreover, a person may enroll in a college anywhere in the nation, take such a course, and then apply for an examination in the state of California.[22] An applicant for a certificate may attend an in-state institution to take such a course to meet this requirement. A person may also study the Constitution independently and then take the examination. No tuition need be paid to any California institution of higher learning if other ways are utilized to meet this requirement.

On the opposite side of the continent, the commonwealth of Florida has made the following enactment:

618. Examination on the Constitution of the United States. All persons applying for certificates authorizing them to become teachers in the public schools of this State, shall, in addition to existing requirements and before receiving such certificates, be required to pass a satisfactory examination upon the *provisions and principles of the Constitution of the United States,* and *shall also satisfy the examining power of*

[18] Letter to the author accompanying Rules and Regulations from H. E. Hendrix, Superintendent of Public Instruction, Phoenix, Arizona, January 5, 1939.

[19] M. J. Hurley, Department of Public Instruction, Phoenix, Arizona. Letter to the author, February 19, 1939.

[20] Regulations Governing Granting of Credentials and Certificates for Public School Service in California. State of California, Department of Education Bulletin, No. 12, June 15, 1935, p. 16.

[21] The Commission of Credentials of the State Department of Education issues credentials by authority of the State Board of Education. A teacher, upon accepting a position, submits his credentials to the county board of education in order that a certificate may be issued authorizing service within the county. School Code sections 5.120–5, 122 and 5.160.

[22] Letter to the author from Evelyn Clement, Chief, Division of Teacher Training and Certification, Department of Education, Division of Teacher Training and Certification, Sacramento, California, January 18, 1938.

*his or her loyalty thereto;** Provided, that this section shall not apply to graduates of higher institutions of learning approved by the State board of education, said graduates having completed a course of six semester hours in American history and government, including the Constitution of the United States.[23]

A course with a different title from that given in the laws will be accepted if the content is fairly equivalent.[24] No residence requirement or resident study in a Florida institution is required by this particular law if the requirement is met in other ways. By the word "satisfactory" is meant a grade of eighty-five per cent or better in the examination.[24] The requirement is not waived,[24] and the examination must be passed or the course taken before a teacher may have his certificate, so the requirement is restrictive in practice.

In the Southwest, Texas requires the Constitution of the United States in addition to the Constitution of the State of Texas,[25] both offered as a two-semester-hour course which may be taken in residence in a senior college or junior college in the state or may be taken by correspondence with a senior college in Texas. The original enactment follows:

Teachers' Certificates. No person hereafter shall be certified to teach in the public schools of the State of Texas until he has secured credit for the course in both *Federal and State Constitutions* of the grade of instruction upon which he is applying for the certificate, that is, either of the sub-college or of the college work; or in lieu thereof shall have passed an examination set by the State Superintendent of Public Instruction on the Constitution of the United States and of Texas.[26]

An applicant may offer six semester hours in the field of American Government completed in or accepted by a Texas institution of higher learning in lieu of the unit in Constitutions.[27] The require-

* Italics are the author's.

[23] School Laws of Florida, Chap. 10256, Acts of 1925, Sec. 3; Chap. 11908, Acts 1927, Sec. 1. As amended by Acts of 1937.

[24] Letter to the author from Joe Hall, Supervisor of Certification, Department of Public Instruction, State of Florida, Tallahassee, May 4, 1939.

[25] Public School Laws of State of Texas, Sec. 346, 2663b, Sec. 4. Teachers' Certificates. (Became effective 1930.) See also Public School Laws of the State of Texas, Bulletin State Department of Education, 1938, Vol. XIV, No. 2, Austin, Texas, February, 1938. Article 2886, pp. 169–170. Also Acts 1924, Thirty-ninth Legislature, Chap. 124.

[26] Public School Laws of State of Texas, *op. cit.* Italics are the author's.

[27] Letter to the author from C. L. Kuykendall, Chairman, Texas Board of Examiners, May 3, 1939.

ment may be met after contracting for a position. Furthermore, a four-month temporary certificate is granted if a person has a position promised him in the state.[28] A person planning to meet this requirement during the first four months of teaching in Texas would be certificated on the same basis as a person meeting the requirement before applying for a certificate. This requirement, therefore, is not restrictive.

In Nevada, teachers must meet the requirement in the Constitution of the United States, but may take an examination on the subject within one year. In Wyoming, a satisfactory examination in the Constitution of the United States must be passed or an equivalent course taken before a certificate can be issued. It is apparent that the commonwealths wish to retain the authority to give the examinations required on the United States Constitution. One phrase in the Florida requirement previously quoted is revealing:

> (that) . . . persons . . . be required to pass . . . examination upon the provisions and principles of the Constitution of the United States, and shall *also satisfy the examining power of his or her loyalty thereto. . . .*[29]

Such promises and oath laws provide a basis for much controversy, into which this study cannot enter, although it has attempted to reveal in part the purpose and intent of the groups sponsoring the requirement.

State

STATE CONSTITUTION

Texas has included a requirement of the Texas State Constitution in addition to the Federal Constitution. In the last quarter of the nineteenth century such state constitutional prerequisites were common, although they were not usually offered in college courses. The applicant for a certificate usually took an examination in each of several subjects, which sometimes numbered forty or more, including a series of questions on the constitution of the particular commonwealth. The oldest of these requirements now in force appeared in

[28] *Ibid.*, December 13, 1937.

[29] Public School Laws of State of Florida, *op. cit.* Italics are the author's.

Washington in 1889; another in the adjoining state of Idaho in 1911. Later "The State Constitution" became the title of a college course offered in an institution of higher learning of the respective state. Arizona, Wyoming, and Nevada have since followed suit with a similar requirement.

The theories behind such course standards may have been similar to those which prompted the initiation of the requirement of the United States Constitution. A knowledge of the constitution of the state in which one is teaching would be invaluable, although certain requirements related to such standards are open to question. For example, several commonwealths require an applicant to take such a course before he may begin teaching in the state regardless of how well qualified he may be otherwise. The following details relate to the various standards pertaining to state constitutions.

Specifically, Arizona, in conjunction with its requirement of the Constitution of the United States, requires a "satisfactory examination upon the provisions and principles of the Constitution of the State of Arizona." [30] The questions for this examination are not sent outside the state, and the requirements are not waived for any applicant regardless of his residence within or outside the state.[31, 32] This particular requirement is restrictive because of the fact that it requires persons to come to the state for the examination, bringing such a requirement within the scope of the definition of restrictions.

As indicated previously, Texas also requires a combination course including the Constitution of the State and the United States Constitution.[33] Individuals already under contract within the state who have not completed this course may receive an emergency certificate at the request of the city or county superintendent with whom they have contracted.[34] This certificate is good for four months, during

[30] Rules and Regulations Governing the Certification of Teachers in Arizona. Effective October 1, 1936.

Letters to the author from H. E. Hendrix (January 5, 1939), and from M. J. Hurley (February 19, 1939).

[31] Letter to the author from M. J. Hurley, Director of Certification, Department of Public Instruction, Phoenix, Arizona, April 8, 1938.

[32] Usually, application to take this examination must be made to the County School Superintendent ten days prior to the examination date. The examinations themselves are conducted in the offices of the County School Superintendent on the second Saturday of each month. (See footnote 17.)

[33] See footnotes 25 and 26.

[34] *Ibid.*

which period the individual must meet the requirement by taking the course in both constitutions.[35] If other standards are met a person planning to meet this course requirement during the first four months of teaching would be given a certificate on the same basis as the person who had satisfied the requirement before requesting a certificate.[36] This standard is seldom waived, a few exemptions being made under certain conditions. It is not restrictive because of the possibility of a temporary certificate being offered.

Wyoming requires that applicants pass ". . . a satisfactory examination upon the provisions and principles of the Constitution of the United States and of this State, or submit evidence of having pursued a course equivalent to that required in Sections 1 and 2 of this Act."[37] This examination must be taken within the confines of the State of Wyoming,[38] and no person may take such an examination under supervision of any other state. Although no phase of this requirement necessitates attendance at a college or university in Wyoming, a substitute for the examination is a course in the State Constitution in a college within the state. This requirement, which must be met by every applicant for a certificate regardless of his place of training or residence, is restrictive.

Nevada will give one year's time for a teacher otherwise qualified to meet the requirements in the State Constitution.

It is apparent that the "pressure groups" that initiated such requirements as these have affected the certification of thousands of teachers. Whether the restrictive effects were anticipated is doubtful, but the effects remain.

Because of these specific state requirements, prospective teachers are required to go to a particular commonwealth for an examination, for a college course, or for residence within that state. This group of requirements therefore is subject to the same criticisms which Cubberley made with reference to the certification requirements, practices, and restrictions in the first decade of the twentieth century.

[35] *Ibid.*

[36] *Ibid.*

[37] Certification Laws, State of Wyoming, 1931, 99–142. See also, Certification of Teachers, Regulations adopted by the State Board of Education, Cheyenne, Wyoming, Bulletin No. 8, Series B., 1937.

[38] Letter to the author from R. L. Markley, Commissioner of Education, Cheyenne, Wyoming, February 8, 1938.

The details are different and the purposes of their inception vary, but the effects are similar.

STATE SCHOOL LAW

The passing of the state constitution certification requirements set a precedent. The way had been cleared for the legislating of additional types of specific state requirements. Different social and professional organizations helped in some commonwealths to pass requirements, this time in state school law. At first in Washington, this was merely school law. Later in other states it was changed to include the name of the state requiring it, such as Idaho School Law. Altogether, ten states have passed such requirements. Apparently these ten commonwealths, or groups within them, thought that all teachers in the state school systems ought to understand the provisions of the school law. It is not questioned that it would be helpful for teachers to have this information. If a teacher had moved from Nebraska to Idaho, for example, and was acquainted with the Nebraska school laws and not with those of Idaho, some of his activities and concepts would be based on what is, in Idaho, inaccurate information where the laws of the two states differed.

Seven of these ten commonwealths evidently regard state school law as an important prerequisite for public school teachers. Idaho[39, 40] requires such a course at the University of Idaho at Moscow of every teacher except a few that are brought into the state in an emergency. Kansas,[41, 42] Montana,[43, 44] Nevada,[45, 46, 47, 48] New

[39] The state of Idaho requires residence or correspondence course credit from the University of Idaho in Idaho School Law. This requirement must be met before a person may begin teaching in this state, and it must be satisfied by every person regardless of experience or training, with the exception of a very small number of teachers sometimes brought into the state in an emergency. School Laws of the State of Idaho, Article X, pp. 47–48. As amended by the Twelfth Session of the Legislature, 1911. Issued by authority of Grace M. Shepherd, Superintendent of Public Instruction, State of Idaho. Although an opportunity is given for correspondence course credit, in practice this requirement is restrictive.

[40] Letters to the author from Miss Douglas Hilts, Certification Clerk, Department of Education, State of Idaho, Boise, Idaho. May 8, 1938, and October 24, 1938.

[41] Kansas includes school law in the course "School Organization, Administration, and Kansas School Law," permitting people to take the course from a Kansas college or through correspondence work.—Kansas School Laws, Revised, 1937. See Chapter 5, Certificates.

Under date of June 4, 1938, the State Board changed the requirement, removing the phase of state law. The course can now be taken from any accredited institution

Footnotes continued from page 135

in any state wherever the course is available.—Letter to the author from Miss Louie Lesslie, Secretary, Department of Education, State of Kansas, Topeka, Kansas, January 13, 1939.

[42] The same requirements are made for out-of-state persons as for in-state teachers, but in practice, this requirement is restrictive. (This requirement was changed in 1938 to a course of Educational Administration without Kansas School Law—making it nonrestrictive.)

[43] Montana requires "Evidence of a working knowledge of Montana school law, acquired by taking work in residence at a division of the greater University in the State by correspondence, or by examination."—Out of State Teaching Requirements, sent by Miss Ruth Reardon, State Superintendent of Public Instruction, Helena, Montana. January 11, 1938. Regulations of the Montana State Board of Education, Extract from Minutes dated December 14, 1931. Passed by the State Board of Education on that date.

[44] If taken by examination, such must be taken within the state. This requirement can be satisfied while an applicant is meeting the nine weeks' residence requirement. Furthermore, this requirement must be satisfied before a person may obtain a certificate. The regulation is never waived and is restrictive.—Letter to the author from Mary Clifford, Deputy Superintendent, Helena, Montana, May 10, 1938.

[45] Nevada asks for "an examination in Nevada School Law within one year." All teachers drawing public school money must meet this requirement.

On March 21, 1921, Assembly Bill No. 284 . . . was approved. Under provisions of this Act, Nevada School Law was included in the list of required subjects for teachers seeking certificates via the examination route.

In 1926, the State Board of Education made a ruling requiring all teachers who had not received their training in Nevada School Law to pass an examination in this subject within one year from the date of the certificate. For the benefit of teachers who have not received credit in Nevada School Law, the School Law examination is given twice a year, the first Saturday in May and the first Saturday in November. All teachers drawing public school money must meet the School Law requirement.

—Letter to the author from Mrs. Pearl M. Elstner, Certification Clerk, Department of Education, State of Nevada, October 22, 1938.

[46] A course in this subject is offered at the University of Nevada both in the Regular and in the Summer School Sessions.—Letter to the author from Mrs. Pearl M. Elstner, Certification Clerk, Carson City, Nevada, October 22, 1938.

[47] An examination in lieu of this course may be taken within one year after beginning to teach in Nevada, if all other requirements are satisfied. Examinations in School Law are given twice a year, the first Saturday in both May and November. A teacher planning to take this examination within one year from the date of application for a certificate is certificated as readily as a person planning to meet the requirement before obtaining the certificate. The examination itself must be taken within the geographical confines of the State.

"It was recommended that teachers from outside the state granted High School Certificates meet the requirement in Nevada School Law. Certificates may be granted provisionally where all other requirements are met; the provision to set some date for an examination in School Law. Upon motion duly made and seconded, it was recommended. Motion unanimously carried."—Taken from the Minutes of a meeting of the State Board of Education held on June 24, 1927.

[48] Attendance at the University of Nevada and the taking of the course at that institution is one way of meeting this requirement, but such is not necessarily demanded, the examination being the alternative. This requirement is not restrictive because it can be postponed one year.—Letter to the author from Mrs. Pearl M. Elstner, Certification Clerk, Carson City, Nevada, December 16, 1938.

Hampshire,[49, 50] Oklahoma,[51, 52, 53] Oregon,[54, 55] Rhode Island, and Texas all have a similar requirement in their respective state law. Some of these requirements are restrictive. In the commonwealths of Kansas, Nevada, New Hampshire, Ohio, Oklahoma, Rhode Island, and Texas, however, this particular type of requirement is not restrictive because of certain details that permit a postponement by the incoming teacher or the subject is not now required.

STATE GOVERNMENT

It seems that the minority groups that sponsored the requirements in state law also thought that those who teach the children of the state ought to know something about the state government. In only one commonwealth, however, has this requirement appeared. Montana requires "Evidence of the working knowledge of Montana Government and History, acquired by taking work in residence at a division of the University of Montana or by examination."[56]

[49] New Hampshire has a requirement in New Hampshire School Law.—Regulations Governing the Approval of Superintendents, Headmasters, Principals, and Teachers in the Public Schools of New Hampshire, New Hampshire State Board of Education, Concord, New Hampshire, 1933, p. 7. See also for January, 1938.

[50] The examination in this subject must be passed within one year after applying for a certificate. The questions for the examinations are set by the State Department, but the examinations are given at the Normal Schools and at the University. Because of the one-year postponement of the examination, the requirement is not restrictive.—Letter to the author from James M. Pringle, Commissioner of Education, State of New Hampshire, Concord, New Hampshire, October 19, 1938.

[51] Oklahoma requires "A two-semester-hour course in general methods and management, including Oklahoma School Law."

[52] Included in the requirements for certification by the Oklahoma State Board of Education (about) 1919.—Letters to the author from L. Norman Duncan, Executive Secretary, State Board of Education, Oklahoma City, Oklahoma, November 9, 1938, and May 8, 1939.

[53] See also Regulations and Requirements for Teachers' Certificates, adopted by the Oklahoma State Board of Education, March 3, 1936. Issued by A. L. Crable, State Superintendent and President State Board of Education, Oklahoma City, Oklahoma.

The requirement in this state is not restrictive because an applicant who has otherwise completed all courses required for state certification in an institution outside Oklahoma may have this school law requirement waived for one year.

[54] Oregon included Oregon School Law with several other factors in a 2⅔-semester-hour requirement taken from a standard college, university, or normal school. The requirement is restrictive.—Oregon School Laws, 1937, Chapter 249. From the Oregon Code, 1930, Oregon Code supplement 1935, and Acts of the Thirty-ninth Legislative Assembly with notes, annotations, and opinions of the attorney generals and decisions of the Supreme Court for use by Government of Directors and School Officers. Requirement went into effect September 1, 1937.

[55] Circular of Certification for the State of Oregon, January, 1938, p. 7.

[56] See footnotes 43 and 44.

STATE HISTORY

Five states apparently consider a knowledge of state history an important qualification of public school teachers. Montana asks for evidence of a working knowledge of Montana history, although it is not stated what a "working knowledge" is and when such is to be obtained. Oklahoma,[57] Oregon,[58] Rhode Island, and Texas also require courses in their respective state histories. In two instances the requirements are not waived and must be met within the state having the requirement, so these two are restrictive.

STATE COURSES OF STUDY, STATE MANUAL, AND STATE PROGRAM OF STUDIES

Although there is considerable controversy as to whether or not a commonwealth should have a state-wide course of study, it is evident that where such does exist the prospective teachers should have some information regarding this course of study. The original requirement in this area was passed by Idaho in 1911, even before a course of study was written, but four years later a course of study was published, after which the requirement was enforced.[59, 60] Although provision is made for correspondence study, the way in which this requirement operates in actual practice is restrictive.

Montana also asks for "Evidence of the working knowledge of Montana Courses of Study, acquired by taking work in residence at

[57] See footnotes 51, 52, and 53.

[58] See footnotes 54 and 55.

[59] See footnotes 39 and 40.

[60] "In 1911 Idaho adopted a new set of certification regulations. These were laws passed by the legislature. One requirement for all Idaho certificates was credit or examination in Idaho school law and Idaho course of study. At that time we did not have a high school course of study, but along in 1915 we had one published, and thereafter those who were going to teach in high school were expected to take the high school course of study. This was a bad regulation and was probably not always checked carefully, but in 1921 we again had a legislative change of certification. At that time high school course of study . . . (was) made (a) positive requirement for everyone who received an Idaho high school certificate. This credit can be earned by examination, by correspondence for the University of Idaho (Moscow), or in residence at any Idaho high school which trains high school teachers."

"At present we have so few people who wish to take the credit by examination that we have discontinued these and expect all teachers to get the subjects by residence or by correspondence. We accept correspondence work from the University of Idaho only."—Letter to the author from Miss Douglas Hilts, Certification Clerk, Department of Education, Boise, Idaho, October 24, 1938.

one of the divisions of the University of Montana or by examination."[61]

Before the turn of the twentieth century states usually listed examinations for teachers in a number of subjects, including a group of subjects like state school law or state constitution. The state of Washington included such subjects in 1889, but in the statutes of 1897, 1899, and 1903 changes were made in the original requirement, and in 1911 the Washington State Manual[62] was added as a requirement. This subject includes the educational organization of that state, the powers and duties of the officers, and information regarding the numbers of students enrolled, the types of education offered, and other data of general information about the administration of the Washington schools. The present purpose of this requirement is to make out-of-state applicants for teaching positions acquainted with the Washington Constitution, School Law, and history of the state. The State Manual is also a requirement for graduation from the teacher training courses in the publicly supported schools.* An examination with a grade of eighty-five per cent or better is required or two semester hours earned in this subject by attendance at any one of the Washington teacher-training institutions or enrollment in correspondence courses offered by these institutions.[63]

[61] The shortest period during which a person may take such a course in the University of Montana is the nine-week summer session. If the examination route is chosen, it must be taken within the state. This requirement, which must be met by every applicant otherwise well qualified, is not waived and is in practice restrictive. See footnotes 43 and 44.

[62] Certification of Teachers, State of Washington, September 1, 1937. See also letter to the author from Andrew Elwick, Deputy Superintendent, Department of Education, Olympia, Washington, November 15, 1938. See also, Session Laws, 1889–1890, Section 12, Chapter XII, Educational, Title III, Board of Education. See also, Session Laws, 1899, Chapter CXLII, Section 21. Sundry amendments to the School Code, Olympia, Washington. See also, Session Laws of the State of Washington, 1897, Chapter CXVIII, Title II—Officers, Their Powers and Duties. Chapter 9, Article 1, Section 141. See also, Session Laws, 1903, Chapter 104, Section 34. See also, Session Laws 1911, Chapter 16, Section 4.

* Letter to the author from Andrew Elwick, Deputy Superintendent, Department of Education, Olympia, Washington, November 15, 1938.

[63] The examination, if such is chosen by an applicant among the possibilities, must be taken within the state. The course, if chosen, must be taken in an in-state institution. A one-year temporary certificate is given a person who has satisfied every other requirement except this State Manual. A person who has been graduated from an out-of-state institution must have a position promised him in Washington before a certificate will be issued to him. The requirement of State Manual is not restrictive because of the possibility of a one-year postponement.—Letter to the author from

Very similar to the requirements of a state course of study is that found in New Hampshire entitled "Secondary Program of Studies." A satisfactory examination must be passed in this subject within one year after a person begins to teach in this commonwealth. The subject therefore is not restrictive[64] and represents a desirable type of certification requirement, inasmuch as persons may begin to teach in the state without first passing the examination, and yet within a period of one year must have this needed information. Teachers are not restricted but they obtain the required information. This situation avoids the effects of restrictions and accomplishes what the subject requirement was intended to do.

STATE ORGANIZATION AND ADMINISTRATION OF SECONDARY SCHOOLS

There is little question but that teachers within a state, drawing their salaries from that commonwealth, should know about the state organization and the administration of the secondary schools. It is questionable, however, whether such a requirement should be restrictive. Utah has a course requirement including these two general areas. According to the official requirements, this course in school organization and administration should include: "(a) A study of the Utah school law and means and agencies by which the law is being administered; (b) the relationship of the federal government to state and local units.[65, 66, 67] Though the information is of value, the course is restrictive.

STATE PROBLEMS OF EDUCATION

Two commonwealths apparently consider it of importance to inform their teachers of the status, details, and problems of education within their boundaries.

Andrew Elwick, Deputy Superintendent, Department of Education, Olympia, Washington, February 7, 1938.

[64] See footnotes 49 and 50.

[65] Requirements for Certification of Teachers, Supervisors, and Superintendents, State of Utah. Department of Public Instruction, C. N. Jensen, Superintendent, Salt Lake City, Utah, 1925.

[66] Utah State High School Certificates (mimeographed list of requirements). A. C. Matheson, Chairman, Certification Committee, State Board of Education, Salt Lake City, Utah, 1939.

[67] See also letters to the author from A. C. Matheson, Chairman, Certification Committee, State Board of Education, Salt Lake City, Utah, February 23, 1938, and May 10, 1939.

Rhode Island has a requirement in Rhode Island education.[68] The requirement can be satisfied within one year after provisional certification is granted so the requirement is not restrictive.

New Mexico requires a course in "Problems of Education in New Mexico."[69, 70] This requirement became effective for applicants after July 1, 1938, and is restrictive. A companion requirement in New Mexico asks for six semester hours of credit earned in an approved New Mexico institution of higher learning, so this course in "Problems of Education in New Mexico" can be taken while fulfilling the resident study requirement.

STATE SYSTEM OF EDUCATION

At least one commonwealth considers information regarding its entire system of education important enough to include as a qualification of teachers for certification. Oregon asks for a minimum of 2⅔ semester hours in a course covering the Oregon system of education and related subjects mentioned elsewhere and asks that this course be taken at a standard college, university, or normal school.[71] Inasmuch as no postponement is possible and the requirement must be satisfied before certification, the requirement is definitely restrictive. Apparently Oregon wants its teachers to have this information regardless of the restrictive aspects of such. The objective might be accomplished and the restrictive effect avoided if this course were required within the period of one year and not demanded before teaching begins.

Resident Study in an In-State Institution of Higher Learning

Several courses just discussed contain information that would undoubtedly be of benefit to prospective teachers of the respective commonwealths. Three states apparently considered these courses

[68] Certification of Teachers, Department of Education, State of Rhode Island and Providence Plantations, Rules and Regulations. Revised and in effect January 1, 1938, pp. 11, 15.

[69] Rules and Regulations Governing the Certification of Teachers in New Mexico, adopted by the State Board of Education, effective September 1, 1937, p. 13.

[70] See Session Laws for State of New Mexico, 1933, Chapter 77 (House Bill No. 81, approved March 14, 1933). See also Session Laws, 1935, Chapter 196 (House Bill No. 210. Approved February 25, 1935), Section 1.

[71] See footnotes 54 and 55.

insufficient and took a further step to require *resident study in a state institution of higher learning*. There are other reasons and purposes behind such requirements, however; namely, to keep state positions for state people and to restrict out-of-state applications. The first resident study requirement was passed by the Montana State Board of Education in 1931, the first of this type in the history of the United States.[72] One year later Idaho, in passing a similar requirement, stated emphatically that:

> . . . surrounding states have devised means of reserving educational positions for teachers who are residents of their respective states, and trained in the educational institutions of said respective states, and . . . Idaho has adopted no such protective measures for Idaho teachers. . . .[73]

This is clearly in retaliation for a similar requirement in Montana, or some other surrounding state or states, and was devised *to keep teachers from other states out of Idaho*. From time to time other evidences of similar laws have been apparent. The details of these requirements follow.

Idaho now requires "six weeks' attendance in an Idaho educational institution with credit for a full term's graduate work."[74] It is intended that the several specific state requirements be taken while the residence is being satisfied. This requirement must be met by every out-of-state person before he may begin teaching in this state, with the possible exception of a few persons brought into the state in case of an emergency. Regardless of training or experience, every person must meet these requirements, which are not waived for anyone regardless of residence. For those who have had twelve hours of work in an Idaho post-high-school institution, however, such requirements are waived.[75] For all those who have attended any Idaho undergraduate college, university, or normal school, such a requirement would not need to be satisfied because these people would already have taken these courses. This requirement is definitely restrictive.

[72] State Board of Regulation, enacted December 14, 1931. Extract from Minutes of State Board of Education of same date. See also footnotes 43, 44, and 61.

[73] Excerpt from minutes of State Board of Education, November 23, 1932. Went into effect January 1, 1933.—Letter to the author from Miss Douglas Hilts, Certification Clerk, Department of Education, State of Idaho, Boise, Idaho, October 24, 1938.

[74] See footnotes 39, 40, 59, and 60.

[75] Letter to the author from Miss Douglas Hilts, October 24, 1938.

The near-by commonwealth of Montana, however, asks for "Nine weeks' residence in one of the divisions of the greater University of Montana with a reasonable and appropriate amount of work."[76] This requirement must be met by all persons regardless of training or experience and is not waived for any teacher otherwise qualified. Inasmuch as this requirement must be satisfied before teaching is begun in the state, the requirement is restrictive.

New Mexico also requires "Six semester hours of satisfactory work in a New Mexico institution of higher learning."[77] The implications of this type of requirement are serious when it is considered that education is really a national service. Undoubtedly the purposes for such requirements were good. Nevertheless, some states are definitely restricting the interstate mobility of all out-of-state teachers, screening out many persons of low ability but also restricting teachers of considerable professional ability and promise. It is paradoxical that such requirements should arise in a nation whose very constitution provides so carefully for interstate freedom of movement in other ways.

Other Courses Adapted to State Needs

Unique problems arise in some states, partly because of their geographical location and partly because of their financial status or for other reasons, which apparently require state-wide support to solve. Two commonwealths, Florida and Louisiana, have required courses in their certification standards to help solve problems peculiar to these states.

Florida stipulates a course in the conservation of natural resources.[78, 79] The waste of natural resources in the state led members of the legislature to require the course for certification in the belief that the teachers' knowledge in this area would have a carry-over to

[76] See footnotes 43, 44, and 61.

[77] Rules and Regulations Governing the Certification of Teachers in New Mexico, State Board of Education, effective September 1, 1937, pp. 1–2.

[78] State of Florida, Handbook for Teachers, Section 1, 1936–37. Department of Public Instruction, Tallahassee, Florida.

[79] "INSTRUCTIONS IN CONSERVATION OF NATURAL RESOURCES. That on and after September 1, 1936, all of the higher State Educational Institutions shall give instruction in nature study and the conservation of natural resources, including the study of fish and game, soil fertility and erosion, forests and minerals, and all students in said institutions preparing to be teachers shall be required to take such course of instruction." Laws of Florida, Acts of 1935, Section 1, Chap. 17030.

the children who would then be trained to help develop such resources. A course with a different title but with fairly equivalent content would suffice to meet this requirement, which is limiting.

Louisiana requires "Nine semester hours of Health and Physical Education."[80, 81, 82] This requirement must be met before a person may begin to teach in this state, and is not waived for any teacher, regardless of experience or training, with the exception of a new teacher coming into a school system where she is not required to give instruction in health and physical education because a full-time teacher is employed in those subjects.[83] Teachers from a great majority of colleges and states would find it virtually impossible to meet the detailed spread of this health and physical education requirement.

Of forty-three specific state requirements in eighteen commonwealths, eighteen are found to be restrictive and twelve are limiting in nine states. Reference to Table IV will review the type and location of these restrictions and limitations.

In addition to these specific state requirements, there is a small, heterogeneous group of requirements not yet discussed, such as minimum age limits of applicants, United States citizenship, race, color, political affiliation, and other detailed stipulations which, in no instance, were found to be limiting or restrictive for most qualified teachers. A list of these details can be found in the state requirements. No factor exists with regard to the race, color, religion, or political affiliation of an applicant for certification that is related in any way to most state boundaries and therefore to restrictions and

[80] State Board Regulation Requirements passed in 1935 and became effective for every teacher, September 1, 1940.

[81] Certification of Teachers, State Department of Education of Louisiana, see Bulletin No. 322, August, 1936, and Bulletin No. 370, April, 1938.

[82] Authorization as classroom teacher will be noted on the basis of this minimum requirement of nine semester hours; as special, part-time teacher, eighteen semester hours; as full-time special teacher, forty semester hours. See also letter to the author from Jess W. Hair, State Supervisor of Health and Physical Education, October 20, 1938. Department of Education, Baton Rouge, Louisiana.

[83] In-state teachers are not certificated until they have met this full requirement. Persons are not required to take these nine hours in Louisiana colleges, but it is important that the nine hours be spread approximately among the recommended divisions of the requirement. Regardless of their major field subject or probable teaching position, this requirement must be met by all applicants. A person meeting such requirements in out-of-state institutions is certificated on an equal basis with the in-state persons. This requirement is not restrictive, but it is limiting.

See also letter to the author from J. E. Lombard, Director of Certification, Department of Education, Baton Rouge, Louisiana, May 3, 1939.

limitations. In community employment practices, such matters may be of importance, but not in the matter of state certification. Investigation revealed that forty-six states certificated persons without regard to race or color.[84] Forty-seven of the commonwealths certificate persons, who meet other requirements, without regard to religion. Twenty-five states certificate without regard to the applicant's political party or views. Twenty-three states did not answer the question asked with regard to this last factor of the political viewpoint of the applicant. Of those that did reply, however, there was unanimity in regard to the lack of importance of such a factor in certification.

In this entire study of certification requirements, beginning with the study of degrees, and including investigation of academic courses, professional standards, practice teaching, and finally specific state requirements, this factor of residence has been stressed. The expressions "in-state" and "out-of-state" have been used time and again with reference to applicants for certification, and in the interpretation of requirements.

The factor of residence is important with reference to restrictions and limitations.

Several complex problems exist in relation to residence. With reference to the definition of restrictions, it must immediately be recognized that identical requirements for certification must be satisfied by persons whether they live inside or outside any given commonwealth. However, if a certification requirement in one state differs from comparable standards in another, such variations constitute *limitations* for the interstate mobility of teachers, according to the original definition. Furthermore, if a requirement, policy, or practice in one commonwealth cannot be satisfied by courses or degrees in accredited colleges in other states, demanding that a person meet the standards within the particular commonwealth having the requirement, *restrictions* immediately become apparent. This is true because of at least five reasons: (1) financial, (2) the time element, (3) "place utility," (4) difficulties in obtaining a position, and (5) inflexibility of certification requirements. These will be discussed in this order, with the somewhat different effects of limitations and restrictions upon inexperienced and experienced teachers indicated.

[84] Question 25, State Certification Data Sheet. See Appendix A.

Financial. The young, inexperienced but trained teacher just graduated from college has probably incurred some debts during his four-year program. Often he has exhausted almost all his available resources, saved, earned, or borrowed. Any differences in certification requirements, therefore, which he must meet *after* his four-year program is ended are a financial hurdle which he often cannot successfully clear. Slight differences in semester hours between courses he has taken and courses required for certification as well as qualitative differences in the courses, all require additional summer school work, which in turn demands financial outlay. The specific state requirements, including residence, especially require that the prospective teacher travel to the commonwealth making the requirements.

This travel means additional outlay, which in some instances is considerable. It involves expenditure of money to make the trip and to pay for board and room away from home. It entails tuition expenses, and money for other items, such as books and materials. Then, too, while this prospective teacher is going to summer school trying to meet certification requirements, he is foregoing any earning possibilities that he may have had if he had not gone to summer school. This extra money is important because even if he obtains a position he will usually need to pay in advance for room rent and board before his first salary check is received, and to buy new clothes and books. These details mean that the out-of-state prospective teacher is limited by variations in certification requirements and is restricted by specific state requirements often because of financial reasons, and not because of any lack of merit or professional ability to teach. The prospective teacher may be a decided professional addition to a commonwealth, but he is restricted from teaching in the state because of the very requirements by which the state hoped to attract the best persons. For this reason the employing groups within the state do not see all or even a large part of the best applicants who wish to apply for certification and employment because they are eliminated by the state's requirements before they can even be interviewed by the prospective employers.

The time element. When a student needs to attend a summer school to meet a specific state requirement, he is in a difficult situation for reasons other than financial. This time element is basic.

The prospective teacher looking for a position must see prospective employers, have conferences in connection with his credentials, write letters, obtain recommendations, and at the same time attend summer school to meet the varying requirements and to take the specific state courses referred to in this and the preceding two chapters. Summer school is often considered a good place in which to meet possible employers. Sometimes, however, the teachers needed for next year may already have been employed before summer school started. Enforced attendance at summer school often may keep the prospective teacher from doing the very things he needs to do to obtain a teaching position for the next academic year.

Place utility. There is a certain utility because of a person's living within the state that does not accrue to out-of-state persons—hence the term "place utility." Persons living within a particular state having a restrictive requirement have had in most instances an opportunity to take the required courses before being graduated from high school or college in that same commonwealth. In one instance, persons are required to take the same course in high school that is later required for certification. *Persons in institutions in all other states do not have the same opportunities of taking these courses.* In some other cases, a person's attendance at a high school or a college within the respective state makes that person exempt from the course requirement which restricts persons from other commonwealths. Indirectly, therefore, certain requirements tend to discriminate between in-state and out-of-state applicants.

Difficulties in obtaining a position. With competition for positions often very keen, and with qualifications for several leading applicants for a position somewhat similar, an employing official may prefer the applicant who already has his state certificate or has the written assurance he can obtain one.* The person who has yet to attend summer school to meet certain limiting or restrictive requirements *may be fairly sure* he can obtain a certificate, but there is always some doubt, even though sometimes slight, that he will obtain it. This situation is aggravated by the fact that most states stipulate that all their requirements be satisfied before a person may be certificated. The employing officer sometimes cannot take the risk involved, for if something unforeseen should occur and the certifi-

* Question 29, State Certification Data Sheet, Appendix A.

cate is not issued, the school official would need to look for another person all over again, and this somewhat late in the season. *More likely than not, it is the out-of-state person who is in doubt about his state certificate, not the in-state applicant for the teaching position.* The employer wants to avoid any irregularity or uncertainty attendant upon certification; this is understandable when it is considered that the school in which an uncertificated teacher is employed may lose its accredited status. In the practical, matter-of-fact competitive situation, therefore, specific state requirements or limiting certification factors of any type may restrict or limit, respectively, out-of-state persons.

Inflexibility of certification requirements. The standards in each commonwealth must usually be met completely before any person, in-state or out-of-state, may be certificated.* If a person has taken a course for two semester hours and a particular state requires three, that applicant must obtain that extra semester hour somewhere. If a person has had one course and the state requires a somewhat related but yet a different course, that applicant must take that separate course. This situation becomes involved when a person tries to meet requirements in more than one state. Whether a teacher is inexperienced or has had several years of teaching experience in the classroom, he is required to meet completely the certification requirements, item for item, in most commonwealths, regardless of other qualifications. An institution cannot hope to offer courses to meet adequately the requirements of more than a few states. The wide variety of teacher-training institutions, the great differences in their program offerings, and the inflexibility of certification requirements all combine to make a decidedly limiting or restricting situation for the applicant for a teaching position. The situation, however, is much more restrictive and inflexible when a teacher must go to an institution of higher learning *in a particular state* to take a specific course *given only in that state* and cannot obtain even a provisional certificate without that course. Inflexibility is inherent in this situation, especially when other qualifications are not considered.

Specific state requirements seem to operate with greater restrictive power against trained but inexperienced recent graduates than against trained, experienced teachers. At every point it seems that the

* Question 12, State Certification Data Sheet, Appendix A.

former has the advantage over the latter where limiting and restricting certification requirements are concerned. The experienced teacher has probably accumulated enough money to pay his debts and perhaps even to save some money, so finance may not be such a pressing problem as with inexperienced recent graduates. The experienced person, with a position and an income, can be more poised, more definite, and more confident in his planning. The difficulties in securing another position are considerably lessened because such a person has already had teaching experience, which is one of the important assets in obtaining a position. The experience of an applicant affords the prospective employer one of the best criteria available for determining a teacher's professional ability. With inexperienced persons this criterion is absent and the risk of employment may therefore be greater. Inflexibility of certification requirements affects the experienced teacher also but perhaps to a less degree because the importance of obtaining *another* position is not so great as obtaining *a* position.

The Factor of Residence

Plainly, this factor of residence is of great importance in this study of limitations and restrictions. The five major factors just discussed are reasons why residence is so fundamental in the total picture of certification and employment. Basically, it is often an advantage to be a resident of a state in which one wishes to teach. But a person technically cannot be a resident of more than one state at the same time. How then can he overcome these barriers to out-of-state persons and how can he become a resident of a state? In trying to answer these questions, one finds that the matter of residence is exceedingly complex. Some factors tend to favor directly in-state residents, with other factors favoring such residents only indirectly. Three pertinent questions are involved in this problem:

What is meant by the term "residence"?

How many people counteract any differentiation, favoritism, or discrimination between an in-state and an out-of-state person?

If a person may avoid such restrictions by establishing residence:

How long must a person reside within a state to establish residence for purposes of avoiding any such factors named above?

It was necessary to ask each of the forty-eight state attorney-generals the following pertinent questions on this matter of residence: How long does a person need to reside in your state to become a legal resident of your state? Answers were received from thirty-seven attorney-generals. The replies contained a variety of complex legal definitions of terms, as well as some direct answers regarding the time necessary to establish residence in each state. Table XVII gives the answers obtained.

TABLE XVII

*Length of Time Needed to Establish Legal Residence for Voting Purposes in Each of Thirty-Seven States, January, 1939**

Length of Time Needed to Establish Residence	Number of States with Such Requirement
Six months	9
One year	24
Two years	4
No answer to this question	11
	48

* Letters to the author from thirty-seven state attorney-generals or officials designated by them, January, 1939. State laws prevent some attorney generals from giving an opinion to any persons except their own state officials. See Appendix D.

One-half of all the states in the Union, therefore, require that a person live one year in residence within a state to establish his legal residence in that state. This residence requirement is for voting purposes, however. There are many other types of residence, each state having its own definitions. Some of the different kinds of residence are related to the following:

1. Voting
2. Educational facilities
3. Taxation
4. Divorce
5. Eligibility to hold office
6. Pauper laws
7. Probate
8. Administration of estates
9. Right of naturalization
10. Relief
11. Old age assistance
12. Right to defend self in suit of law
13. Aid to blind and dependent children

The purpose of residence, therefore, controls in most instances the length of time required to establish residence. In no instance is there a residence law or ruling stipulating when a person may become a resident of a state so as to avoid any differentiating policies or practices established by the certification officials. Direct questions with regard to this problem were not answered. The nearest approximation to the length of time needed to establish residence to avoid any differentiation by certification officials is here considered to be the time needed to establish voting residence. So many definitions of residence exist among the states that there is little value in giving them here. To add to the confusion, three terms are often used interchangeably: abode, domicile, and residence.

The *intent* of a person seems to be the crux of this entire problem of residence. The attorney-general of North Dakota gives a typical answer that seems to apply to many of the states:

> I must state that whenever a person who is under no legal disability enters this state in good faith with the intention of establishing his residence here, he is a resident for all practical purposes. . . .[85]

Arizona is briefly specific on this point:

> In order for a person to become a resident of this state, there must not only be an actual act of removal to this state, but also an intention to acquire a new residence within this state, and both must concur.[86]

In most instances, the union of act and intent makes for residence. If, for any reason whatsoever, a person wanted to be known as a resident of a state to avoid any differentiation in certification proceedings, he could move to the state in which he wanted certification, *but his intention would have to be that of remaining to become a permanent resident. A person often is required to spend a definite, specified length of time in a state before he can claim residence. Some would say that he could not legally or ethically enter a state merely for the period of residence to become known as a resident of the state with the intention of moving away from the state after establishing his so-called residence.* However, no one can question the intent of another person, except as it is actually portrayed by external factors. A person might have the intention of becoming a permanent

[85] Letter to the author from P. O. Sathre, Special Assistant Attorney-General, State of North Dakota, Bismarck, January 10, 1939.

[86] Letter to the author from Joe Conway, Attorney-General, State of Arizona, Phoenix, January 10, 1939.

resident of a state and, after a period of residence is up, find that he must move from that state. In the practical situation, few, if any, would even investigate to see if a person were a resident of the state, especially if his inquiry were postmarked within the state in which he wanted a certificate. A notarized certificate of residence similar to the type required for some Civil Service positions may help satisfy inquiries about residence. However, if a person intends to become a resident of the state, the moment he settles in that state with the intention of remaining to make it his home, he becomes a resident and is entitled to any privilege in connection with such residence.

Fundamentally, if a person were to move to a state to become known as a resident, that very moving to the state is restrictive, coming very clearly within the scope of the definition of restrictions. Then, too, it should not be necessary to reside in a number of different states in order to escape certain differentiating factors in state certification. An applicant from another state should be able to obtain a position in a commonwealth solely on the basis of teaching merit. Teaching in the public schools is rapidly becoming a national service, and its problems are nation wide in scope and importance. No peculiar aspect of any geographical section, state, or community has unique demands sufficient to restrict or limit people from other states. From the broader viewpoint, such factors as restrictions and limitations tend to make teaching other than a profession.

Conclusions

Originating partly because of the activities of vocal minority groups outside the field of education and partly because of vested interests within education, the specific state requirements constitute a source of strong restrictions and limitations. Numerically not great, these requirements are nevertheless found in sixteen commonwealths, and on the basis of expert opinion ten more states are considering the adoption of such restrictive standards within the next few years. Though small in number, these restrictions are not easily removed. They have been accumulating as statutes and regulations since 1889; a few have been dropped, more have been added from time to time.

These specific state requirements are, in the main, found in the

Northwest, the Far West, and the Pacific Coast region, with representative requirements appearing in the Southwest, the Midwest, the deep South and the New England states. The purpose of restricting out-of-state teachers is clearly and unequivocably written into the laws of some of these standards; it is reasonable to assume this same purpose is behind still others though not so clearly designated.

These specific requirements tend to restrict certain groups of teachers from entering states, with the restrictions based on several factors such as the lack of ability to finance further studies rather than upon the professional ability of the prospective teachers. In the main, it seems safe to generalize that the restrictions fall with greater severity upon the inexperienced than upon the experienced person. Though certain values exist for the subject matter of these specific requirements, a one-year postponement when all other standards are met would not restrict teachers and yet would ultimately be of almost as much value as though they had been required at the time of certification.

Though all persons must meet every requirement regardless of residence, the matter of in-state residence is a factor in this problem. The in-state person has opportunity to take such requirements while attending high school or college, and he is "on the ground" without needing to travel a great distance. The out-of-state person has these factors operating against him as restrictions.

If a person needed to establish legal residence within a state, he would need in at least one-half of the states to remain one year within that commonwealth. In moving to a state to become a resident, however, a person thereby comes within the scope of the definition of restrictions, so, in moving to a state to eliminate any distinctions based on residence he would thereby be meeting a restriction.

The potential teaching field is so narrowed by specific course requirements that the employing groups within a state do not see some of the best teachers. Those who can make the financial hurdle demanded by these specific state requirements can obtain certification in these respective states. *The criterion of selection seems to be the ability to pay to meet detailed requirements rather than professional promise and teaching ability.* Groups of applicants are therefore screened out by these restrictions and limitations before they can even appear before the employing groups.

CHAPTER VI

RESTRICTIONS AND LIMITATIONS IN LOCAL EMPLOYMENT POLICIES AND PRACTICES

TEACHERS encounter certain restrictions and limitations to their free interstate mobility in areas other than certification, some of these being in the employment policies and practices of community school systems. While it is the state that certificates teachers, it is the local community school system that employs them. It is reasonable to assume that if a person applies for a teaching certificate in a state he wishes to teach in that commonwealth. If the series of steps leading from state certification to community employment is broken so the applicant does not obtain a position, the certificate is not of much practical value, and the applicant has not accomplished his objective of obtaining a teaching position in that state. Often when a person wants *certification* and *employment* in another commonwealth, he is unable to obtain both, even though his qualifications are equal or superior to those of the successful applicants. Of many possible causes for his unsuccessful application for employment, one may be that there is an oversupply of qualified teachers; second, another may be that a person is considered better qualified; and third, there may be differentiation by the employing officials of the school system *on the basis of residence in the community.* To illustrate, the following statement represents the third type:

> No candidate shall be considered eligible to take examinations unless he was a resident of *this city,* or whose parents were residents here *two years* prior to January first of the year in which the candidate takes the examinations. All data submitted on the candidate's residence will be checked.[1]

In the non-local group not eligible for employment in this community is the group of persons from other communities in the same com-

[1] City in Massachusetts; printed pamphlet usually sent in reply to inquiries from teachers regarding possibility of employment.

Words in italics are author's additions or substitutions for name of city.

monwealth as well as *the larger group from all other states.* Because all out-of-state persons are in this excluded group, this investigation can logically consider community employment restrictions.

No one knows the extent of such community employment restrictions or of their importance; neither does anyone know about the many forms in which these restrictions appear. It seems reasonable to break down this larger problem into its several phases and examine them carefully. This investigation, in meeting its third original objective, endeavors to answer the following questions:

A. What is the present situation with regard to the number of
   1. local, and
   2. out-of-state persons on the staffs of city school systems, as well as
   3. the number of teachers who have received their training in out-of-state training institutions?

B. What is the trend in regard to the employment of local or nonlocal persons and thereby the community restrictions and limitations?

C. What are the current restrictions and limitations in the policies, practices, and attitudes of the employing groups in the community school systems in:
   1. *unwritten* policies favoring local teachers?
   2. *written* regulations favoring local teachers?
   3. preferences shown for graduates of local or nearby colleges?
   4. other phases of this problem, such as
      (*a*) the attitudes of the superintendents?
      (*b*) the attitudes of the school board and those of the community?
   5. the employment standards of the communities exceeding the state certification minima? and

D. What are the important details of this factor of residence?

To obtain the data needed to answer these questions, five hundred and forty-two data sheets[2] were sent to school superintendents in cities with populations ranging from 14,500 to 100,000. Of the number sent out, three hundred thirty-eight, or 62.4 per cent, were re-

[2] These data sheets were sent out jointly by Harold E. Snyder and the author. Different parts were used by each in separate studies. See the Bibliography.

turned, giving a relatively large sampling upon which to base the discussion. In the main, it can safely be assumed that these figures represent the total situation.

THE PRESENT EMPLOYMENT SITUATION

1. *Wide variations occur in the percentages of local teachers on the staffs of community school systems.*

The employment of non-local teachers by the responding communities does not follow a decided trend one way or the other. Table XVIII shows the percentage of local teachers in the 315 cities studied.

TABLE XVIII

Percentage of Local Teachers in 315 Cities Ranging in Population from 14,500 to 100,000,** April, 1938* [1]

Percentage Range of Local Teachers	Number of Cities with Population of: 14,500–29,999	30,000–49,999	50,000–74,999	75,000–100,000	Total	Total Cumulative Upward
0– 9.9	16	7	3	0	26	315
10– 19.9	31	7	4	1	43	289
20– 29.9	33	14	3	2	52	246
30– 39.9	27	6	4	0	37	194
40– 49.9	26	14	3	2	45	157
50– 59.9	22	7	4	2	35	112
60– 69.9	15	9	4	0	28	77
70– 79.9	11	9	4	3	27	49
80– 89.9	7	2	3	0	12	22
90–100.00	8	0	2	0	10	10
Total	196	75	34	10	315 ***	
Question not answered but Data Sheet returned	10	5	6	2	23	
					338	

[1] Question I-A-5, Data Sheet on Employment Policies and Teachers' Residence. See reproduction of Data Sheet in Appendix B.

* Local here means that the teacher has been graduated from the secondary school of the particular community.

** Data for this table came from Question 5 of Part I-A, Current Status and Practices, General Information, of the Data Sheet sent to all United States Cities between 14,500 and 100,000 population. These figures include the cities of these ranges in Massachusetts, which is the only generally decentralized state in certification matters in the Union. See Appendix B.

*** Includes four cities which did not return data sheets but for which information was obtained directly from the superintendents.

Over one-half of the responding communities have less than 40 per cent local teachers on their staffs. The mode falls in the interval with the midpoint of 25 per cent of local persons on the teaching staffs of the cities answering. Only ten communities have between 90 and 100 per cent local persons in the teaching group while sixty-nine communities have less than 20 per cent local teachers employed. Each of the intervals from 0 to 79.9 per cent contains a frequency between twenty-six and fifty-two. In one hundred and twelve cities, more than fifty per cent of the teachers are local.

No one knows what the danger point is in regard to the employment of local persons or the full consequences of the employment of too many or too few local residents. If the figures in Table XVIII are a reliable indication of the present situation with regard to the employment policies of local teachers, the restrictions to the employment of non-local persons had not been too great up to the time of this investigation. However, the word "local" here means that the teacher has been graduated from the secondary school of the particular community. Persons born and reared in the community but graduated from some other community's high school would not be regarded as local residents, neither would those who were graduated from a high school in some other city and who then moved to the city to live. More teachers may actually be locally reared and educated than is indicated here, therefore.

Of the non-local persons employed, some are from near-by communities, others from more distant communities in the same state, and others from outside the commonwealth. It is of importance in this study to know what percentages of teachers were employed from other states. These figures will tend to reveal how many of this non-local group were in-state and out-of-state persons at the time of employment.

2. *Comparatively few teachers were, at the time of their initial employment in the responding communities, residents of other states.*

A large number of communities have a very low percentage of out-of-state teachers on their staffs, as shown in Table XIX.

Over one-half the total number of cities responding had between 0 and 9.9 per cent of out-of-state teachers on their staffs, thus having over 90 per cent in-state persons in their teaching groups. Furthermore, over 78 per cent of the communities had less than

TABLE XIX

Percentage of City Teachers Who Were, at the Time of Their Initial[1, a] *Employment in the Several Communities, Residents of Other States, April, 1938*

Percentage Range of Out-of-State Teachers	Number of Cities with Population of: 14,500–29,999	30,000–49,999	50,000–74,999	75,000–100,000	Total	Total Cumulative Downward
0– 9.9	101	34	18	2	155	155
10–19.9	48	23	6	5	82	237
20–29.9	15	7	4	1	27	264
30–39.9	10	2	4	0	16	280
40–49.9	6	3	2	0	11	291
50–59.9	2	4	0	1	7	298
60–69.9	4	0	0	0	4	302
70–79.9	0	0	0	0	0	302
80–89.9	0	0	0	0	0	302
90–99.9	0	0	0	0	0	302
Total	186	73	34	9	302[b]	

[1] Question I-A-3. Data Sheet on Employment Policies and Teachers' Residence. See Appendix B.

[a] Includes nineteen Massachusetts cities and all other responding cities in the United States of population between 14,500 and 100,000.

[b] An approximate number was requested as it is conceivable that the data are not available in accurate up-to-date form in some instances. The teaching staffs of the cities answering this question have proportionately few teachers from other states represented.

one-fifth out-of-state teachers, having more than 80 per cent in-state persons. Plainly, although communities vary widely in the percentages of local teachers they employ, they tend in the great majority to employ in-state persons for their teaching staffs. Only twenty-two cities of three hundred and two responding had more than 40 per cent out-of-state teachers. The majority of the teachers in these communities responding have come from within the same commonwealth but outside the local community. There are several reasons why non-local persons are employed. One is that persons with the desired type of training may not have been available in the local group of eligible persons, making it imperative for the local school system to employ non-local teachers. Another reason is that a community often requires one year or more of experience, forcing the teachers to go elsewhere, often to rural communities, for the first year or two of experience. Snyder[3] has studied this problem in detail.

[3] Harold E. Snyder, "Educational Inbreeding: A Study of Teacher Residence." Unpublished manuscript.

Many of the persons who are local by definition have received their training in institutions of higher learning in other states, and have thus had the opportunity to study different methods, different types of training, and different approaches to school problems. The next section deals with certain phases of this question.

3. *Relatively few teachers on the staffs of the responding communities received their training in out-of-state colleges or universities.*

Table XX shows that in more than one-half of the total number of cities responding, less than 20 per cent of the teachers had received their training in out-of-state institutions of higher learning.

TABLE XX

Percentage of Teachers Trained in Out-of-State Institutions and Now Employed by 306 Communities Ranging in Population from 14,500 to 100,000, April, 1938 [1]

Percentage Range of Teachers Trained in Out-of-State Institutions	Number of Cities with Population of: 14,500–29,999	30,000–49,999	50,000–74,999	75,000–99,999	Total	Total Cumulative Downward
0– 9.9	58	12	11	1	82	82
10–19.9	50	19	7	4	80	162
20–29.9	35	19	4	1	59	221
30–39.9	25	8	3	1	37	258
40–49.9	17	3	2	0	22	280
50–59.9	4	7	2	1	14	294
60–69.9	4	3	0	0	7	301
70–79.9	2	0	1	0	3	304
80–89.9	1	0	1	0	2	306
90–99.9	0	0	0	0	0	306
Total	196	71	31	8	306	
Question not answered but Data Sheet returned					21	
					327	

[1] Question I-A-4. Data Sheet on Employment Policies and Teachers' Residence. See Appendix B.

Twenty-six per cent of the cities responding had less than ten per cent of the teachers on their staffs who had been trained in out-of-state colleges and universities. Only twenty-six cities of the three hundred and six answering, or 8.5 per cent, had more than one-half of their staffs who had attended out-of-state colleges. Of several reasons for this, one is that persons often find it cheaper to attend their state institutions. Most colleges work for the placement of their graduates, but with the help of their former graduates and others in key professional positions in the commonwealth, the state institutions are in a favorable position to place many of their students in teaching positions. Distance from home is also a major factor in the student's choice of a college. These are some reasons why the number of employed persons graduated from in-state institutions is greater than the number employed from colleges outside the state.

The foregoing data and discussion reveal the present situation with regard to local and non-local teachers on the staffs of the cooperating cities, together with the number of teachers who had attended colleges and universities in other states. What has the employment trend been, however, in the past seven or eight years? Are more or fewer local persons being employed by the communities? What is the direction of the trend and the amount of change? The following section contains a discussion of these problems.

Trends in Restrictions and Limitations in the Employment of Local and Non-Local Teachers

A marked increase in the preference for local residents as teachers has taken place since 1930–1931 in 287 cities of 30,000 population and over.

In 1930–1931, a study was made by the research staff of the National Education Association to determine the policies concerning the appointment of local residents as teachers.[4] At that time 274 cities in the investigation responded with data. In 1937–1938 a similar study was made in which 287 cities cooperated. A comparison based on the data obtained in these two studies as presented in Table XXI reveals a decided trend in such employment policies.

In cities of both population ranges the preference for local residents for teachers increased, the greater increase being in the cities of smaller size, from 30,000 to 100,000 population. The rises in both instances indicate a decided increase in this preference for local residents. In the practical situation this greater preference reveals itself in the employment of local persons and in the refusal to employ those from outside the community or state. This increase therefore reveals

[4] See footnote 1 to Table XXI.

TABLE XXI

Policies Concerning the Appointments of Local Residents as Teachers in 1930–1931 and 1937–1938 [a] [1]

	1930–31		1937–38		Per Cent Increase
	No.	Per Cent	No.	Per Cent	
	Cities Over 100,000 Population				
Policy	68 [b]	80.0	74 [d]	86.0	7.5
	Cities 30,000 to 100,000 Population				
Preference for local residents (as teachers)	146 [c]	77.2	173 [e]	86.0	11.4
Total	214		247		

[1] Policies Concerning the Appointment of Local Residents as Teachers in 1930–1931 and 1937–1938, Educational Research Service, American Association of School Administrators and Research Division of the National Education Association, Circular No. 1, 1938, January, 1938, pp. 4–5. Data are rearranged in slightly different form with differences between the two studies given in percentages.

[a] Ten cities reported practices in more than one district. These cities were counted in this tabulation only when replies from the various districts of an individual city were similar.

[b] Of these sixty-eight cities giving preference to local residents, twenty-nine indicated that this preference is given only if the qualifications of local residents are at least equal to those of outside candidates; fourteen indicated that local residents must meet the minimum training and experience requirements; and one indicated that experience requirements are waived for local residents.

[c] Of these 146 cities giving preference to local residents, sixty-three indicated that this preference is given only if the qualifications of local residents are at least equal to those of outside candidates; and thirty-three indicated that local residents must meet the minimum training and experience requirements.

[d] Of these seventy-four cities giving preference to local residents twenty indicated that this preference is given only if the qualifications of local residents are at least equal to those of outside candidates; nine indicated that local residents must meet the minimum training and experience requirements; four indicated that additional credit is given local residents in competitive examinations or on ranking scale; and eleven indicated that local residents only are appointed.

[e] Of these 173 cities giving preference to local residents, seventy-three indicated that this preference is given only if the qualifications of local residents are at least equal to those of outside candidates; forty indicated that local residents must meet the minimum training and experience requirements; one indicated that additional credit is given local residents; and two indicated that local residents only are appointed.

directly and indisputably the fact of increasing restrictions to non-local and out-of-state teachers.

One reason for the fact that there is a smaller increase in the number of local residents employed in the larger communities may be that the latter are more cosmopolitan and their methods of selecting teachers different in many cases from those methods used in the smaller communities. In the manner of teacher selection, in the routine followed, or the system of examinations in the larger cities, there may be less opportunity to express a preference for a local resident. In the larger cities there may be greater separation of the lay citizen from the Board of Education and the employing groups than in the smaller cities, so the pressures on the part of the lay citizen may be more difficult to apply. In the smaller cities there may be more direct responsibility and sense of ownership or proprietorship on the part of the lay groups than in the larger cities.[5]

A few of the cities granting preference to local residents indicate that preference is given only if the qualifications of local applicants are at least equivalent to those of outsiders. In some school systems preference is given in all cases to local residents.

The economic situation of the past few years has greatly influenced the policy of giving preference to local teachers. Several cities frankly reported an oversupply of local candidates as the determining factor. For this and other reasons, eleven cities over 100,000 in population definitely stated that local city or county residents *only* are appointed, while two of the smaller cities so reported. Occasionally additional credit is given local residents in a competitive examination or on a ranking scale.

In a few cities an effort is made to keep the percentage of local residents and non-residents well balanced. Some superintendents mentioned the danger of "inbreeding."

The data in Table XXI show without question a severe restriction to the possibility of an out-of-state teacher obtaining employment. The teacher finds these employment restrictions in addition to any limiting or restricting factors he encounters in *state* certification.

Some commonwealths require that an applicant for a certificate first have the promise of a position before giving him a certificate. By this practice, the states are saved from issuing a greater number of certificates to applicants who later may not obtain employment. By this practice also the commonwealths *automatically throw the applicant against these non-local employment policies of the community, placing a severe burden upon the applicant's shoulders.* In this connection, it seems that a person might more easily obtain a position if he first has a state certificate than if he first must try to obtain the promise of a position without the certificate. Superintend-

[5] In answer to the questions regarding preference for local residents for teachers, six more cities responded in the larger population range in 1937–1938 than in 1930–1931, and twenty-seven more cities in the smaller population range in the previous study.

ents do not like the uncertainty often accompanying the applicant's obtaining a certificate, choosing to give the position to the person who already can qualify for the certificate or who has one already. This often means that the local or in-state candidate obtains the position for which an out-of-state candidate may have been an applicant.

The present situation with regard to the employment of local and non-local residents has been indicated, as well as the trend from 1930–1931 to 1937–1938. However, what are the policies and practices that will determine the employment of local and non-local persons from the present time into the near future? Although most teachers are employed between May and September of each year, the employment of new teachers is going on continually to replace those who are leaving the school systems because of death, sickness, marriage, retirement, change of location, and other causes. The present attitudes of the employing group and the present employment policies and practices will have a decided effect on the future status of the teaching staffs in the respective school systems because, as teacher turnover occurs, the changes will be conditioned by these present policies and practices. Every teacher employed from now on will be affected in some way by these attitudes and policies of the employing groups of the school systems. The next section discusses the present attitudes and policies of employing groups with relation to restrictions and limitations to teachers and reveals the form which these restrictions take.

Current Restrictions and Limitations in Employment Policies, Practices, and Attitudes in Community School Systems

1. *A great many communities have a consistent policy giving preference to local residents.*

A total of one hundred and eighty seven cities, or 58 per cent of the three hundred and nineteen responding cities, favor local residents in their employment policies, as revealed in the data presented in Table XXII. If a vacancy occurred in the teaching staffs of these cities, it is likely that the employing groups would choose a local resident, if such a person were available. A few cities have a policy

TABLE XXII

Employment Policies Relating to Residence of Teaching Candidates, April, 1938

HAVE FAIRLY CONSISTENT POLICY, NOT PRESCRIBED BY ANY SCHOOL BOARD REGULATION, GIVING PREFERENCE IN THE EMPLOYMENT OF NEW TEACHERS TO ONE OR MORE OF THE FOLLOWING GROUPS, APRIL, 1938 [1]

Policy of Giving Preference to:	Cities with Population of: 15,000–29,999	30,000–49,999	50,000–74,999	75,000–100,000	Total	Total Cumulative Downward
a. Local residents[2]....	114	48	23	2	187	187
b. Residents of other communities in state	17	8	1	0	26	213
c. Residents of own state	54	22	7	2	85	298
d. Residents of one or more adjacent states	9	2	1	0	12	310
e. Residents of distant states...........	1	1	0	0	2	312
f. Other type of regulation............	5	1	1	0	7	319
Total..........	200	82	33	4	319	

[1] Question I-B-1. Data Sheet on Employment Policies and Teachers' Residence. See Appendix B.
[2] The letters *a*, *b*, *c*, etc., refer to Data Sheet items.

favoring residents of other communities within the state. A total of eighty-five of the responding cities favor residents of their own commonwealth, but this group may be limited to local residents. Altogether, two hundred and ninety-eight communities of three hundred nineteen responding, or 93 per cent, have policies favoring in-state people. Preference is heavily weighted in favor of, first, the local teacher and, second, the in-state person. This preference, though intangible, is as much a restriction to out-of-state teachers as a high tariff or a physical barrier and perhaps even more difficult to surmount.

These preferences for local residents operate as restrictions and limitations in several ways. One very effective way to restrict non-local persons is to print a statement of the policy regarding preference for local teachers and then send this statement to persons who have inquired about employment possibilities. Such information is discouraging and restricting in that it tends to keep non-local persons even from applying for positions, thus effectively keeping them out of the employment situation. The following statements from Pennsylvania districts are typical of such statements of policy sent in response to employment inquiries:

> The Carbondale School District has a rule that only local applicants will be placed in teaching positions. . . .
> We regret you are not eligible.[6]

From Augusta, Pennsylvania:

> . . . Our Board of Education requires us to employ local people insofar as we can find them who are qualified to fill local vacancies. . . . We very seldom find difficulty in filling vacancies locally.[7]

Another statement, even more restrictive in character, is given at the beginning of this chapter, and there are others very similar. Such statements differentiate among applicants on the basis of residence and are severely restrictive in intent and effect.

Another effective way in which such a policy favoring local residents reveals itself is in the voting for candidates or in the so-called selective process of "weeding-out" the applicants. In the beginning of the competition, or near the end of it, when the applicants for a position are narrowed down to a few persons, it is a mere matter of voting to favor the local candidate. Sometimes the Board of Education will not even consider the nomination made by the superintendent of schools if the nominee is a non-local teacher.

Such restrictive policies sometimes help the superintendent of schools and the Board of Education to "sell" their policies and practices to the community because, it is pointed out, the residents are "protected" in the basic problem of obtaining positions for their sons and daughters in the local school system, the largest employing group in most communities. The school officials can far more easily go to the public for financial aid for operating the school system because of the presence of these restrictive policies against the non-local teachers than if other policies were followed.

[6] The Superintendent of Schools, Carbondale School District. Letter to the author, December 12, 1938.

[7] The Superintendent of Schools, Augusta, Pennsylvania. Letter to the author, December 15, 1938.

Certain negative effects of such restrictive policies have been pointed out by several students of the problems resulting from localized or provincial employment practices. The peculiar "inbreeding" effects of such "restrictive policies" have been referred to time and again. Snyder, in his study of the local teacher problem, reveals some of the results of these policies.[8] The Lynds mentioned them in their second book on Middletown.[9] Mort and Cornell pointed out in their study on adaptability that new ways of approaching educational problems, new ideas, and different methods were essential in a city's adapting itself to changing conditions.[10] These new and desirable ideas are screened out partly by restrictive employment policies. Ebey made a study of a phase of this problem in St. Louis, Missouri.[11] Lewis has given several arguments pro and con regarding the employment of local persons.[12] Although no one knows what the limits of such restrictive employment policies should be or the complete results of provincial employment procedures, students of the problem agree that the contrasts, different methods and attitudes of non-local and out-of-state teachers are, to a certain extent, of value to any school system. Different approaches to professional problems often stimulate a teaching staff or school system.

2. *Some communities have written regulations with regard to restrictions to non-local teachers.*

Community *policies* have been indicated as restrictive phases of community employment. What, then, is the extent of restrictions in *written regulations* of school boards? If there are any preferences at all for local persons, there are advantages in having these preferences as unwritten policies that can be more or less changed as conditions change. Written regulations tend to resist the changing situations and have a "lingering quality," remaining long after their need or usefulness is past. By their very presence, regulations offer an argument for obedience to their mandates. Investigation, however, in-

[8] Harold E. Snyder, *op. cit.*

[9] Robert S. Lynd and Helen M. Lynd, *Middletown in Transition.* Harcourt, Brace and Company, New York, 1937.

[10] Paul R. Mort and Frances G. Cornell, *Adaptability of Public School Systems.* Bureau of Publications, Teachers College, Columbia University, New York, 1938.

[11] George W. Ebey, *Adaptability Among the Elementary Schools of an American City.* Contributions to Education, No. 817. Bureau of Publications, Teachers College, Columbia University, New York, 1940.

[12] Ervin Eugene Lewis, *Personnel Problems of the Teaching Staff.* The Century Co., New York, 1925.

dicated that of the total group of cities responding, only sixty-four reported that they have regulations regarding the employment of local residents as teachers. Of these, forty-seven cities give preference to local persons while thirteen give preference to in-state teachers.[13]

Apparently, although nearly one-fifth of the total number of cities responding express their restrictive employment practices as regulations, by far the majority have unwritten policies in regard to this problem.

3. *Preference by communities for graduates of local or in-state institutions of higher learning as teachers is not marked.*

Sometimes preference for local or non-local persons is not expressed directly on the basis of residence but indirectly on the basis of the institution attended. Of the 243 cities responding on this question, ninety-two reported that they had no institutions in or near them.[14] Of the remaining 151 cities, only forty-five stated a preference for graduates of certain more or less near-by teacher-training institutions. When asked whether they preferred graduates of in-state colleges or universities, 250 cities responded with answers which showed a slight preference for graduates of in-state institutions. One hundred and thirty-three communities give preference to graduates of in-state colleges and universities while 117 cities do not. Seventeen cities expressed a preference for graduates of out-of-state institutions. It was found that if a person desired later to become a teacher in any particular one of 133 responding communities, he would have the odds in his favor if he attended a teacher-training institution within the same state as the respective community. With regard to his obtaining employment in 117 cities, it would make little or no difference in what state he attended an institution of higher learning.

4. (a) *A majority of city school superintendents think the present proportion of in-state and out-of-state persons on their teaching staffs is about right.*

What the attitudes of the superintendents are toward the present proportion of in- and out-of-state teachers is considered important

[13] Question I-B-2. Data Sheet on Employment Policies and Teachers' Residence. See Appendix B.

[14] Question I-B-3. Data Sheet on Employment Policies and Teachers' Residence. See Appendix B.

in this study. Present attitudes sometimes can change the present situation entirely; often, however, because of opposing forces that hinder or prevent any changes, these attitudes mean but little. Sometimes the superintendent, the professional leader of the community, is not able to carry out the policies he thinks are best for the community or the school system. Table XXIII reveals the expressed attitudes of 273 city school superintendents.

TABLE XXIII

Attitudes Toward the Problem of Teacher Residence

ATTITUDES OF CITY SCHOOL SUPERINTENDENTS TOWARD THE PRESENT PROPORTION OF IN-STATE AND OUT-OF-STATE TEACHERS IN THE CITY SCHOOL SYSTEMS, APRIL, 1938[1]

Attitudes of Superintendents	Cities with Population of: 15,000–29,999	30,000–49,999	50,000–74,999	75,000–100,000	Total
a. Proportion is about right in terms of local conditions	107	39	24	8	178
b. Favor much higher proportion of out-of-state teachers	19	3	3	3	28
c. Favor slightly higher proportion of out-of-state teachers	38	18	5	1	62
d. Favor slightly lower proportion of out-of-state teachers	2	0	0	0	2
e. Favor much lower proportion of out-of-state teachers	2	1	0	0	3
Total	168	61	32	12	273

[1] Question II-3. Data Sheet on Employment Policies and Teachers' Residence. See Appendix B.

Of the two hundred and seventy-three superintendents responding, a total of one hundred and seventy-eight, or 65 per cent, thought that the present proportion of local and non-local persons was about right. The proportion, however, although large, is not two to one in favor of the status quo. Twenty-eight superintendents favored a *much higher* proportion of non-local teachers while sixty-two favored a *slightly higher* proportion of the non-local group. Ninety superintendents desire more out-of-state teachers on their staffs. That these administrators want more out-of-state teachers indicates that whatever differences such persons bring to a school system, these are wanted in the cities responding to this question. It also indicates that some factors, somewhere, are operating to prevent the superintendents from doing what they think is the professionally desirable thing to do for the community school system in employing out-of-state teachers.

Whatever the attitude of the superintendent, is it in line with the prevailing attitude of the community? Or of the school board?

4. (b) *The attitudes of the superintendents of schools differ from those held by the community and the school board on this problem.*

Quantitative data have not yet been given to indicate an apparent underlying conflict between the professional desires of the superintendent and the prevailing sentiment of the community or the school board itself. Usually the superintendent is the one desiring more non-local teachers, with the school board and the prevailing groups in the community wanting more local persons employed. The data presented in Tables XXIV and XXV reveal the situations in the responding communities.

In more than one-third of the cases, the attitudes of the superintendents with respect to the desirability of employing local or non-local, in-state or out-of-state persons, differ from the prevailing views of the community. In 102 communities the superintendent's employment policy would be different if the community sentiment would permit. In 102 cities there is more or less conflict in attitudes regarding this problem of employment. In several instances the superintendents reported their "hands were tied" insofar as personnel employment is concerned and that they were considering resigning to go elsewhere because of this conflict.

Twenty-two per cent of the responding superintendents differed in their attitudes on the problem of employment from those held by the school board. The fact that so many superintendents refer to the existence of conflict with regard to this policy suggests considerable conflict beneath the surface. Some school boards do not consider the superintendent's recommendations for teaching positions unless the candidate is a local person. Residence rather than merit often is the basis of selection by the board. If the training and experience of the local persons are as good as those of a non-local person, few would raise objections to the employment of local residents. Where persons are selected on the basis of residence, regardless of merit, such policies can be seriously challenged.

Superintendents notice the changes in public opinion and the

TABLE XXIV

Attitudes Toward the Problem of Teacher Residence [1]

DIFFERENCES IN THE PREVAILING ATTITUDES OF THE SUPERINTENDENT AND THE COMMUNITY TOWARD THE DESIRABILITY OF EMPLOYING LOCAL, OR NON-LOCAL, IN-STATE, OR OUT-OF-STATE TEACHERS, APRIL, 1938

	Cities with Population of:				
	15,000–29,999	30,000–49,999	50,000–74,999	75,000–100,000	Total
Superintendent's views differ from prevailing attitude in community..............	65	20	12	5	102
Superintendent's views do not differ from the prevailing attitude in the community....	112	50	20	7	189
Total.................	177	70	32	12	291

[1] Question II-5. Data Sheet on Employment Policies and Teachers' Residence. See Appendix B.

TABLE XXV

Attitudes Toward the Problem of Teacher Residence

DIFFERENCES IN THE PREVAILING ATTITUDES OF THE BOARD OF EDUCATION AND THE SUPERINTENDENT TOWARD THE DESIRABILITY OF EMPLOYING LOCAL, NON-LOCAL, IN-STATE, OR OUT-OF-STATE TEACHERS, APRIL, 1938

	Cities with Population of:				
	15,000–29,999	30,000–49,999	50,000–74,999	75,000–100,000	Total
Prevailing attitude of the Board of Education differs from that of the Superintendent...............	40	14	9	1	64
Prevailing attitude of the Board of Education does not differ from that of the Superintendent...............	138	50	25	10	223
Total.................	178	64	34	11	287

"pressure" brought to bear upon them regarding the employing of local persons.

Of one hundred and sixty-two superintendents responding, one hundred and eighteen, or 72.8 per cent, noticed changes in the social "pressure" brought to bear on them, forcing the employment of local teachers from 1929 to 1938.[15] The greatest pressure has apparently been experienced since 1929, particularly in the year 1930 and since 1937. The pressure is still strongly in favor of employing local residents as teachers.

Restrictions and Limitations in Community Employment Standards or Requirements other than Residence or College Preference

5. *Many communities exceed the state certification requirements in setting up their employment standards. This is professionally desirable, but the manner in which this is done may create restrictive or limiting factors.*

Investigation of the employment standards of communities revealed that many cities utilize the state certification requirements as their minimum essentials and proceed to add other requirements for teachers for their own school systems. In this procedure the communities are following in some respects the policy of financial equalization in which a minimum financial program is established, below which the community may not go and above which it is free and urged to go. Professionally, it is a desirable thing for cities to raise their employment standards above the certification requirements of the commonwealth. One peculiar result is, however, that if cities raise their requirements above the state certification standards, the certificate does not have state-wide validity. The anomalous situation arises in which the state certificate is not acceptable within the commonwealth itself. Persons legally qualified to teach in one city are not qualified to teach in another city in the same state. Many cities exceed the certification requirements; still other communities have the increase in standards under consideration. This study could not go into this matter in detail even though it is recognized that it is

[15] Question II-6. Data Sheet on Employment Policies and Teachers' Residence. See Appendix B.

a problem related to the whole problem of restrictions and limitations. Brief reference to this matter and a few data resulting from the study will be given, however, to indicate the extent of the problem. Table XXVI shows the number of cities responding that exceed the state certification requirements.

TABLE XXVI

Numbers of Cities Exceeding the State Certification Requirements or Training Standards, April, 1938[1]

	Cities with Population of:				
	15,000–29,999	30,000–49,999	50,000–74,999	75,000–100,000	Total
Cities exceeding the state certification requirements.......	89	38	13	5	145
Cities not exceeding the state certification requirements....	96	45	21	7	169

[1] Question I-B-5. Data Sheet on Employment Policies and Teachers' Residence. See Appendix B.

Of three hundred and fourteen responding communities, one hundred and forty-five, or 46 per cent, exceed in some way the state certification requirements. Most of these cities specified the particular areas in which they had higher standards. These include certain professional and academic courses, teaching experience, and practice teaching in that order.

In exceeding the states' minimum standards, cities usually follow one of two procedures, both of which have importance in this investigation. These procedures are as follows:

1. The city may require the usual academic or professional courses or teaching experience in addition to the state's minimum requirements. Persons may meet these additional standards in any city or state where the facilities are available.

2. The city may require (*a*) unusual or specific courses peculiar to the city itself, (*b*) graduation from or a fifth-year program administered by a local teacher-training institution, or (*c*) examinations for which the applicant must come to the city itself. Persons usually can meet these types of standards only within the particular cities requiring them.[16]

[16] In this investigation, questions were asked about the requirements for certification and employment, not for the manner of conducting examinations and the pro-

Cities following the first procedure are raising their standards in a highly desirable manner professionally, limiting the teachers of poorer quality and yet not restricting the teachers who can meet the higher standards. In fulfilling the requirements of one community that has gone beyond the state requirements, a person may also be obtaining the training that would be useful to him in meeting standards elsewhere. No restricting factors exist in this type of additional requirement and very few limiting factors.

Communities following the second procedure are raising their standards but are also adding more limitations and restrictions in the three factors described below:

A. If a person is required to meet specific community requirements unique for each city in which he applies for a position, not only interstate but also intrastate freedom of teachers' mobility will be restricted. If cities exceed the state minima with unique requirements demanding that an applicant come to the city or take a particular course or examination, a type of provincialism or localism is evident in such procedures, which definitely come within the scope of the definitions of restrictions.

B. If an applicant for employment in a given community is required to attend a local or near-by normal school or college, he would need to select the community in which he wished later to teach, and then attend that particular teacher-training institution. This type of requirement closes the doors of employment to most if not all teachers from other cities inside and outside the state and graduates of all other institutions of higher learning. *Few plans have contained within them more provincial aspects or restrictions than this.* Often, however, teaching experience is accepted in lieu of graduation from a local college. Furthermore, some of the specified institutions are of a professionally high caliber. Because of alert leadership and adequate financial support of a local college, the city's employment of only graduates of local institutions might be entirely satisfactory from a professional standpoint. The factor of restrictions and limitations still exists, however, with the in-bred conditions that come with it. It may be better professionally for some cities to employ a certain proportion of their teachers from non-local col-

---

cedures followed. Consequently, no data are presented with regard to these areas. This is one part that had to be delimited.

leges or school systems. Unless safeguards are provided few factors stagnate the teaching staff as does the predominance of locally reared and locally trained teachers.

c. By requiring persons to take examinations for city employment, communities are going back to the older method of certification, but with new and improved techniques. The certification procedures followed by states and localities early in this nation's history are now being used by many cities as a basis for employment. More skillful techniques and better interpretation or use of the examination results are some of the improvements made. City examinations, however, come within the scope of the definitions for both restrictions and limitations. It seems in some cities that the examinations are merely a routine, a professional "smoke screen" behind which the employing groups may take shelter after choosing teachers on other bases than the examination.

In certain speech tests given applicants, the examiners are often overly sensitized toward certain accents or pronunciations. While the giving of speech tests is a very desirable procedure, there are certain sections in this nation in which people have different ways of speaking that are not grammatically or culturally undesirable but are merely different. Applicants from the South or from other sections are sometimes penalized by speech tests.

Examinations usually request specific information and ignore other qualifications which may be more important. "By watching carefully the trees, the examiners may ignore the forest itself." Then, too, the time required for the series of examinations may be so great or they may come when persons from other cities or states cannot take them or cannot even apply for them. It seems in some cases that the cities are driving away the very talent which they wish to attract.

The Factor of Residence in Relation to Restrictions Is a Complex Problem

The factor of residence is very important in the matter of community employment. If persons are to be favored because they are residents of a community or if they are to be differentiated on the basis of residence, it is important for the teachers to know just how residence can be established, and, second, how restrictive factors favoring local residents can be counteracted by establishing such residence. Obviously, if any factor whatsoever favors local residents as against non-local residents, then it is important to know how that differentiating factor can be met and eliminated. The following questions are involved in this problem:

1. What is residence?
2. How long must a person reside within a community to establish residence for purposes of avoiding or counteracting any differentiating factors?

As indicated in the preceding chapter, a letter was sent to the attorney-general in each of the forty-eight states with questions on the matter of residence.[17] One of the two questions has already been given; the other is as follows:

> How long does a person need to reside in a community in your state to become a legal resident of that community, assuming that the day he entered the community he intended to become a legal resident of that community?

Answers to this question involved a variety of definitions of terms and answers as to the length of time needed to establish residence. The length of time a person needs to spend in a community to establish legal residence for voting varies from thirty days to one year. For example, four states require thirty days, two demand sixty days, eight ask for ninety days, one asks for five months, seven require six months, and two ask for one year's residence.

In most instances the union of act and intent makes for residence. If a person wanted to be known as a resident of a community to avoid any possible differentiation that may exist, he could move to the community in question. His intent would have to be that of remaining to become a permanent resident. He could not legally or ethically enter a community merely to become known as a resident and then move away; however, no one can judge the intent of another except by his actions, his written or his spoken word. By merely moving to a community, a person might thereby become known as a resident for many intents and purposes.

[17] See Appendix D.

Establishing residence within a community involves different problems from those involved in establishing one's residence in a state. A community is much smaller and more compact sociological unit than the state. A person moving into a community becomes the cynosure of many eyes. A "new" neighbor becomes a topic of conversation for many persons. It would be difficult to establish one's self as a resident by the mere fact of moving into a community because more is involved than the factor of legal residence. A person's moving into a city to establish residence to escape any possible differentiation or restriction would in the course of events be asked how long he had lived in the community, what his address was, and other questions about his residence. If the data in his application for employment were checked at all, the information about his residence would perhaps come to the attention of the employing groups. The *fact* of legal residence may be a hollow argument on which to base an applicant's defense of his statement about residence.

By going to a community to establish residence to avoid restrictions, a person comes within the scope of the definition of restrictions as established by this investigation.[18] Then, too, while establishing his residence in one community, he cannot at the same time be trying to establish his residence in another city to escape restrictions by the employing groups. The very practical question arises as to how a person moving from place to place will in the meantime earn his bread and butter. Moving to a community or going from one to another to establish residence to be considered eligible for employment as a teacher should not be at all necessary in any occupation or profession. Professional ability or promise should be the main criterion, not geographical residence. It is detrimental and ignoble for any occupation or profession to require the kind of situation to exist in which residence rather than ability is the main consideration.

In some cities the legal phase of this question of residence does not enter inasmuch as the community itself stipulates a period of time in which the applicant for a teaching position or his parents must have lived in the community. One such illustration is given at the beginning of this chapter; there are many others. In these instances, residence does not depend upon the state's interpretation of residence but is a matter of community policy or board regulation.

[18] See definitions in Chapter I.

Employment policies and practices such as those just discussed are distinctly restrictions to the free interstate movement of teachers. They bar non-local and out-of-state persons from entering the community as thoroughly as very high tariff walls or physical barriers. The young, inexperienced teacher meets such restrictions—so do the older, trained, experienced persons. Some applicants may be conscious of the fact of restrictions in some cities. Others are aware only that they have no opportunity for employment in particular communities. The latter perhaps do not realize that it is geographical residence, not the quality of their professional ability, that deprives them of an opportunity even to apply for employment, let alone be considered for any position. There are few factors that could be discovered or used that restrict non-local persons as effectively as many of these employment policies.

Some commonwealths contain a number of communities which have very restrictive employment policies and practices regarding non-local teachers. Gradually the reputation of the state becomes such that persons regard it as restrictive, the inference being that it is restrictive in certification, whereas the restrictions arise from the community employment policies, not from the state certification requirements, policies, or practices. Mrs. Clements, of the California State Department of Education, says on this point:

> . . . Quite widely prevalent throughout the country is the idea that California maintains barriers against out-of-state teachers, through credential regulations. . . . Actually the case is far different.[19]

The certification procedures and standards of the state may be liberal and free from restrictions, yet because of the community restrictions in employment the state becomes known as a "closed" or a restrictive commonwealth to out-of-state teachers.

Conclusions

Present situation. Community employment policies and practices provide some difficult and complex restrictions and limitations of out-of-state teachers, with the responding cities favoring, first, local

[19] Evelyn A. Clements, "The Employment of Out-of-State Teachers," *School and Society,* L (July 15, 1939), 87–89.

residents, second, in-state teachers, and, third, persons from other commonwealths. More than a third of the cities have 50 per cent or more local persons on their teaching staffs. Over half of the communities have less than 10 per cent out-of-state teachers employed. Fewer than one teacher in five in approximately half of the responding cities had been trained in out-of-state colleges, while only one in ten of the teachers in 25 per cent of the cities had attended out-of-state institutions of higher learning.

Ninety superintendents of two hundred and seventy-three cities favored slightly greater or much higher proportions of out-of-state teachers on their staffs, while one hundred and seventy-eight thought the present proportion was about right. In almost half of the two hundred and ninety-one responding cities, the views of the superintendent differ from the prevailing community attitude toward the employment of local or non-local, in-state or out-of-state persons. Nearly one-fourth of the superintendents differed from their own boards of education in regard to this same problem.

Trend in employment of local persons. A decided trend toward greater preference for local residents as teachers is revealed by an investigation conducted by the Research Division of the National Education Association.[20] This gain is 7.5 per cent in cities of over 100,000 population and 11.4 per cent for the smaller communities. These figures reveal severe limitations and restrictions for out-of state teachers insofar as their obtaining employment is concerned. If these figures represent the total situation, some additional and extensive restrictions are present.

Of those communities favoring local residents for teachers, most express such preference in unwritten rather than written form. Ninety-three per cent of the communities favor in-state persons as teachers and use diverse ways of showing this preference. Sixty-four cities of the three hundred and nineteen responding had written regulations giving preference to local or in-state persons. Preference for graduates of in-state and out-of-state colleges was about evenly divided.

One hundred and forty-five communities of three hundred and fourteen responding cities exceed in their employment standards the state minima in some manner. Some cities require resident study in

[20] See footnote 1, Table XX, page 159.

a local or near-by teacher-training institution or some other institution of higher learning or ask that the applicants for positions pass locally given examinations. These definitely come under the scope of the definitions of restrictions.

Residence factor. To avoid any residence restrictions, applicants wishing to establish residence within a community would need to live within the cities from thirty days to one year. By going to a community to establish residence, however, a person automatically comes within the definition of restrictions. Such action is restrictive.

Sometimes this factor of community employment restrictions becomes so powerful that the reputation of the state is established as being restrictive in its certification policies. Actually, the commonwealth may be relatively free from certification restrictions or limitations, with the restrictive community employment policies causing this reputation as a "closed state" to persons from other commonwealths.

CHAPTER VII

WAYS OF OBTAINING MORE INTERSTATE FREEDOM OF MOBILITY FOR TEACHERS; COMMENTS AND RECOMMENDATIONS

THIS investigation has pointed out limitations and restrictions to the free interstate mobility of teachers and has discussed some of their probable effects upon trained inexperienced and experienced teachers. It seems reasonable and desirable that some positive suggestions be made that, if put into effect, will reduce or eliminate these limiting and restrictive factors and prevent additional ones.

This study does not reveal any *one* method by which all the varied and numerous restrictions and limitations in certification and employment can be removed. There is no single panacea or cure for these defects. As a matter of fact, a different solution may be needed for each of several types of restrictive or limiting problems in each particular commonwealth or community. Solving such problems usually requires that the causes be known so that they can be removed or their effects nullified or changed in practice. It is not possible to isolate the real causes of many of these restrictions and limitations because of frequent changes in community and state personnel, lack of written materials, variance between stipulated and real causes, the length of time some of these factors have been in operation, and the social character of the restrictions. A sweeping hypothesis maintaining that economics is the sole reason for restrictions and limitations is not correct in those instances where partial causes can be ferreted out. Unquestionably economics is one of the fundamental causes of restrictions, but it is not the only cause. There is no gainsaying the difficulties involved in advancing workable solutions to such problems as restrictions, for these are imbedded deeply in the social, political, and economic character of the community and the state. Regardless of the inherent difficulties and with full cognizance of the complexity of the problem, this study, having revealed conditions that are susceptible to treatment, can reasonably point the way to at least a partial solution of this complex problem of restrictions. There are several factors to be considered in any plan suggested to eliminate or reduce restrictions and limitations, whether in state certification or community employment.

Factors in State Certification Requirements

1. *Education is at present considered a state function and responsibility.*[1]

Any plan submitted to reduce or eliminate restrictions and limitations must be considered on the basis of states' rights, which are inferred from Article X of the United States Constitution:

> The powers not delegated to the United States by the Constitution, nor prohibited by it to the States, are reserved to the States respectively, or to the people.[2]

The authority inferred from this Article has been further expressed in state constitutions, amplified by statutory provisions, and augmented by judicial decisions.[3] The concept of state responsibility for education is fundamental, so much so that any type of federal aid is frowned upon if it involves in any way an infringement upon the rights and control of education by the state.[4]

[1] See Educational Policies Commission, *The Structure and Administration of Education in American Democracy,* Chapter III. National Education Association, 1938.

[2] United States Constitution, Amendments, Article X, Rights of the States under Constitution.

[3] John Richard Emens, "A Study of State Administration of Teacher Personnel." Unpublished doctoral dissertation, University of Michigan, Ann Arbor, 1938.

[4] With forty-eight separate and different commonwealths administering certification, their obvious differences will produce variations in certification with resulting limitations. In defense of limitations from this viewpoint, it must be said that the present way to increase certification requirements is to have an individual commonwealth take the lead in increasing its standards, with other states gradually swinging into line in increasing or improving their own requirements. With each increase in requirements, which is highly desirable from the professional standpoint, come additional limitations. Are states then to refrain from raising their standards just to avoid limitations? Not at all. The state should raise its standards as high as is consistently possible. However, a cooperative attack on this entire problem of restriction could be made by the states to increase standards and yet minimize limitations.

In further defense of limitations that exist because of variations in requirements among states, it has been said that if a person wants to teach in a given commonwealth, he should pay the price required to meet its certification standards. If he does not want to meet the other state's particular requirements, let him remain

From another viewpoint, however, the following General Welfare clause in the constitution is considered to indicate national responsibility for education:

> The Congress shall have power:
>
> To lay and collect taxes, duties, imposts, and excises to pay the debts and provide for the common defense and general welfare of the United States; *but all duties, imposts, and excises shall be uniform throughout the United States.*[5] [Italics are the author's.]

This so-called General Welfare clause has been interpreted by some to mean that education was intended to be more of a federal responsibility than is ordinarily thought. Some problems are admittedly too large to be taken care of by a cooperative group of the states or by the state governments. This problem of restrictions may be one of these. It is true that it is difficult to say just what constitutes *general welfare.* Would it be better to have a plan whereby limitations and restrictions in state certification are eliminated, or would it be more desirable to retain the status quo? But education is *now* a state responsibility. Elsbree sums up the matter as follows:

> The licensing problem is accentuated by the fact that, legally, education is a state function rather than a federal one. It would be a relatively simple procedure to substitute a federal certification plan for the forty-eight separate and distinct state arrangements which are now in force, were it not contrary to the fundamental principles upon which our government was established. Improvements and reorganization can come only through leadership and cooperation. . . .[6]

These points are fundamental, therefore: Any plan of removing or reducing restrictions and limitations that is of broader scope than the state must be a system of *qualifying only* and not of *certification.*

---

in the commonwealth where he is. If he is to receive the benefits and salary monies from a community in another state, he should be willing to meet any and all certification standards set up. This concept, however, avoids the basic problem of restrictions.

Then, again, it has been said that states should not assume a colorless uniformity by having similar requirements in education. Each state has its own unique conditions and needs. Each commonwealth should be free to enact whatever requirements it sees fit.

[5] United States Constitution, Section 8, Powers of Congress, paragraph 1.

[6] Willard S. Elsbree, *The American Teacher,* pp. 357–358. New York: The American Book Company, 1939.

State acceptance of any plan must be *voluntary,* not *required,* because of the state responsibility of certification under the present organization and administration of education. Any improvements can come only through leadership and cooperation by the state.

2. *The plan to reduce or eliminate restrictive factors must be practical and must therefore take into consideration the present situation.*

Although theory often runs ahead of present practice, and is expected to do so in many instances, any plan by which restrictions are to be reduced or eliminated must be well grounded in the present situation or it will be too theoretical to use. This adds to the difficulty in that so many different situations are present among the states that what may be applicable in one commonwealth may not be at all useful in another. So many vested interests, differences in policy, in practice, and in governmental structure exist that no plan could be put into practice in all the states except after years of sustained effort.

3. *Plans to reduce or remove restrictions and limitations must include both state certification and community employment.*

In this complex problem of restrictions there are at least two separate and distinct phases, one, the restrictions and limitations in state certification; and, two, the restrictions and limitations present in community employment practices and policies. Separate suggestions must be made for each of these distinct phases of this problem of restrictions.

4. *Any plan should take into consideration the details, advantages, weaknesses, and positive suggestions of plans used by other occupations and professions in solving a comparable problem. Allowance, however, should be made for basic differences among the professions.*

Other occupations and professions have met this same type of problem of interstate restrictions more or less successfully. These other groups operate on the same constitutional bases as education and therefore have a similar problem of forty-eight separate and different licensing bodies. Although interstate variations among the professions exist, some of the plans and ideas used by them may be helpful in solving a comparable problem in education.

5. *No plan need be administered for all teachers.*

Any plan submitted would not need to be created for *all* teachers, inasmuch as there are many who would obtain a position in a given city or state to remain there for their professional lives. A plan could be made to parallel or to be superimposed on the present system of certification, with the states legally empowered to *accept* such a plan on a *voluntary* basis. For many teachers the usual state administration of certification may suffice.

These five factors are fundamental in any consideration of plans for avoiding, reducing, or eliminating restrictions and limitations to the free interstate mobility of teachers. Any plan offered has its advantages and disadvantages. In each of the following suggestions there will be included a brief statement of the plan, some arguments for and against it, and some statement as to its feasibility and worth. These suggestions have grown directly out of this study of restrictions and limitations, as well as a comprehensive survey of plans to assist with the free interstate mobility of members by other occupations and professions, namely, law, medicine, and architecture.

Suggested Plans to Remove Restrictions and Limitations in State Certification

1. *Develop certification so that every requirement of any state can be satisfied by study in accredited teacher-training institutions in several of the other states. The courses should be of such nature that out-of-state institutions could reasonably be expected to include them in their curriculum.*

By following this plan, states would eliminate any course of a unique character that requires resident study or attendance in any particular institution within the borders of the respective states. They would also refrain from adopting any other restrictive requirement. This procedure would necessitate twelve commonwealths that have specific state requirements eliminating the restrictive aspects of such standards, by giving teachers *otherwise qualified* an opportunity to obtain a provisional certificate. These teachers could be allowed to teach one year without previously meeting these specific requirements. The commonwealths that would be directly affected by this plan are as follows: Arizona, Florida, Idaho, Kansas, Louisiana, Montana, New Mexico, Oklahoma, Oregon, Utah, Washington, and Wyoming. In addition, if the State of Rhode Island were to follow this suggestion, it would permit teachers to meet the practice teaching requirement in institutions of higher learning in other states, or allow a leeway of one year in which to meet the total requirement. In this latter instance, Rhode Island could give a provisional certificate on the basis of a certain number of semester or clock hours of practice teaching, then demand the rest of the requirement within a given period of time.

If all states followed this plan, no additional commonwealth would enact any specific state courses or residence requirement or any other type that required applicants to attend an in-state institution of higher learning before receiving a provisional certificate. If such standards are enacted, it will be with the understanding that teachers *otherwise well qualified* may teach the first year without having to meet such a restrictive and specific requirement.

One argument for this plan is that at the present time in several states persons from other commonwealths are restricted by reason of one or two courses or six to eight weeks of resident study, even though such persons may have had one or two years of training beyond that actually required by these commonwealths. Such requirements usually equal from 2 to 4 per cent of the total amount of training required for a certificate. For a very small percentage of the total requirements, therefore, commonwealths now restrict out-of-state applicants for teachers' certificates. The states having these specific requirements tend to discount competency or training by accepting only those applicants for certification who have taken the restrictive courses or filled the residence requirements. There are thousands of unusually competent teachers in this nation who have never had Idaho law, for example, who would add professionally to the teaching group in Idaho, yet who would not be obtainable under these present requirements. Professional competency and specific state requirements do not necessarily go together. By requiring the latter, the states tend to ignore the former. With this plan in effect, employing officials in a community would have the opportunity of interviewing applicants for positions who are at present restricted or limited by such specific requirements or restrictive courses such as practice teaching taken within the respective state.

A possible argument against such a plan is the fact that some of the information given in certain specific courses is useful to a person beginning teaching in a given state. Information regarding state school law, state history, and other similar courses aids in the orientation of a new teacher, acquainting him with the commonwealth in which he may later teach. This plan would not deprive him of the opportunity to obtain this information but suggests that he obtain it during or after his first year of teaching.

After considering the arguments for and against such a plan, it is believed that the state will gain rather than lose by permitting an otherwise well-qualified person to teach at least one year without first having to meet such specific and restrictive courses. The state can admit competent teachers rather than restrict them, and at the same time see that each teacher has the needed information before a second year begins. This plan would reverse the present situation in which the state restricts persons who might stay a long time as well as those who plan to stay only a short time, such as a year. Those who plan to stay a considerable length of time within the state will consent to meet specific state requirements after their first year. These teachers will constitute the professional backbone of the commonwealth. Those who do not plan to stay but choose to drift may leave the commonwealth after the first year.

The several states would need to change their certification requirements somewhat to follow this suggestion because certification is a state function. This plan is practical. It already has been put into practice by California, Nevada, New Hampshire, Oklahoma, Rhode Island, and Texas, for example. This suggestion would not cause too much disturbance in the current certification situation and would eliminate the most prolific source of restrictions. A similar requirement does not exist in other professions, so a comparison cannot be established.

2. *Require a total amount of professional and academic training without specification of detailed courses and the number of such courses within that total.*

It is not only the *total* number of semester hours of professional courses that limits or restricts out-of-state teachers, but also the detailed requirements and amounts *within that total.* Such a plan of requiring a given number of hours of professional work from an accredited institution without the detailed enumeration of titles and particular number of semester hours may be helpful in obtaining more interstate freedom of mobility. In many of the *academic* requirements for certification there is no specification as to course titles and *detailed* amounts of semester hours for the several academic courses. In the core requirements and in some few of the academic requirements, there is some stipulation as to definite titles and numbers of semester hours but not in most of the states' academic requirements. Such a plan could be followed with professional courses.

An argument for this plan is that it would remove a great number of the interstate differences in courses and semester hours. A teacher, by taking certain professional courses, may thereby be meeting part or all of the professional requirements in most of the commonwealths.

One argument that might be advanced against this plan is that it does not insure breadth of training. A person may, under the provisions of this plan, take all his professional work in one area, for example, in History of Education or Principles of Education, and may not take such courses as Educational Psychology and Educational Philosophy. A person specializing too much in any given area would lack the professional preparation desired by most states. Lack of specification at least in part of the courses would not insure the needed breadth of training unless the burden of guidance were placed upon the teacher-training institutions. This would not be feasible.

An argument for this plan is the fact that at the present time several states have already listed their requirements in accordance with it. These include: Florida, Idaho, Nebraska, North Dakota, South Carolina, and Tennessee. In these commonwealths, if a person has the required total of semester hours and the desired quality of work, he can meet the professional requirements for certification. This argument, of course, would be sound only if the plan were successful where it is in effect. There are indications that it is, up to a certain point.

This arrangement is practical, but the disadvantages seem to outweigh the advantages. Adopting such a plan would cause considerable disturbance in that most of the states now definitely require particular courses in a given number of hours. No other profession has a comparable type of requirement so no comparison with another profession is possible. It would seem from a professional standpoint that this plan would not be feasible at this time for most states. However, if modified to some extent, it does have some excellent features. The discussion of plans number three and four offers suggestions for modifications.

3. *Require a total amount of professional and academic work, specifying requirements in semester hours in several broad content areas rather than in specific courses.*

Under this arrangement, several *broad areas* of professional work could be required with a total number of semester hours within each. There would not appear in the specification a number of *particular* courses required, each with a definite number of semester hours. There would be, however, specifications in certain broad areas to insure breadth of professional training by the candidate. This plan would remove the objections to plan number two. To satisfy the requirements in each broad area a person could offer one or more of several different courses of varying amounts of semester hours. The choices would be broad, permitting a person to study widely within a given area. By way of illustration, a state could require twenty-four semester hours in professional work, as a total, to include six semester hours in each of the following four fields:

1. Social and historical foundations of education.
2. Psychological and philosophical foundations of education.
3. Tests, measurements in general and specific fields, research methods, statistics, methods of teaching.
4. Administration, organization, and supervision of education.

The total requirements could be different, as could the broad areas required and the amounts in each. All four areas or any three of a given number could be required. The total requirement and a given variety of subject areas would need to be satisfied, yet a person could do this by taking courses of widely different titles and content.

An argument for this plan is that it would eliminate many of the interstate differences now in existence and would insure, at the same time, the breadth of training that is so necessary. Competency to a certain degree would be assured, yet limitations to out-of-state teachers would not be created or maintained to the extent they are at present.

Another argument for such a plan is that if a state raised its professional certification requirements, the increase in requirements would come within one or more of these particular areas so teachers, by meeting the requirements in any given commonwealth, *would thereby be assisting themselves to meet the higher requirements in any other state.*

An argument against such an arrangement is that it would be difficult to obtain wide agreement upon any particular professional subject areas for certification. Another negative argument is that it would be difficult to administer in those instances where courses do not fit into any particular category. Such an arrangement, however, has more to recommend it than it has arguments against it. It seems feasible and worthy of consideration. It is a step toward the elimination of overly detailed requirements and limitations among the states; at the same time it insures breadth of training. Such a plan is practical, although it may cause some disturbance when the changes it necessitates are being carried out. Again, no such type of requirement is present in any other profession which has attempted to solve this problem of limitations and restrictions.

4. *Break down the national problem of certification into smaller sectional problems in such way that groups of states geographically near or adjacent to one another can set their requirements in broad areas or bodies of knowledge.*

In every part of the United States there are states close together geographically which have similar problems to meet insofar as education is concerned. In many of these smaller clusters of states there is similarity within the groups in their ability to finance education; in others there may be dissimilarity. Several bases could be used on which the states could combine and attack a common problem in groups instead of on a nation-wide scale. By agreeing on certain broad fields which they will commonly require, these small groups of states can eliminate many of the interstate differences.

An argument for this plan is that it will tend to provide a somewhat comparable basis among a small group of states which have common problems to meet and thus tend to insure greater cooperation and better understanding than if the problem were to be attacked on a nation-wide scale.

Another argument in favor of this plan is that it has already been worked out by the Federal Reserve Banking System[7] for other purposes and on other bases but with this group idea of attacking an important problem. Once the problem had been attacked successfully in small groups of states, the plan might later be used to combine groups to meet the problem of restrictions on a nation-wide basis.

There are several arguments against such a plan. One is that the groups may include states widely dissimilar in many factors, such as ability to finance education. States with very high requirements might be included with commonwealths having very low certification requirements. Unequal groupings may interfere greatly with such an arrangement. Again, once sectional groups are established to meet this problem, these groups may "freeze" their own requirements and thus interfere with the solution of the problem on a national scale. Then, too, some of the existing restrictions have been established in retaliation by one state for the enactments of requirements by another state. Small groups of states may contain these dissenting commonwealths which may tend to break up such a plan. On the other hand, such grouping may invite cooperation not now present. This plan is now being followed in the Midwest and the South.[8]

5. *With small groups of states, develop a sectional certificate with higher requirements than those in any state within the group of commonwealths so each state can accept this higher certificate in lieu of its own.*

Under such an arrangement, the states could group themselves as in plan four, and could cooperatively set up the standards for a certificate that exceeds in its requirements those of any included commonwealth or that equals the requirements of the highest type certificate in the group.

Such a plan would bring even higher standards to groups of cooperating states than are now present, yet without the limitations and restrictions so prevalent. Interstate mobility could be provided within groups of these states. At the same time between and among these small groups of states, there may develop a somewhat comparable plan so as to obtain wide freedom of mobility for teachers. By accepting a certificate with even higher requirements than their

[7] See Board of Governors of the Federal Reserve System, "The Federal Reserve System." The National Capital Press, Washington, D. C., 1939.

[8] See Chapter I.

own, the states would not be lowering their standards in any way but would be inviting competency on a higher plane than before. If any state increased its requirements, such would tend to close the gap between the former requirements for that state and the higher standards of the sectional certificate. From time to time the states could increase the requirements for this sectional certificate to keep ahead of any individual commonwealth.

One difficulty in this plan is the fact that it would require a great amount of cooperation, which, in some instances, would be difficult to obtain. Again, such a plan may "freeze" the arrangements within the small groups and prevent a national solution to the problem later. It may even bring regional restrictions. On the other hand, it may be a step toward a national solution. The costs of the state representatives meeting together and of administering the plan may be greater than could be taken care of by the present budgets. Another disadvantage is that each state on the fringe of a given region or group is also a border state for still another group or region so, in solving the problems with one group, some of the states would also be meeting problems with other near-by or adjacent states outside the particular group attacking the problems. One state may therefore be meeting the problems of one group of which it is a member yet at the same time be encountering restrictive or limiting problems in other states also adjacent or near-by which are outside the group.

Such a plan seems workable, but to accomplish it would require considerable time and effort. It is practical if planned on a voluntary basis. It would cause a number of changes in the present situation, which may tend to prohibit its adoption. It is worthy of consideration by educational officials.

6. *Establish a national norm or average requirement in each large certification area or group of subjects.*

By establishing a national norm or mean average in each of the several certification requirements or areas, it may be possible to create a certificate that would be accepted by most states. Under this arrangement, approximately one-half of the states now exceeding the norm would accept, provisionally, these standards, and within a given period of time would require the applicant to meet the individual state's requirements which are higher than the national mean average. The other half of the states would need to increase their requirements to meet such a mean average requirement. These national mean averages could be either the average certification standard at present required, or the average amount of work taken by teachers in the nation. Such mean averages, established by this study and by a nation-wide survey by Evenden, Gamble, and Blue in 1933, are given in Table XXVII.

TABLE XXVII

Average Requirements for National Certification of Teachers

	National Average in the State Certification Requirements (in semester hours)	National Average of Work Taken by Teachers (in semester hours)	Mean Average of the Two Median Averages of Certification Requirements and Amount of Work Taken (in semester hours)
Degree or total training	Slightly higher than a baccalaureate degree	[a]	Slightly higher than a baccalaureate degree
Academic requirements	31*	30** [1, 2]	35 [6]
Professional requirements	17.4 [5]	24 [3]	21 [6]
Practice teaching	5 [5]	5 [4]	5 [6]

[a] No data.
* Mean average of major and minor and particular requirements together. See Table VIII.
** Does not include core requirements.
[1] Edward S. Evenden, Guy C. Gamble, and Harold G. Blue. *National Survey of the Education of Teachers*, Vol. II, p. 55, Table XVI, Column 8; English as selected example. State medians taken.
[2] Figure taken for English as sole field of teaching. Other figures are 33 for principal field of teaching and 24 for English as a next main field of teaching.
[3] *Ibid.*, p. 58, Table XVII, Column 7. Means of medians taken from data given.
[4] *Ibid.*, Vol. II, p. 60, Table XIX, Column 14. Mean of medians taken from data given.
[5] See Table X.
[6] Nearest round numbers used.

If such a plan were adopted, the following changes would need to be made by the several commonwealths in each of the broad categories of certification requirements. Those states with higher requirements than the mean could give a provisional certificate to those meeting the mean average requirement, then require the rest during or after the first year of teaching. Those with less than this mean average would need to increase their requirements, perhaps giving provisional certificates also to those otherwise qualified and permit the persons to meet the remaining requirements during or shortly after the first year of teaching. (See Table XXVIII.)

One disadvantage of this plan is that it would require a total of seventy changes in increasing state requirements in academic, professional, and practice teaching requirements, in addition to sixty-three changes where requirements are higher than the mean average of the states' requirements. In this respect, these states, as suggested previously, could give provisional certificates the first year provided the teachers meet the national mean. The teachers could then meet the individual state's requirements during or shortly after the first year. In some of the commonwealths, however, the requirements are considerably below or above the mean, necessitating rather large adjustments. This plan would be workable only if plan number three were used with it; otherwise, the total requirements would be similar but the inside details would be greatly different.

It should be noted that this plan does not include a provision for specific state requirements. If it were adopted, specific state requirements would need to be eliminated or provisional certificates given for a year during which the applicant could take such specific courses as required (plan one). One disadvantage is that those states with high requirements should not be forced to lower their standards in any way, even provisionally. The fight to increase standards is a very difficult one over a period of years, and the profession would lose much if the leading states were to lower even partially their standards.

It would be advantageous if thirty-eight states increased in seventy instances their several requirements to equal the mean average among the commonwealths. The raising of standards on this plan would not only remove some limitations but would also raise standards materially.

The danger of uniformity underlying this plan is great, and the restrictions on initiative too markedly present. The plan would interfere greatly with state responsibility; many states would not ever agree to the necessary arrangements; still others might agree but would not be able to adopt the plan because of negative or slow legislative action. The plan will cause considerable disturbance. No plan of this type has been used in other professions. It is feasible but would be difficult in active practice.

TABLE XXVIII

Changes Required of the Forty-Eight States in the Certification Requirements in the Adoption of Plan Six in Meeting National Norms or Mean Averages of Requirements to Eliminate Limitations and Restrictions

	(31) Changes in Academic Requirements		(17) Changes in Professional Requirements		(4) Changes in Practice Teaching Requirements	
	plus	minus	plus	minus	plus	minus
Alabama	..	11	..	7	1	..
Arizona	..	8	..	7	..	1
Arkansas	13	..	1	..	..	1
California	..	5	..	7	..	..
Colorado	25	..	..	3	..	..
Connecticut	10	..	11	..	..	2
Delaware	13	..	..	1	4	..
Florida	7	..	..	1	..	2
Georgia	7	..	..	1	1	..
Idaho	31	..	2	..	4	..
Illinois	..	17	2	..	4	..
Indiana	6	..	..	2	1	..
Iowa	..	4	2	..	1	..
Kansas	16	..	..	1	1	..
Kentucky	..	29	..	1	..	2
Louisiana	19	..	..	1	..	..
Maine	31*	..	..	1	4	..
Maryland	7	..	1	..	..	..
Massachusetts	..	5	5	..	4	..
Michigan	..	23	..	3	..	1
Minnesota	31*	..	2	..	1	..
Mississippi	1	..	..	1	..	5
Missouri	7	..	..	1	..	..
Montana	31*	..	2	..	4	..
Nebraska	..	..	..	1	1	..
Nevada	31*	..	..	1	..	..
New Hampshire	..	5	5	..	4	..
New Jersey	..	17	..	1	..	2
New Mexico	..	8	..	1	..	..
New York	13	..	..	1	..	..
North Carolina	7	..	..	1	1	..
North Dakota	31*	..	1	..	4	..
Ohio	..	14	..	..	..	..
Oklahoma	1	..	2	..	..	..
Oregon	31*	..	2	11	2	..
Pennsylvania	13	..	..	1	..	2
Rhode Island	31*	..	..	3	..	6
South Carolina	31*	..	..	1	4	..

TABLE XXVIII (*Continued*)

Changes Required of the Forty-Eight States in the Certification Requirements in the Adoption of Plan Six in Meeting National Norms or Mean Averages of Requirements to Eliminate Limitations and Restrictions

	(31) Changes in Academic Requirements		(17) Changes in Professional Requirements		(4) Changes in Practice Teaching Requirements	
	plus	minus	plus	minus	plus	minus
South Dakota	..	8	2	..	1	..
Tennessee	7	..	..	1	2	..
Texas	..	5	..	7	..	2
Utah	..	1	..	1	..	1⅔
Vermont	31*	..	5	..	1	..
Virginia	19	..	..	1	..	2
Washington	..	17	1	..	1⅓	..
West Virginia	7	..	..	3	..	1
Wisconsin	..	23	..	1	..	1
Wyoming	16	..	1	..	2	..
Total changes	30	17	16	31	24	15

Total plus changes = 58. Total minus changes = 36.

* Where amounts of academic training are not specified outright. Often such amounts are left to accrediting associations or the training institution.

7. *Create a national examining or certification board to examine teachers, evaluate their credentials, and issue certificates higher in caliber than those in any commonwealth and therefore acceptable to most states.*

In establishing a national certifying board with requirements for a national certificate higher than those of any commonwealth, the differences among the states can be minimized or removed altogether, and yet professional standards can be maintained or improved. A national certificate would be acceptable to the state boards or certificating groups only on a *voluntary basis* as the administrative organization, the constitutional and legal development would preclude any other arrangement. If professional standards are maintained or improved with no federal control exercised, the states may find it to their advantage to accept such a national certificate in lieu of their own.

This idea of a national certificating board is not new in the history of this nation. As early as 1906 Cubberley said that, if other means could not be found to obtain interstate freedom in the mobility of teachers, the states had better work for national uniformity by establishing a national examining and certificating board that would examine teachers, pass on credentials, and issue certificates of such high standards that the states would be forced to accept them.[9] The essential features of such a plan follow:

1. A national board to examine, evaluate and issue certificates.
2. Certificates of a higher status than those in any state.
3. Voluntary acceptance by the states, but with requirements for this national certificate so high that in the very interest of high professional standards the states could not ignore them.
4. The use of this higher certificate to overcome interstate differences in certification requirements.
5. The ability and legal right of a teacher so certificated by the national certificate to enter any state without further need of meeting any detailed standard.

This plan of a national board has a counterpart in several other professions. The one used by the medical profession is fairly typical. After an examination of the plans used in law, engineering, architecture, accounting, medicine and nursing, it was found that from the standpoint of successful operation and the numbers of persons involved, the methods used by the medical profession were of most value in this study. A brief outline of this plan is presented in the following section.

The National Board of Medical Examiners

In the early twentieth century, the medical profession found that the various state requirements for medical licenses severely curtailed the physician's field of practice by holding him within the boundaries of one state. These various state requirements also limited markedly the medical school's curricula, the schools finding it almost impossible to train their students to meet all the requirements of all the states. The independent licensure regulations made it necessary for

[9] Ellwood P. Cubberley, *The Certification of Teachers.* In National Society for the Scientific Study of Education, Fifth Yearbook, Part II, p. 74. The University of Chicago Press, Chicago, 1906.

a practitioner to pass a state board examination whenever he moved his practice across a state line. (This situation is duplicated today in the educational profession with these licensure limitations and restrictions to the free interstate mobility of teachers, the limitations to schools' curricula, and the nullifying of a teacher's training and experience by state boundaries.) The Federation of State Medical Boards was organized in 1912 to aid the forty-eight states in harmonizing their laws and licensure regulations and in developing uniform requirements in medical education. The plans for the National Board of Medical Examiners were later set up.[10]

The National Board of Medical Examiners was organized in 1915, and chartered March 17, 1922, under the laws of the District of Columbia. Its purpose was to establish in this country a qualifying examination of such character that successful candidates could be admitted to the practice of medicine by state boards of medical licensure.[11] Further light as to its purpose is gained from the certificate of incorporation:

> . . . The objects of said corporation shall be . . . to elevate the standard of qualification for the practice of the profession of medicine, surgery, or any branch thereof; to provide for the admission of qualified persons to the practice of medicine, surgery, or any branch thereof, in any State, Territory, or Dependency of the United States without further examination by licensing boards thereof, by means of an examination and certification, or in the case of persons already qualified under the laws of any other jurisdiction, by tests approved by the National Board of Medical Examiners, by means of certification alone, acceptable to such licensing boards in lieu of their own . . . ; to adopt a constitution, by-laws, and regulations to carry out its purposes, not inconsistent with the laws of the United States.[12]

Its constitution provided for a membership of thirty, including six members representing the Federal services, five members nominated by the Federation of State Medical Boards of the United States, three members nominated by the Association of American Medical

[10] Everett S. Elwood, State Board and National Board Relationships. Paper read before the Annual Congress on Medical Education, Medical Licensure and Hospitals, Chicago, February 16, 1932.

[11] Medical Licensure Statistics for 1938, p. 1724.

[12] Constitution, By-laws and Charter, National Board of Medical Examiners, pp. 13–14, Philadelphia, November, 1934.

Colleges, two members nominated by the Council on Medical Education and Hospitals of the American Medical Association, and fourteen members elected at large, special attention given to their geographical distribution.[13]

Examinations of the National Board of Medical Examiners

The examinations given by the National Board are three in number, two written and one oral or clinical. They are searching and thorough, and result in an average of 9.7 percentage of failures among the candidates.[14] Because of their difficulty, they are considered somewhat in the nature of an honors examination. Candidates applying for interneship in hospitals after completing their academic training frequently ask the National Board to certify to the hospitals in question the grades which they made in the first part of the National Board's examinations. The Board's certificate is also considered in making appointments to hospital staffs and to the lower positions of the faculties of medical schools. In selecting their new medical examiners, the medical departments of some of the leading insurance companies give preference to those who have successfully passed the National Board examinations. Authorities in medical schools sometimes use the grades in these examinations as a check on their own grading and the training offered. The National Board also furnishes the state boards with photostatic copies of the candidate's medical credentials as well as a transcript of his grades on examinations.[15, 16]

Altogether, in 1938, there were six hundred and eighty-two medical students who successfully passed the National Board examinations. In all, 2,306 persons, including students and all others, passed these examinations in 1938.[17] In the same year 9,493 licenses[18] were issued on the basis of examinations, reciprocity, and endorsement of credentials by the forty-eight states, the District of Columbia, United

[13] Circular of Information, Bulletin No. 3, Revised January 1, 1937, National Board of Medical Examiners.

[14] *Ibid.*, p. 1726.

[15] J. Steward Rodman, M.D., and Everett S. Elwood, Comments on Examination of the National Board of Medical Examiners, pp. 3–7.

[16] See footnote 10.

[17] Medical Licensure Statistics for 1938, p. 1726.

[18] *Ibid.*, p. 1697, Table 1.

States Territory, and her possessions, with 6,252 of these being additions to the medical profession.[19] It is thus seen that only 24.2 per cent of all who were licensed passed the National Board's examinations; 60.6 per cent of all new additions to the medical profession did the same. Those successful in passing the examinations, or diplomates as they are called, were registered in 1938 in thirty-eight states.[20] The licensing boards of forty-four states, however, recognized the certificate of the National Board of Medical Examiners in 1938.[21]

This National Board is a qualifying board solely and would never have licensing power; therefore, the state board's licensure powers and enforcement duties could not be encroached upon in the slightest degree. State boards originally doubted the legality of their accepting the National Board's examinations in lieu of their own licensing examinations or requirements.[22] Elihu Root, one of the great legal minds of the nation, gave the decision that this procedure would be entirely proper and legal if the state medical practice laws were so framed as to give their boards of licensure discretionary authority to accept the certificate of a National Board in lieu of their own examinations and requirements.[23]

The fundamental point is this: Any physician who has demonstrated his ability in such an examination as the National Board gives is qualified to practice medicine anywhere in the United States and should be given that privilege on the basis of competence established.

There are other ways by which the members of the medical profession obtain freedom of interstate mobility. One of these is through the establishment of reciprocal relations between states, which permits a person, on the basis of his license in one state, to obtain a license in another. This method was tried by the education profession, with the peak of such reciprocal relations being reached by 1921, at which time thirty-eight states had some form of reciprocity agreements with at least one or more other commonwealths. Then occurred a decided drop in the number of states using reciprocal agreements so that by 1938 only seven states had such arrange-

[19] *Ibid.*, p. 1710, Table 8.
[20] *Ibid.*, p. 1705.
[21] *Ibid.*, p. 1726.
[22] See footnote 10.
[23] *Ibid.*

ments. Even then, because of qualifying conditions, it was as easy to obtain a new certificate as it was to obtain one through reciprocity.

Restrictions in the Medical Profession

It is interesting that, in spite of the elaborate plans which the medical profession has developed to obtain interstate freedom of mobility of its members, there are restrictions and limitations present in many commonwealths. These follow:

1. Five states did not in 1938 accept the certificate of the National Board of Medical Examiners although they have indicated that they are willing and ready to do so as soon as the proper legislation can be put through. Applicants must therefore take the examinations given by each of these states unless reciprocal relations have been established with the particular state. These examinations differ from state to state and come within the scope of the definition of restrictions.[24]

2. In one commonwealth an admittedly well-trained physician who has all the essential qualifications and who has demonstrated his ability by passing a thorough, searching National Board examination, is required to wait one year before receiving his license or is required to take the state examination in addition. This ruling practically nullifies the effect and purpose of the National Board's examination, as few persons can afford to wait a year before beginning to practice. This is a restrictive practice.[25]

3. Another factor that disturbs the National Board relationships with the states is the matter of examination fees. Some charge all diplomates the full reciprocity fee for their licenses. These fees range from $25 to $100 although the fees for the state licenses to those taking the state examinations range from only $10 to $25.[25] It is not difficult to explain to the satisfaction of medical students and diplomates that the state board must charge for every license issued whether the applicant is examined or not, because in many states the fees received are the board's only income. It is difficult, however, to convince a diplomate that he should be asked to pay $100 fee for a license without examination when a license given after a successful

[24] States which do not accept the certificate of the National Board of Medical Examiners are: Florida, Idaho, Louisiana, Texas, and Wisconsin.

[25] Elwood, *op. cit.*

completion of the state examination could be obtained for a $25 fee. The young physician who has been through eight to ten years of college, medical school, and hospital in fitting himself for his profession has often so exhausted his financial resources that any additional tax is a burden. Then again, some states differentiate between young physicians just entering practice and older experienced physicians applying for a license.

4. Interneships are required by medical licensing boards in many of the states and not in others. Those differences are limitations rather than restrictions because a medical student may take his interneship in an accepted hospital in any state in most instances. The list of those states requiring interneships for licensing are as follows:[26]

Alabama	New Hampshire	South Dakota
Delaware	New Jersey	Utah
Idaho	North Dakota	Vermont
Illinois	Oklahoma	Washington
Iowa	Oregon	West Virginia
Louisiana	Pennsylvania	Wisconsin
Michigan	Rhode Island	Wyoming

This type of requirement is highly desirable, however, and is limiting, not restrictive. During a crisis, such as a war, some states may temporarily eliminate this type of requirement.

5. There are some states which do not reciprocate with any other commonwealths under any conditions; these include Florida, Idaho, Massachusetts, and Rhode Island. All applicants must meet certain requirements and pass examinations for licenses regardless of residence. Two of these states are those which have restrictions in the education profession as well.[27]

6. Some states have established certain examinations which they require of applicants regardless of other qualifying examinations they may have taken. Others of these commonwealths accept the certificate of the National Board of Medical Examiners in lieu of such examinations. The subjects in which the examinations are conducted in the respective states number eight in all, including anatomy, bac-

[26] Medical Licensure Statistics for 1938, p. 1713, Table 12.
[27] Medical Licensure Statistics for 1938, p. 1705.

teriology, chemistry, diagnosis, hygiene, pathology, physiology, and hygiene and public health. The states having these basic science laws are as follows with the date of enactment:[28]

States Having Basic Science Laws, and the Year of Enactment

Arizona	1933	Nebraska	1927
Arkansas	1929	Oklahoma	1937
Colorado	1937	Oregon	1933
Connecticut	1925	South Dakota	1939
Iowa	1935	Washington	1927
Michigan	1937	Wisconsin	1925
Minnesota	1927		

The states which do not accept the examination of the National Board in lieu of their own examination in the basic sciences are creating restrictions to the free interstate movement of medical practitioners and so are raising problems that will need to be solved. Thus it is seen that the medical profession, which of all the professions has apparently created the most successful plan for obtaining interstate freedom of mobility for its members, has not escaped entirely from the problem of restrictions and limitations, although it must be said that this group has been quite successful in its attempt to solve this difficult problem. That the national board and the state board relationships are proceeding in a very acceptable manner is indicated in the following statement:

> . . . the relations existing between the state boards of medical licensure and the National Board of Medical Examiners are, in the main, harmonious and highly effective. . . . The interlocking memberships of the Federation of State Medical Boards and the National Board, accompanied by a clear appreciation and understanding on the part of each other and value of the other, bespeak continued cooperation.[29]

There are several reasons for the establishment of a National Board of Educational Examiners, many of these being similar to the reasons for which the National Board of Medical Examiners was created. Free interstate mobility of teachers could be made possible in most if not all states, thereby avoiding the restrictions and limitations present with forty-eight separate certification bodies among the

[28] *Ibid.,* p. 1723.
[29] Elwood, *op. cit.*

states. Such a National Board would make it possible for the teacher-training institutions to meet the certification requirements in a more thorough manner without the severe burden imposed by forty-eight separate and distinct certification systems with different course requirements. The plan would certainly offer selective procedures which would insure persons of such high caliber that successful teachers could readily be admitted into all states without further question. Those successful in passing an examining system set up by a National Board would be highly selected and would provide a group from which many of the best teachers in any school system might be taken.

Furthermore, a series of highly reliable, valid examinations properly interpreted and correctly used would remove an often invalid and even fallacious basis of certification. The basic assumptions of certification by the acceptance of evidences of training have been: that it is known what qualities and characteristics are desired in teachers, that it is known how to recognize these qualities and characteristics, and that by present methods of certification these factors are obtained. All these assumptions are, to a certain degree, false. The irrelevances of unit, credit, and time requirements have long been apparent. Prescribed units, credits, and other factors used as bases of teacher certification or training have failed to maintain professional standards in the past, if the results and interpretations of a recent series of examinations[30] are correct. According to this investigation,[31] many students who now fulfill all the unit and credit requirements for certificates are not of high professional caliber in intelligence, culture, or personality. If attention were transferred from unit and time requirements to the ascertaining of the professional promise and qualifications of individual candidates, better results might be obtained. Time spent in classrooms may not be a good index of intelligence, culture, personality, or other professional qualities considered desirable.[32]

There are several arguments against the plan of a National Board of Educational Examiners. Examinations as a main basis for the selection of teachers are not considered with favor by many educa-

[30] Ben Wood, "The Student and His Knowledge."
[31] *Ibid.*, p. 9.
[32] *Ibid.*, pp. 9, 10.

tion officials because so many other important yet intangible factors must be considered. Examinations usually stress subject matter information and therefore miss much of value in the other qualities desired and needed in a teacher. Once used for state certification, examinations for this purpose have been gradually eliminated, with evidences of training in institutions of higher learning being substituted as a basis for certification. New techniques and more valid and reliable examination measures, however, may do away with many objections to this method. As Wood indicates:

> It is obvious that many qualities other than academic intelligence and achievement are essential for good teaching, and these qualities should be considered and estimated or measured as accurately as possible. But their importance does not detract from the importance of the qualities measured by the objective tests. . . . However, well endowed with personality qualifications a candidate may be, he cannot teach mathematics or foreign languages, or English or history or science unless he has at least a minimal mastery of one or more of them.[33]

Only a small percentage of teachers would take such an examination, if the medical profession is a criterion of the numbers who take the National Board examinations, so the plan would not serve a great majority of teachers. This cannot be said, however, to be a leading argument against the plan. Such a National Board may be costly to maintain. Even so, the cost may be offset by the successful operation of the board and its resulting freedom from interstate restrictions. Unless the professional life of the average teacher in this nation becomes of longer duration, such a board may be superfluous. Furthermore, as revealed by the experiences of the National Board of Medical Examiners, the plan does not remove all interstate restrictions and limitations.

Then, again, the very mention of a National Board may arouse opposition to such a plan. Many persons are so fearful of federal control in even the slightest degree that such a plan may be killed before its benefits are well considered. Many fearful connotations would be gleaned from the very idea of a federal board which might in some way cause the states to lose control of their cherished rights that there would be little value in suggesting this plan. It may not be considered

[33] Ben D. Wood, "Teacher Selection"; reprinted from *The Educational Record,* XVII, July, 1936, 374–387.

by the opponents that the states would retain their states' rights entirely and that they would accept a National Board certificate only on a voluntary basis. However, there may be the additional danger of such a board becoming a political or an economic racket if dominated by unprofessional leaders.

Differences between Education and the Medical Profession

Certain differences between education and the medical profession may not make it feasible to compare the plans used by medicine and the suggested plan for education. These differences include the following: Education is financed from public funds, whereas the medical doctors are paid, in the main, from private or corporate incomes rather than from state or community taxation. Education is institutionalized, whereas medicine is largely personal. The professional career of a medical doctor is usually lifelong, whereas that of a teacher is, on the average, markedly shorter. Education has both state and local autonomy, whereas medical licensure is largely state controlled. Education is not basically competitive within the community once the teacher has his position, whereas medicine is often highly competitive for each case. Education has more teachers within its ranks than medicine has doctors. Teachers are employed for the period of at least one year, subject to good behavior, whereas doctors are employed for a single performance. Usually, however, if a doctor is successful, he is retained for a much longer period of time. One of the most important differences between education and medicine as professions is that the National Board of Medical Examiners account only for state restrictions and limitations, whereas in education some of the strongest restrictions are not in the state licensing at all but in the community employment policies and practices. A National Board of Educational Examiners, however, could account for many of the limitations and restrictions in state certification, and therefore would be worth while in these respects.

The similarities between education and medicine, however, are marked. Both medicine and education licenses are given by the state. In each case the state authority is inferred from the same constitutional basis. In both professions this same problem of interstate restrictions and limitations has arisen with similar difficulties for both the experienced and the inexperienced trained persons. In both fields the various state requirements and limitations are restricting the curricula of teacher-training institutions and proving to be a burden to many of these institutions. Both professions exist under the same economic conditions, although the manner and time in which each is affected by fluctuations may differ.

8. *Classify all colleges and universities into "A," "B," and "C" groups, then accept the baccalaureate degrees only from the grade "A" institutions in lieu of the certification requirements as at present constituted.*

The plan could be worked out this way: carefully examine and classify all colleges as to their ability to educate young men and women. Bases of classification could be cooperatively arrived at so as to sift out the weak colleges and keep those which are strong and which do the best possible job of training people for the education profession. Classify the colleges and universities as "A," "B," and "C" institutions, then accept the baccalaureate degree from the "A" colleges in lieu of the specific certification requirements as now constituted. Provision could be made so those institutions of lower caliber in the "B" and "C" groups could grow into the "A" group, but until they do, their degrees would not be acceptable for certification by the states. As the requirements continue to increase, with the trend toward a master's degree or a fifth year of study, the master's degree could be accepted as minimum requirement for certification in the secondary schools. This plan would eliminate many weak schools, but, on the positive side, would give the colleges an opportunity to educate their students instead of attempting to meet the detailed certification requirements, which, in the end, do not actually guarantee ability anyway. The medical profession long since adopted this procedure, apparently with profit to the profession, and improvement in preparation of medical doctors and in curriculum offerings of the training institutions. The number of teachers that are needed may not be readily obtainable; considerable supervision would be needed during the classification and after to maintain standards; and considerable difficulty would be faced in setting up criteria. Such a plan would eliminate some colleges, in fact, numerous institutions would have to close their doors; but in the long run, it can be argued rather successfully that the profession would gain from such a step. This plan would arouse enormous opposition, but it may be workable.

Recommendations

After considering the differences and similarities between education and medicine it is thought that the National Board plan for qualifying persons for the education profession is feasible. Such a plan would not need to be substituted for the forty-eight state requirements but could be used in addition to the present requirements for those who wished to take advantage of it. Furthermore, such a National Board would be a qualifying board only, with the states accepting or rejecting the plan on a voluntary basis. The states could still maintain their individual certification requirements and departments. There are thousands of teachers who would probably not move from positions in their home communities or elsewhere. Other thousands would wish to be certificated in only one commonwealth and remain there. On the other hand, there are many who would take advantage of the National Board plan and thus avoid restrictions and limitations in the various states. Besides removing many limitations and restrictions, the plan may also raise the standards of the teaching profession with regard to the scholarship and ability of the teacher personnel.

If this National Board of Educational Examiners plan were adopted by the several states, it would probably be superimposed upon the present administration and organization of certification. On a voluntary basis the states may accept in toto the examinations and qualifying statements of such a National Board; however, unless this acceptance were in toto, several requirements that now are restrictive may still remain, such as the specific state requirements. If states reserved any of such requirements, there would need to be the adoption of plan number one, by which all standards requiring resident study within the respective states are abolished. Furthermore, no state would pass, according to this plan, any restrictive requirement that demands that a person attend an in-state institution of learning or establish in-state residence. This combination of plans would remove several weaknesses that have appeared in the system used by the National Board of Medical Examiners, whereby restrictions are growing in spite of the elaborate cooperative methods set up.

If the National Board plan were adopted, there would still remain possible corrections or weaknesses in the individual requirements for certification, as the states now administer it. Changes could be made in the state organization and administration of certification to reduce or eliminate other limitations and restrictions. The requirement of definite amounts of training in several broad areas of subject matter rather than specifically detailed courses, as given in plan number three, could be used. This plan is of a high order in the reduction of interstate limitations in certification requirements. It is a flexible plan, it is practical, and it can be of great help in this problem.

By way of summary, requiring a total amount of training, without any specification of subject matter areas as given in plan number two, is hardly feasible, nor will it provide for permanent growth in certification proceedings. It is a reaction from the overly detailed requirements in many states at this time, is too flexible to be of much use, and provides too much leeway for misuse in actual practice. Even so, it is now in use in some states.

Plan number five, the breaking down of the national problem into sectional ones, and the provision of a certificate higher than that of any state in a group for cooperative acceptance by the group, may be a step in the right direction if adopted by several groups of states. However, inasmuch as this plan is similar to the National Board plan and may require as much work and time to put into effect as the larger plan, it may be that the National Board plan would be the one to adopt rather than this smaller scale plan of grouping the states.

It is thought that plan number six entails too many changes in the creation of a certificate based on national norms or means of present requirements and the providing of temporary certificates for a period of a year in which persons might meet the total requirements of any particular state. This idea has merit but does not seem to be practical, especially in comparison with the other plans mentioned.

It may be that certain combinations of plans would best serve the needs of cooperating groups. The breaking down of the larger problem into smaller sectional ones as given in plan number four, could be combined with the specification of definite amounts of training in broad subject categories rather than detailed courses, as indicated by plan number three. The removal of specific requirements as in plan number one could also be used in this combination to provide for greater interstate mobility.

Other Needed Administrative Changes

1. *Develop administration of certification in such manner that the certification requirements are enacted by state board regulations rather than state legislative statutory proceedings.*

This change is sorely needed inasmuch as many state certification systems are now so organized that even the minute details of certification requirements and practices are enacted by the state legislature. This not only places the laws on the statute books to "freeze" long past the time when they are desired, or needed, but also places the authority for such professional administrative activity in the wrong hands. The legislature should be the policy forming body, with the state board and its professionally trained leaders the administrators of these policies. As now legislated, certification requirements lag far behind the states' needs because of the difficulty involved in having the legislature act. Usually law-making bodies are slow, cumbersome, and lacking in professional training needed to place into force such things as certification requirements. The latter require a trained, alert group to make and enforce them after continuing research and study of the needs of the respective commonwealths.

The present situation also brings the possibility of certain "pressure groups" and their lobbying practices. These often influence legislatures to enact requirements which may be far different from those useful or valuable to the state. Many specific state requirements which prove restrictive are the results of such lobbying by pressure groups. Although there is no proof that state board members and their trained professional leaders may not also be subject to lobbying pressure, nevertheless, these groups may be better trained for their work and may be made more responsible in direct manner for the results obtained. It is reasonable to assume that state board members would be freer from such lobbying practices and pressures than legislators. Then, too, the regulations once passed can be changed as conditions change without the lingering tendencies for which many statutes are notorious.

2. *Initiate and maintain continuing research into the certification needs of the state and the supply of and demand for teachers in various subject areas and school levels.*

This change in administrative function is sorely needed inasmuch as very few states have the data necessary before administering or passing certification requirements. Most states are actually "blind" insofar as knowing the requirements of the states, how many teachers are needed in certain areas, or what the supply of teachers is. This "blindness" on the part of the educational officials is a result of not having a plan of continuing research and data-gathering on pertinent problems of certification. Much of the state's action with regard to certification is taken without adequate knowledge of the needs or trends of the state educational and certification functions.

For example, Emens, in a study of state administration of teacher personnel,[34] found that the data-gathering of most states was hopelessly inadequate. He found that eighteen states had no provision for keeping a permanent, continuous record of teacher personnel within the state office. In these eighteen states it is necessary, if information about teacher personnel is needed, to go to the teacher-training institutions, other state officers, employees, or the teachers themselves. Eighteen other commonwealths have no complete individual records, but some information is available although perhaps filed in different files or offices within the state education department.[35] Only six states have complete records in a collection of items that are filed in a central office. Only five states keep single, complete, continuing personnel records of each teacher in matters comprising personal, educational, certification, placement, and employment data.* Emens' study reveals an astonishing lack of even partially complete information about certification. The supply data are woefully inadequate, as are the figures showing the demand, the placement of teachers, employment, and other personnel data.[36]

It is astonishing how states can proceed with such fragmentary

[34] John R. Emens, "A Study of State Administration of Teacher Personnel." Unpublished Doctoral dissertatión, University of Michigan, 1938.

[35] *Ibid.*, p. 99.

* No reply from one state.

[36] *Ibid.*, pp. 97–115.

information as they possess regarding the personnel of the teaching group within the state or of certification. Of course, the personnel[37] of state departments are subject to tenure and financial controls; so is the research division. It may not be possible for many states to do all that they have planned to do or thought necessary for the professional advancement of the state. Nevertheless, the situation reveals a definite lack of information about the needs of the state—a decided "blind spot" in the matter of certification administration. After considering the lack of data and the almost total lack of continuing research or even or records, it is surprising that certification is administered as well as it has been in some states. There are great needs in this entire area which must be met before certification affecting almost one million teachers can be greatly improved, but a start must be made; hence this administrative suggestion.

Factors to be considered in reducing or eliminating restrictions and limitations to the free interstate mobility of teachers in community employment policies and practices.

As indicated in Chapters III, IV, and V in this study, the applicant for a teaching certificate meets restrictions and limitations in state certification practices and policies. Plans for reducing or eliminating these have just been given. Chapter VI reveals that teachers also meet restrictions and limitations in community employment policies and practices. Suggestions for reducing or eliminating such restrictive factors from the community practices must consider several factors.

1. Teacher employment is a community responsibility, not a state function.[38]

It is the community which employs teachers, although in most instances the person employed must either have a certificate from the state or have made adequate arrangements for such, if the community does not want to be penalized for employing a non-certified teacher. It is in the community policies and practices that restrictions

[37] *Ibid.*, pp. 116–117.

[38] See Educational Policies Commission, *The Structure and Administration of Education in American Democracy,* Chapter II. In some instances the state as well as the federal government conducts employment offices, but it is still the community that usually employs its own teachers.

or limitations to the out-of-state teachers must also be reduced or eliminated.

2. Professional merit or ability should be the main criterion of teacher selection, not the geographical residence of the applicant.

To remove the community restrictions to non-local and out-of-state teachers, the factor of residence as a qualification of the applicants must be reduced in value or eliminated entirely from consideration by the employing groups. If the local teacher has training, experience, and professional ability or promise equal to or similar to that of applicants from other cities or states, there can be little objection to the employment of the local teacher. On the other hand, if local teachers are chosen because they are local persons when they are not as well qualified as non-local or out-of-state applicants, the situation is one that can be seriously challenged.

It is distinctly to the advantage of employing officials in the school system to engage the best possible teachers for school positions. With the best available teachers, improvements can be carried out, better instruction given, and a higher morale maintained among the teaching staff, other factors being similar. It is reasonable to assume that students would profit from having superior teachers in the classroom situation. The quality of education which a child receives is the ultimate criterion of the school's efficiency. The superintendent and the board of education can ill afford to employ teachers other than the best available. In considering the non-local and the out-of-state residents as well as local, the employing officials in communities thereby widen their selection.

Any plan to remove restrictions and limitations from the employing procedures of community school systems must offer the possibility of finding merit and must remove any possibility of residence influencing unduly the employment practices. There are many types of plans considered feasible. One of these is based upon the practices now usually followed in employing a person. The other is based upon examinations with improved techniques and wider sampling of information. Both have weaknesses and advantages. Either could be used in eliminating employment restrictions, though care must be taken to be sure that additional restrictions are not created.

Suggested Plans to Remove Restrictions and Limitations in Community Employment

1. *Weight certain factors of training, merit, and experience among the several bases of teacher selection to remove the factor of residence.*

A plan can be arranged whereby such factors as training and experience, and numerous other items are weighted so as to remove or reduce considerably the factor of local residence of the applicants for teaching positions. Degrees, courses taken, years of experience, ratings of personality and character, attitude, appearance, and similar factors could be considered on a point basis in this procedure. The residence of the teacher could either be ignored entirely or given a very small weighting so it would not overbalance other factors.

Every experienced superintendent has developed techniques and ideas of his own in the selection of teachers. Each looks for different factors and considers different points of greater or less importance than others. Nevertheless, such a plan could be created and followed in many instances so there can be definitely weighted factors considered. In Providence, Rhode Island, teacher selection has characteristics of such an objective plan.[39]

The Providence Plan of Teacher Selection *

The plan is briefly as follows:

Every candidate should possess certain broad educational qualifications, including general culture, scholastic aptitude, and professional preparation. All candidates must take objective examinations in these fields. In addition, each candidate should be a master of at least two subject fields of instruction in the curriculum of the public schools and through objective examinations must demonstrate scholarship in these fields sufficient to justify his appointment to teach them. The result of each of these five examinations is translated into a percentile rank, indicating exactly where the candidate would rank in a group of one hundred teachers. These percentile ranks are added and the total examination marks count a possible five hundred points out of a total of one thousand.

[39] Ben D. Wood, *Teacher Selection,* pp. 12–15. Data supplied by Dr. R. D. Allen.

* The by-laws of the School Committee and the statutes of the State of Rhode Island require the Superintendent to nominate teachers and report upon their qualifications. During the school year 1931–32 the Superintendent and his staff adopted a plan for the testing and rating of candidates for teaching positions in order to select from the many available candidates those who were clearly superior in the essential and desirable elements that make for successful teaching.

Naturally the desirability of any system of examination depends upon the quality, fairness, reliability, method of correction, and method of administration of the tests. Much of the success of the present program is due to the fact that at the time of its inception a new series of tests was made available through the efforts of the American Council on Education and the generosity of the General Education Board. The examinations are of the new-type, objective form, easy to correct, and comparable from year to year. New forms are guaranteed for ten years. The examinations have been prepared by some of the foremost technical experts in the country and are entirely free from commercial motives, since they are available at cost through the foundation.

Three special advantages of these examinations are worthy of note:

1. The objective nature of the examinations makes it possible for each candidate to have the privilege of examining his corrected test to satisfy himself concerning its proper scoring.

2. No teacher who is a college graduate should object to taking the subject examinations that are required of high school and college students.

3. The impartial nature of the examination and its removal from a local setting is highly desirable. Special arrangements insure that no candidate may secure a copy of any test before the date of the examination.

Of the remaining five hundred points, the two hundred which evaluate training and experience are also impersonal and objective, since they are determined by a scale of values and are based upon a questionnaire which each candidate files by number without his name attached. Thus seven hundred out of one thousand points are determined on the basis of examinations and facts, all of which may be reviewed and challenged by the candidates and all without involving the names of the candidates.

The remaining three hundred points represent a group rating in teaching personality. The rating is made by a group of principals and assistant and deputy superintendents who determine the relative desirability of each candidate as a member of a school faculty, as a wholesome influence with growing young people, and as a positive asset in the life and work of the school. A relative rating on personality is spread on a three hundred point scale and added to the ratings on experience, general qualifications, and special qualifications, to obtain a grand total score. When the candidate has been trained in our schools, the record of training is a very important phase of the rating.

When these steps have been taken, the candidates then are listed in subject fields in the order of their total scores and appointed in order as they appear on the list. During the past three years this procedure has been followed. Preference in appointment is given to local candidates.* Every candidate is informed concerning his own rating. All records are open for inspection by any person who has a legitimate interest in them,

* Presumably where qualifications were equal on the examinations.

and all candidates who desire further information have been interviewed by the Director of Research or his assistants.

The present plan prevents any suspicion of discrimination on the basis of religion, nationality, race, or political considerations. It places entrance to the teaching profession in Providence upon a high professional plane which considers only the selection of persons best qualified to serve the needs and interests of children and the community. The record of appointments for the past three years speaks for itself in the growing confidence of the teaching staff and of the public in the method and its administration.[40]

Wood states:

There may be some who would demur at the use of objective tests of subject matter achievement in selecting teachers. In the Providence Plan the objective tests are assigned five hundred of the one thousand points on the basis of which the candidates are placed in preferential order. It is obvious that many qualities other than academic intelligence and achievement are essential for good teaching, and these qualities should be considered and estimated or measured as accurately as possible. But their importance does not detract from the importance of the qualities measured by the objective tests used in the Providence Plan. However well-endowed with personality qualifications a candidate may be, he cannot teach mathematics or foreign languages, or English or history or science unless he has at least a minimal mastery of one or more of them.[41]

One advantage of such a plan is that it offers definiteness in the solution of a very difficult problem and that it helps to remove this matter of residence of the applicant as a *major* factor. Where comparable ability is revealed by these tests, preference is given to the local resident. This kind of arrangement would consider professional ability and experience as main criteria, not residence. Another argument is that the results of such a plan can be defended adequately if challenged. Local residents cannot complain if the superintendent attempts to choose the teachers on the basis of merit because it is the children of the residents of the community who may be expected to profit. The board of education cannot view entirely negatively any plan by which ability and merit are recognized and by which better teachers are brought into the school system. A much larger group of teachers can thus be considered if ability and merit are the main criteria.

[40] Ben D. Wood, "Teacher Selection," p. 14.
[41] *Ibid.*, p. 15.

An argument against such a plan is that it might tend to try to make objective the selection of teachers, which is generally conceded to be largely a subjective matter. So many intangible factors enter the picture that it is difficult or impossible to make the selection of teachers an entirely objective matter. However, some large cities have successfully used objective measures.[42]

A second argument against such a plan is that the examinations might be used as a smoke screen, with the applicants chosen for the available positions on the basis of local residence anyway.

Another argument against such a plan is that, in the last resort, when the superintendent recommends the appointment of certain persons, the school board may not elect those who are not residents of the community in spite of the very good reasons for having the best possible teachers in the school system. Having a paying position is a matter of bread and butter for members of the community. The schools are a community enterprise and are supported by the community. It is only natural that local residents should want the money-paying positions to go to local persons, so the money paid out by the community goes to members of that group. Such a plan as indicated above, however, may have many advantages to counteract this possible negative factor.

Local "pressures" for employing local persons are strong and often very audible and urgent, whereas the "pressures" for non-local candidates may not be very strong. The superintendent is usually anxious to please the strongest or most insistent of the local residents. The plan suggested may therefore be very difficult to administer.

Then again, such examinations may require a too great expenditure of money, time, and effort by the community and the applicants for teaching positions. A very important objection is that such examinations would immediately erect limitations and restrictions for non-local people. If every city had such an examination, a person could be required to take as many examinations as he had applications for positions in different cities. This would be disastrous and prohibitive. At one time city examinations were held by many com-

[42] John C. Coulbourne, *The Selection of Teachers in Large City School Systems.* Bureau of Publications, Teachers College, Columbia University, New York, 1938. Contributions to Education, No. 740.

munities, but the plan was later dropped during the development of education in this country. Why should education return to such a plan now?

After considering the advantages and disadvantages, it is thought that there is some merit to such an arrangement in the employment of teachers but that there is danger of heavy limitations and restrictions. There may be as many different plans as there are superintendents of schools, yet, basically, if the factor of residence is removed or reduced in value and teachers appointed on the basis of ability or merit, such an idea may aid in reducing or removing these employment restrictions to non-local and out-of-state persons.

2. *Establish comprehensive and reliable examinations on a national scale, using the results of such as the major criterion of teacher selection.*

In the attempt to find the best teachers, one suggested plan is to establish a thorough, comprehensive, valid, and reliable examination for teaching applicants, the results to be used as one of several criteria of selection. Such a plan has already been in operation for two years—the National Teacher Examinations, administered by the National Committee on Teacher Examinations of the American Council on Education.[43] The Cooperative Test Service of the American Council prepares the tests and examinations.[44]

The Committee frankly recognizes the importance of the teacher in the educative process, as well as the complexity of the teaching function. Admittedly, if the qualifications of a prospective teacher are to be adequately judged, a comprehensive picture of the candidate is required. Those responsible for the choice of teachers must weigh the total pattern of characteristics of each applicant.[45] Some of the factors making up the total picture of the teacher considered are: personal and social characteristics, such as age, appearance,

[43] Committee consists of the following: A. J. Stoddard, Chairman, Philadelphia; Ben G. Graham, Pittsburgh; Leslie R. Gregory, Fredonia; James L. Hanley, Providence; H. E. Hawkes, New York: E. W. Jacobsen, Pittsburgh; Charles H. Lake, Cleveland; Carroll R. Reed, Minneapolis; and George F. Zook, ex-officio, Washington, D. C.

[44] The Cooperative Test Service is a nonprofit service agency established in 1930 with the aid of a grant from the General Education Board.

[45] Report of the First Annual Administration of the National Teacher Examinations and Announcement of the 1941 Examinations, National Committee on Teacher Examinations of the American Council on Education, p. 23.

personal adjustment, and organization of personality; intellectual abilities and accomplishments, including aptitudes, ability to understand and express ideas, general cultural knowledge, professional educational knowledge, and special competence in the teaching field; instructional efficiency or classroom effectiveness; experience; training; potentialities for professional growth, and physical fitness.[46] The Committee looks upon the examination as *one phase* of teacher selection because such tests do measure essential elements of teaching ability more accurately and more economically than they can be measured by any other presently known devices or methods.

The Committee, however, according to their statement, was and is keenly aware, and must advisedly be so, of the great importance of other vital factors in teacher selection, such as health, training, experience, interest in children, social sensitivity, character and personality traits.

At the request of a number of school teachers and administrators throughout the country, the American Council on Education, in the spring of 1939 appointed this National Committee on Teacher Examinations. The Council sponsored the project after consultations with superintendents indicated a crucial need for an examination service which would avoid the costly duplication and uncertainties of locally assembled examinations for teacher candidates; which would give reliable and valid measures; and which would be comparable from year to year and from one school system to another. Helpful in the selection of new teachers, such an examination is at the same time of advantage to the candidate and to teacher-preparing institutions because of the opportunity to "register" certain types of abilities on a national scale in terms of widely comparable units. On March 29 and 30, 1940, a comprehensive battery of specially constructed examinations was given in twenty-three official examining centers throughout the United States to a total of 3,726 candidates for teaching positions.[47] The 1941 examinations were administered on March 14–15, 1941. The tests comprising the National Teacher Examination Battery and the time limits for each are given below:

[46] *Ibid.*, p. 3.

[47] For further details of the origin, report, and announcement of the further work of the National Committee on Teacher Examinations, write the National Committee on Teacher Examination, 15 Amsterdam Ave., New York, N. Y.

Common Examinations, which are recommended for all candidates on the theory that admission to the profession in any capacity should be restricted to those above a certain minimum of intelligence, culture, and professional preparation.

Reasoning . . . . 40 minutes
English Comprehension. . . . . 40 minutes
English Expression . . . . 40 minutes
General Culture . . . . 180 minutes
- Current Social Problems
- History and Social Studies
- Literature
- Science
- Fine Arts
- Mathematics

Professional Information . . . . 120 minutes
- Education and Social Policy
- Child Development and Educational Psychology
- Guidance, and Individual and Group Analysis
- Elementary School Methods or Secondary School Methods

Contemporary Affairs . . . . 60 minutes

Optional Examinations (examinations to show mastery of the subject matter to be taught). It is recommended that candidates for elementary school positions take number 1, and candidates for high school positions any two others.

1. Education in the Elementary School . . . . 120 minutes
2. English Language and Literature. . . . . 90 minutes
3. Social Studies . . . . 90 minutes
4. Mathematics. . . . . 90 minutes
5. Biological Sciences . . . . 90 minutes
6. Physical Sciences . . . . 90 minutes
7. Spanish . . . . 90 minutes
8. French . . . . 90 minutes
9. German . . . . 90 minutes
10. Latin. . . . . 90 minutes

Two particularly significant facts which have been recognized for some time and which are further proved by a review of the 1940 examination results are: first, the candidates for teaching positions are not equally well qualified; and second, a fairly long and varied battery of examinations is necessary to describe the candidates adequately. Although all the individuals taking the tests had satisfied the legal certification requirements and had accumulated the necessary credits, some of them knew almost nothing about the fields covered by the tests whereas others made nearly perfect scores. It is in the light of such differences in intellectual ability among seemingly equally well qualified prospective teachers that the National Teacher Examinations can contribute to school superintendents in the teacher selection process, according to the sponsors.[48]

It is in the use of the examination results, however, that the greatest values and interests lie in the removal of local residence as a sole factor in teacher selection. The methods of selection as employed in three different cities are outlined below:

SCHOOL SYSTEM I

Information concerning the candidate is combined on the basis of a total possible number of points of one thousand. Five hundred points on the one thousand point scale may be contributed by ratings of training, experience, and personality. In this system the remaining five hundred points are determined by examination results. The examinations are divided into "general" and "special" examinations. The "general" examinations, given to all teachers ("Common Examinations" of National Teacher Examination battery), are intended to measure qualifications common to all the teaching candidates regardless of the particular positions for which individuals may be applying. The "special" examinations consist of a test of the candidate's major field and examination in at least one minor field selected by the candidate (National Teacher Examination "Optional Examinations"). When the final group ratings and examination scores have been obtained, they are combined and candidates are selected in the order of their combined rating within the subject classification.

SCHOOL SYSTEM II

The scale upon which candidates are ranked in this system consists of one thousand possible points. Personal and social characteristics (as determined by interview and rating methods) account for a total possible three hundred points. Instructional efficiency contributes three hundred points; of this, training receives one hundred points, demonstrated teaching ability one hundred points, and experience one hundred points. The remaining four hundred points are allotted

[48] *Ibid.*, p. 17.

for intellectual qualifications. Of this amount aptitude contributes one hundred points, general knowledge one hundred points, and mastery of a special field two hundred points.

SCHOOL SYSTEM III

In this system the candidate's scores and ratings on all factors for which the school has data, including the test results, are converted to a common scale, and a "profile chart" is constructed for each candidate. Members of the administrative and supervisory staff subjectively judge these profiles in determining the most desirable pattern of ability, training, experience, personal and social characteristics, etc., for the particular position open. The candidate whose pattern is such that he seems best for the position is selected.

It is of peculiar significance to the present study that by means of some such weighting device the local residence factor be reduced or eliminated in the selection of candidates, and that ability be made a main criterion. There is always the danger, however, that such favoritism would not be removed by such machinery and examinations. Each local school system should determine the use made of the examination results and assign relative weights desired to the several factors contributing to the final ranking of the candidates.

It is the present plan of the National Committee on Teacher Examinations to conduct research in two types of activities: first, to carry on a continuous program for the improvement of the tests, and, so far as the resources permit, to study ways of improving the appraisal of the factors not covered by the objective examinations; and, second, to lend all possible aid to the initiation and coordination of long-range research programs in the cooperating centers. In addition, a central file will be maintained for the examination results, which will be kept in strict confidence and results made known only to those whom the applicant designates in writing.

It is important to note that the National Committee has not proposed to provide a teacher SELECTION, but rather a teacher EXAMINATION service as an aid to teacher selection. If these examinations are used in any way in teacher selection, care must be taken to guard against several potential dangers, including, among others, the following:

1. The examinations may eventually influence the curriculum of teacher-training institutions in the direction of undesirable rigidity and resistance to change.

2. Less emphasis on classroom techniques and on qualities of initiative and imagination on the part of the teacher may result. The examinations or supplementary ones may not test or reveal many character traits essential for teaching success.

3. Administrators may accept the ratings as an "easy way" of selecting teachers, or may be influenced wholly by test results, to the neglect of other important factors involved in teacher selection.

4. The possibility exists that candidates may cram or be coached even though cramming is purported not to be essential.

5. The examination system may become a commercial enterprise.[49] This last point is fundamental. Objections are now being raised to such examinations on these grounds.

On the other hand, arguments in favor of such examinations may include the following:

1. In terms of the findings of this study, such a type of examination would aid superintendents in their efforts to select new teachers and would, if used with other indispensable factors, be a basis for the elimination of local residence as a factor of selection or reduce its importance.

2. Prospective teachers would be provided an opportunity to demonstrate their qualifications objectively on a national scale in terms of widely comparable units.

3. The examinations may be useful in improving instruction in teacher-preparing institutions of widely different types. Results of graduates' taking these tests would provide invaluable data to such institutions.[50]

4. Such examinations would serve to identify the strong applicant better than does the present system of college transcripts and letters of recommendation. Other essential factors would, of course, have to be considered as vital items in the selective process.

5. Such tests challenge the applicant to do his best, and, if successful, to develop self-confidence.

Fundamentally, the plan contains highly debatable issues for the several types of institutions now training students. Any expression of opinion on this proposal should await further developments. If these examinations become of value to the profession as have

[49] Carter V. Good; summary presented to the National Council of Education, Atlantic City, February 24, 1941. Mimeographed, 8 pages.

[50] See *The Student and His Knowledge* by William S. Learned and Ben D. Wood. The Carnegie Foundation, New York, 1938.

those of the National Medical Board of Examiners, eventually their results may be of service in other ways besides employment and certification. The test results may be used, together with scores or marks by institutions, as measures of evaluation of the caliber of academic work done by the student. In this way the examinations may supplement the institution's measure of a student's abilities. Some institutions use the National Medical Board examination results in considering a student's ability to graduate, as well as in the selection of instructors and minor officials for positions in medical schools. In the medical group, these examinations have become similar to honors work and are eagerly sought and taken. Administrators can perhaps use such results to evaluate their own teaching.

Those who know of the New York Regents' Examinations are of divided opinion as to their worth. Some would eliminate these examinations entirely, while others would modify and retain them. Some regard the Regents' Examinations as one of the big stumbling blocks to New York's progress, preventing the optimum improvement of that state's school curriculum. The problem is indeed a complex one. Though the objectives of those in charge of the Regents' Examinations and of the National Teachers' Examinations differ, similar criticisms and comparisons might be made of them. The experiences obtained from working with the Regents' tests should be utilized by those in charge of the National Teachers' Examinations as factors in the consideration of the whole program.

3. *Elect a highly trained professional leader of the community schools, arrive at a conclusion as to the proper division of the work of the board of education and the superintendent, and then give the superintendent support in his professional leadership of the schools.*

Many communities, as indicated in Chapter VI, elect a superintendent of schools and then bring so much pressure to bear on him or on the board of education that the superintendent is controlled or blocked in his educational leadership. A highly trained professional leader who is alert and vigorous can, with the sincere backing of the board of education, do a great amount of good for any community's school system. This kind of superintendent will use his best professional judgment as to the kind of teacher he employs. He knows the dangers of "teacher inbreeding." He is also aware of the advantages of new ideas and different ways of approaching professional problems which can come through a diversified, trained staff composed of persons chosen primarily on the bases of merit and professional ability rather than residence. He will use his best judgment in this important problem of teacher selection. If the board of education and the community will support him, he will go a long way toward removing the restrictions and limitations which out-of-state or non-local teachers find in the community employment policies and practices in the cities of this nation. Such a leader will have his own devices and techniques of choosing teachers on the bases of their training, experience, personality, and professional ability. Given full support, he will do more than any other one factor in eliminating the restrictions discussed in Chapter VI. *With* such a leader, no other plan would be absolutely necessary. *Without* such a leader, few other plans would operate successfully.

Conclusions

The plans whereby restrictions and limitations might be reduced, eliminated, or avoided in state certification and community employment were arrived at by an analysis of the results of the entire investigation and by a study of the plans used in other professions. These suggested plans are sufficiently general to be adaptable to specific situations and yet definite enough to be meaningful and helpful.

The suggestions of this chapter, once put into operation, may provide effective instruments for the removal of restrictions and limitations to the free interstate mobility of teachers. There is no gainsaying the difficulties involved in any change of certification. However, the ends may justify the means. It should be remembered, also, that no plan or law, regardless of how perfectly framed, can alone produce the desired results. Good school administration can do more than anything else to make it possible for teachers from other states to obtain certification and employment without undue restrictions and limitations to their free interstate mobility.

BIBLIOGRAPHY

AMERICAN COUNCIL ON EDUCATION STUDIES. *Major Issues in Teacher Education.* Series 1, Vol. II, No. 4, February, 1938. Pp. 44.

AMERICAN MEDICAL ASSOCIATION. Medical Licensure Statistics for 1938. *Journal of the American Medical Association,* April 29, 1939, 1697–1730.

ASHBY, LYLE W. *The Efforts of the States to Support Education.* Washington, D. C.: National Education Association, 1936. Pp. 63.

BARRETT, RICHARD C. "Reciprocity in Licensing Teachers." *National Education Association Journal of Proceedings and Addresses,* 1902. Pp. 299–305.

BLODGETT, JAMES H. *Legal Provisions of the Various States Relating to Teachers' Examinations and Certificates.* U. S. Bureau of Education. Report of the Commissioner of Education, 1897–1898, Vol. 2. Washington, D. C.: Government Printing Office, 1899. Pp. 1691.

BOARD OF GOVERNORS OF THE FEDERAL RESERVE SYSTEM. *The Federal Reserve System.* Washington, D. C.: The National Capital Press, 1939. Pp. 128.

BOWERS, HOWARD J. "Ten Principles of Teacher Certification." *American School Board Journal,* XCVI, 41–42, June, 1938.

CLEMENTS, EVELYN A. "The Employment of Out-of-State Teachers." *School and Society,* L, 87–89, July 15, 1939.

COOK, KATHERINE M. *State Laws and Regulations Governing Teachers' Certificates.* U. S. Bureau of Education, Bulletin No. 22. Washington, D. C.: Government Printing Office, 1921. Pp. 244.

COOK, KATHERINE M. *State Laws and Regulations Governing Teachers' Certificates.* U. S. Bureau of Education, Bulletin No. 19. Washington, D. C.: Government Printing Office, 1927. Pp. 296.

COULBOURNE, JOHN C. *The Selection of Teachers in Large City School Systems.* New York: Bureau of Publications, Teachers College, Columbia University, 1938. Pp. 177.

CROOKER, JAMES F. *Forty-first Annual Report of the State Snperintendent of Public Instruction, State of New York,* 1895, Vol. XI.

CUBBERLEY, ELLWOOD P. *The Certification of Teachers.* Fifth Yearbook of the National Society for the Scientific Study of Education, Part II. Chicago: University of Chicago Press, 1906. Pp. 88.

CUBBERLEY, ELLWOOD P. *State School Administration.* Boston: Houghton Mifflin Co., 1927. Pp. 773.

DRAPER, A. S. "Life Certificates." *Thirty-third Annual Report of the State Superintendent of Public Instruction.* Albany, N. Y., 1887, p. 14.

DRAPER, A. S. *Thirty-fifth Annual Report of the State Superintendent of Public Instruction.* Albany, N. Y., 1889, pp. 30–32.

DRAPER, A. S. *Thirty-sixth Annual Report of the State Superintendent of Public Instruction.* Albany, N. Y., 1890, p. 832.

DRAPER, A. S. *Thirty-eighth Annual Report of the State Superintendent of Public Instruction.* Albany, N. Y., 1892, p. 35.

EBEY, GEORGE WILLIAM. *Adaptability Among the Elementary Schools of an Amer-*

ican City. Contributions to Education, No. 817. New York: Bureau of Publications, Teachers College, Columbia University, 1940. Pp. 73.

EDUCATIONAL POLICIES COMMISSION. *The Structure and Administration of Education in American Democracy.* Washington, D. C.: National Education Association, 1938. Pp. 128.

ELSBREE, WILLARD S. *The American Teacher.* New York: The American Book Company, 1939. Pp. 566.

ELWOOD, EVERETT S. "State Board and National Board Relationships." Paper read before the Annual Congress on Medical Education, Medical Licensure and Hospitals, Chicago, February 16, 1932.

EMENS, JOHN R. "A Study of State Administration of Teachers' Personnel." Unpublished Doctoral dissertation, University of Michigan, 1938. Pp. 249.

EVENDEN, E. S., GAMBLE, GUY C., AND BLUE, HAROLD G. *Teacher Personnel In the United States.* National Survey of the Education of Teachers, U. S. Office of Education, Bulletin No. 10, Vol. II. Washington, D. C.: Government Printing Office, 1935. Pp. 258.

FAIRLIE, JOHN A. *The Centralization of Administration in New York State.* New York: Columbia University, 1898. Pp. 207.

FLANDERS, JESSIE K. *Legislative Control of the Elementary Curriculum.* Contributions to Education, No. 195. New York: Bureau of Publications, Teachers College, Columbia University, 1925. Pp. 242.

FRAZIER, BENJAMIN W. *Development of State Programs for the Certification of Teachers.* U. S. Office of Education, Bulletin No. 12. Washington, D. C.: Government Printing Office, 1938. Pp. 166.

GILDERSLEEVE, VIRGINIA C. "And Sadly Teach. State Requirements That Discourage Educated Persons From Teaching." *American Scholar,* V, 429, September, 1936.

GOODRICH, CARTER AND OTHERS. *Migration and Economic Opportunity.* Philadelphia: University of Pennsylvania Press, 1936. Pp. 763.

GOODRICH, CARTER, ALLIN, BUSHROD W., AND HAYES, MARION. *Migration and Planes of Living.* Philadelphia: University of Pennsylvania Press, 1935. Pp. 111.

HERBST, R. L. "Statutory Status of Six Professions." *National Education Association Research Bulletin,* Vol. XVI, No. 4, September, 1938.

HOLMES, HENRY W. "The English Teacher and Educational Theory: The Sorry Business of Meeting State Requirements." *School and Society,* XLVIII, 177–179, August 6, 1938.

JACKSON, WILLIAM R. *The Present Status of Certification of Teachers in the United States.* U. S. Bureau of Education, Report of the Commissioner of Education, 1903, Vol. 1. Washington, D. C.: Government Printing Office, 1905. Pp. 519.

JAGGERS, RICHARD E., Director of Teacher Training and Certification, Kentucky. "The Education and Certification of Secondary Teachers," *Report of the Eleventh Annual Meeting of the South Carolina Association of Collegiate Registrars,* May 12, 1939. Pp. 22–29.

JONAS, RUSSEL E. "Progress Report, Midwest Regional Conference on Certification." Des Moines, Iowa, November, 1939. Mimeo.

KENDALL, RAYMOND L. "The Closing Door." *Journal of Higher Education,* IX, No. 5, 529, May, 1938.

LATSHAW, MARY L. "Interchange of Teachers." Unpublished Master's thesis. Washington, D. C.: George Washington University, 1928. Pp. 122.

LEARNED, WILLIAM S. AND WOOD, BEN D. *The Student and His Knowledge.* A Report to the Carnegie Foundation on the Results of the High School and College Examinations of 1928, 1930, and 1932. New York: The Carnegie Foundation for the Advancement of Teaching, 1938. Pp. 406.

LEWIS, ERVIN EUGENE. *Personnel Problems of the Teaching Staff.* New York: The Century Co., 1925. Pp. 460.

LORIMER, FRANK AND OSBORN, FREDERICK. *Dynamics of Population.* New York: The Macmillan Company, 1934. Pp. 461.

LYND, ROBERT S. AND LYND, HELEN M. *Middletown.* New York: Harcourt, Brace and Company, 1929. Pp. 550.

LYND, ROBERT S. AND LYND, HELEN M. *Middletown in Transition.* New York: Harcourt, Brace and Company, 1937. Pp. 604.

MCMULLEN, RAYMOND F. "Reciprocity Among the States in the Certification of Teachers." Unpublished Master's thesis. Columbus, Ohio: Ohio State University, 1932. Pp. 162.

"Midwest Conference on Certification." *School and Society,* XLVII, 746–747, December 12, 1938.

MIDWEST REGIONAL CONFERENCE ON CERTIFICATION. Russel E. Jones, Chairman. *Progress Reports.* Des Moines, Iowa, November, 1929. Foreword, p. 1.

MORT, PAUL R. AND CORNELL, FRANCIS G. *Adaptability of Public School Systems.* New York: Bureau of Publications, Teachers College, Columbia University, 1938. Pp. 146.

NATIONAL BOARD OF MEDICAL EXAMINERS. *Circular of Information.* Bulletin No. 3, Revised January 1, 1937.

NATIONAL BOARD OF MEDICAL EXAMINERS. *Constitution, By-Laws and Charter.* Philadelphia, November, 1934.

NATIONAL EDUCATION ASSOCIATION, Research Division and the American Association of School Administrators. *Policies Concerning the Appointment of Local Residents as Teachers in 1930–1931 and 1937–1938.* Circular No. 1, 1938, January, 1938.

NATIONAL EDUCATION ASSOCIATION RESEARCH BULLETIN. *Population Trends and Their Implications.* Vol. XVI, No. 1, January, 1938.

NATIONAL RESOURCES COMMITTEE. Report of the Committee on Population Problems and the National Resources Committee. *The Problems of a Changing Population.* Washington, D. C.: Government Printing Office, May, 1938. Pp. 306.

NORTON, JOHN K. AND NORTON, MARGARET A. *Wealth, Children and Education.* New York: Bureau of Publications, Teachers College, Columbia University, 1937. Pp. 100.

PIERCE, EDWARD T. "Recognition of Diplomas of Other State Normal Schools in Other Than the State in Which Issued." *National Education Journal of Proceedings and Addresses,* 1897, 715–716.

PITTINGER, L. A. "Raising Certification Requirements." *National Education Association Journal of Proceedings and Addresses,* 1931, 897–911.

RAUP, BRUCE. *Education and Organized Interests in America.* New York: G. P. Putnam's Sons, 1936. Pp. 238.

RODMAN, J. S. AND ELWOOD, E. S. "Comments on the National Board Examinations." *Proceedings of the Annual Congress on Medical Education.* Chicago: American Medical Association, 1936. Pp. 63.

RUSSELL, JAMES E. *Report of the Dean of Teachers College, 1925.* New York: Teachers College, Columbia University.

RUSSELL, JOHN DALE AND JUDD, CHARLES H. *The American Educational System.* New York: Houghton Mifflin Company, 1940. Pp. 854.

SNYDER, HAROLD E. "Educational Inbreeding: A Study of Teacher Residence." Unpublished manuscript.

SNYDER, Z. X. "Reciprocal Recognition of State and Normal School Diplomas by the States." *National Education Association Journal of Proceedings and Addresses,* 1898, 451–454.

STATE BOARDS AND STATE DEPARTMENTS OF EDUCATION. *Rules and Regulations Governing the Certification of Teachers,* 1933, 1936, 1937, 1938, 1939, 1940.

STATE SUPERINTENDENTS' ROUND TABLE. "Interstate Recognition of State Certificates and Exchange of Official Documents." *National Education Association Journal of Proceedings and Addresses,* 1896.

STRAYER, GEORGE, JR. *Centralizing Tendencies in Administration of Public Education.* New York: Bureau of Publications, Teachers College, Columbia University, 1934. Pp. 123.

SWITZER, ENDA. "The Trends in the Certification of Secondary School Teachers in the United States." Unpublished Master's thesis, Washington University, 1930. Pp. 144.

ULLMAN, R. R. *The Prognostic Value of Certain Factors Related to Teaching Success.* Ashland, Ohio: Ashland College, 1931. Pp. 133.

UNITED STATES CONSTITUTION. Amendments, Article X, Rights of the States Under Constitution.

UNITED STATES CONSTITUTION. Section 8, Powers of Congress, Paragraph 1.

UNITED STATES TWELFTH CENSUS, 1900. Vol. 1, p. XXXVII.

UNITED STATES FIFTEENTH CENSUS, 1930.

UPDEGRAFF, HARLAN. *Teachers' Certificates Issued Under General State Laws and Regulations.* U. S. Bureau of Education, Bulletin No. 19. Washington, D. C.: Government Printing Office, 1911. Pp. 269.

VALENTINE, ALAN. "Teacher-Training versus Teacher Education." *The Educational Record,* XIX, 340, July, 1938.

WEBSTER, WILLIAM C. *Recent Centralizing Tendencies in State Educational Administration.* New York: Columbia University, 1897. Pp. 78.

WHITNEY, E. L. *The Prediction of Teaching Success.* Bloomington, Ill.: Public School Publishing Company, 1924. Pp. 85.

WOELLNER, ROBERT C. AND WOOD, M. AURILLA. *Requirements for Teaching Certificates for Junior High School, Senior High School, Junior College.* Chicago: University of Chicago Press, 1938. See also for 1936, 1937, 1939, and 1940. Mimeo.

WOLFE, L. E. "The Recognition of Certificates and Diplomas Granted (a) By State and County Authorities, (b) By Schools of Education." *National Education Association Journal of Proceedings and Addresses,* 1904, 306–307.

WOOD, BEN D. "Teacher Selection." Reprinted from *Educational Record,* XVII, 374–387, July, 1936.

Laws, Statutes, and Minutes, Listed According to States

Arizona

School Laws, 1925, p. 56.

Rules and Regulations—Certification of Teachers, 1936.

California

School Code, 1929.

Statutes, 1923.

Annual Report of the Division of Teacher Training and Certification. State Department of Education, Division of Teacher Training and Certification, May 15, 1937. Mimeo. report, pp. 2, 10.

Certification of Teachers, Bulletin No. 12, 1935.

Florida

School Laws, 1927.

School Laws, 1935.

Handbook for Teachers, 1936–1937.

Acts, 1925.

Laws, 1925.

Idaho

State Board of Education Minutes, December 14, 1931.

School Laws—Certification of Teachers, Article X, as amended by the Twelfth Session of the Legislature, 1911.

Session Laws, 1911.

Kansas

School Laws, 1937.

Louisiana

State Department of Education—Certification of Teachers, Bulletin 370, 1938.

Certification of Teachers, Bulletin 322, 1938.

Massachusetts

General Laws, Commonwealth of Massachusetts, Section 12, Chapter 71.

Circular of Information, Certification of Teachers in State-Aided High Schools, 1937.

Montana

State Board of Education Minutes, December 14, 1931.

Nevada

School Code, 1935.

School Code, Section 25, Elementary Certificates, 1935.

New Hampshire

Regulations Governing the Approval of Superintendents, Headmasters, Principals, and Teachers in the Public Schools of New Hampshire, 1933.

New Mexico

Session Laws, 1933, 1935.

Rules and Regulations—Certification of Teachers, 1937.

Oregon

School Laws, 1937.

Circular of Certification, 1938.

Oklahoma

Regulations and Requirements for Teachers' Certificates, 1936.

RHODE ISLAND
Certification of Teachers, 1938.
State Board of Education Minutes, 1915.

TEXAS
Public School Laws, 1938.
Statutes, 1930.
Acts, 1924, 39th Legislature, Chapter 124, Article 2886.
Public School Laws, 1930.

UTAH
State Board of Education Minutes, 1924.
Requirements for Certification of Teachers, Supervisors, and Superintendents, 1925.

WASHINGTON
Session Laws, 1889–1890, 1897, 1899, 1903, 1911.

WYOMING
School Laws, 1924.
School Laws, 1925.
Certification Laws, 1931.
Certification of Teachers, Bulletin No. 8, 1938.

STATE BULLETINS

ALABAMA. *Certification of Alabama Teachers* (Abridged). State of Alabama Bulletin, No. 5. Montgomery, Ala.: State Department of Education, Division of Instruction, 1939. Pp. 28.

ARIZONA. *Certification of Teachers in Arizona.* Phoenix, Ariz.: State Department of of Education, 1936. Mimeo.

ARKANSAS. *Regulations Governing the Certification of Teachers in Arkansas.* Bulletin No. 11. Little Rock, Ark.: State Department of Education, 1939. Pp. 38.

CALIFORNIA. *Regulations Governing Granting of Credentials and Certification for Public School Service in California.* State of California, Department of Education Bulletin No. 12, June 15, 1935.

COLORADO. *The Law Governing the Issuance of Certificates. Rules and Regulations of the State Board of Examiners.* Denver, Colo. February 21, 1941.

CONNECTICUT. *Rules and Regulations Concerning State Teachers Certificates.* Connecticut School Document No. 3. New Haven, Conn.: State Board of Education, 1940. Pp. 48.

DELAWARE. *Rules and Regulations for the Certification of Superintendents, Supervisors, Principals and Teachers.* Wilmington, Dela.: State Department of Public Instruction, 1941. Pp. 16.

FLORIDA. *Information Regarding Certification of Instructional Personnel and Registration Service.* Tallahassee, Fla.: State Department of Education Bulletin A, 1941. Pp. 19.

GEORGIA. *Certification of Teachers.* Atlanta, Ga.: State Department of Education, 1940. Pp. 15.

IDAHO. *Certification of Teachers.* State Board of Education, 1939–40 Edition. Pp. 15.

ILLINOIS. *State Examining Board.* Circular No. 316. Chicago, Ill.: State Board of Education, 1940. Pp. 23.

INDIANA. *Educational Bulletin,* No. 94. State Department of Education, 1937. Pp. 63.

IOWA. *Certification of Teachers. Laws and Regulations Governing the Issuance and Renewal of Certificates Based upon Training.* Bulletin No. 7 (Revised). Des Moines, Iowa: Board of Educational Examiners, July 1, 1940. Pp. 23.

KANSAS. *Handbook on Organization and Practices for the Secondary Schools of Kansas.* Revised Edition. Topeka, Kan.: State Department of Education, 1939. Pp. 77.

KENTUCKY. *Teacher Education and Certification.* Vol. VIII, No. 3. Frankfort, Ky.: State Department of Education, 1940. Pp. 232.

LOUISIANA. *Certification of Teachers (White).* Bulletin No. 437. Baton Rouge, La.: State Department of Education, September, 1940. Pp. 14.

MAINE. *State Certification of Teachers.* Augusta, Me.: State Department of Education.

MARYLAND. *Certification Requirements.* Baltimore, Md.: State Department of Education.

MASSACHUSETTS. *Standards for the Appointment of Teachers.* Commonwealth of Massachusetts. Boston, Mass.: Recommended by the State Department of Education, December 1, 1940.

MASSACHUSETTS. *Circular of Information,* 1940. Commonwealth of Massachusetts, Department of Education.

MICHIGAN. *Teachers' Certification Code.* Bulletin No. 601. Lansing Mich.: State Department of Public Instruction, 1937. Pp. 21.

MINNESOTA. *Requirements for Elementary and High School Teaching Certificates.* St. Paul, Minn.: State Department of Education, 1940–1941. Mimeo.

MISSISSIPPI. *Teacher Training Requirements.* State Board of Education, 1938–1940. Mimeo.

MISSOURI. *Rules and Regulations Governing the Certification and Qualifications of High School and Elementary Teachers of Missouri.* Jefferson, Mo.: State Department of Public Schools, 1941.

MONTANA. *Montana Teachers' Certificates.* Circular of Information. Helena, Mont.: State Board of Educational Examiners, 1939. Pp. 10.

NEBRASKA. *Certification Digest of Teachers' Certificates.* Lincoln, Neb.: State Department of Public Instruction, 1940.

NEVADA. *Laws and Regulations Governing Certification, Duties, and Retirement Salaries of Teachers.* Carson City, Nev.: State Board of Education, 1939.

NEW HAMPSHIRE. *Regulations Governing the Approval of Superintendents, Headmasters, Principals, and Teachers in the Public Schools of New Hampshire.* Concord, N. H.: State Board of Education, 1940. Pp. 15.

NEW JERSEY. *Rules Concerning Teachers Certificates.* Sixteenth Edition. Trenton, N. J.: State Board of Education, 1937.

NEW MEXICO. *Rules and Regulations Governing the Certification of Teachers in New Mexico.* Sante Fe, N. M.: State Board of Education, 1940.

NEW YORK. *Certificates for Teaching Service.* Certification Bulletin No. 2. Albany, N. Y.: State Education Department, March 1, 1940.

NORTH CAROLINA. *Digest of Requirements for High School Teachers Certificates.* Raleigh, N. C.: State Department of Public Instruction, 1931. Mimeo.

NORTH DAKOTA. *Requirements for Professional and Special Certificates.* Bismarck, N. D.: Department of Public Instruction.

OHIO. *Certification Requirements.* Columbus, Ohio: State Department of Education.

OHIO. *Laws and Regulations Governing the Certification of Teachers in Ohio.* Columbus, Ohio: State Department of Education, 1939. Pp. 24.

OKLAHOMA. *Teachers' Certificates.* Oklahoma City, Okla.: State Board of Education, 1936.

OREGON. *Circular of Certification.* Salem, Ore.: State Department of Education, May, 1939.

PENNSYLVANIA. *Certification of Secondary School Teachers of Academic Subjects.* Harrisburg, Pa.: Department of Public Instruction. Mimeo.

RHODE ISLAND. *Certification of Teachers.* State of Rhode Island and Providence Plantations, Department of Education, 1938, Pp. 16.

SOUTH CAROLINA. *Rules and Regulations for the Certification of Teachers.* State Department of Education, 1925.

SOUTH DAKOTA. *Certification Requirements.* Pierre, S. D.: Department of Public Instruction, 1941. Mimeo.

TENNESSEE. *The Tennessee Educational Bulletin,* Vol. XVII, No. 4 (Abridged.) Nashville, Tenn.: State Department of Education, 1939.

TEXAS. *Certification Requirements.* Austin, Tex.: State Department of Education.

UTAH. *Requirements for Certification of Superintendents, Supervisors, Teachers, School Librarians, and Coordinators.* Salt Lake City, Utah: Utah State Board of Education, 1939. Pp. 23.

VERMONT. *Regulations for Certification of Teachers.* Montpelier, Vt.: State Department of Education, 1940.

VIRGINIA. *Regulations Governing the Certification of Teachers and the Qualifications of Administrators and Supervisors in Virginia.* Richmond, Va.: State Board of Education, Bulletin, Vol. XXII, No. 6, 1940.

WASHINGTON. *Certification of Teachers.* Olympia, Wash.: State Department of Public Instruction, 1940. Pp. 22.

WEST VIRGINIA. *High School Certificates.* Morgantown, W. Va.: State Board of Education.

WISCONSIN. *The Certification of Teachers in Wisconsin.* Madison, Wis.: State Department of Public Instruction, 1939.

WYOMING. *Certification of Teachers,* Bulletin No. 8, Series B. Cheyenne, Wyo.: State Board of Education, 1937.

APPENDIX

APPENDIX A

DATA SHEETS SENT TO STATE CERTIFICATION OFFICIALS

Your general, academic, secondary school certification requirements are typed in red, with questions following regarding some of your procedures in administering these requirements.

STATEMENT OF DEGREE REQUIREMENTS:

---

1. To prepare a student to meet the terms of the above requirement, must an institution of higher learning lie within the geographical boundaries of your State? Yes .... No ....
2. Kindly check below the accrediting groups whose accrediting of colleges and universities you now accept so the graduates of those accredited institutions can meet this above requirement.

American Association of Teachers Colleges ....
Association of American Universities ....
Association of Colleges for Negro Youth ....
Middle States and Maryland Association ....
National University Extension Association ....
New England Association ....
North Central Association ....
Northwest Association ....
....
Southern Association ....
State Department of Education (in your own State) ....
State Department of Education (in the State in which the institution is located) ....
State Teachers Colleges (Your own State) ....
State Teachers Colleges (Other States) ....
State University (Your own) ....
....
Others: ....
....

3. Other qualifications being equal, would you certify a person who has received a degree or who has been graduated from an accredited institution outside your State on an EQUAL BASIS with a person who has received a degree or who has been graduated from an accredited institution within your State? Yes .. No .. ..
4. Do you accept, to meet this above requirement, a degree or a statement of graduation from a non-accredited institution (a) within your State? Yes .... No ..... (b) outside your State? Yes .... No ....
5. What is your policy with regard to an applicant for certification who has a degree or has been graduated from a non-accredited institution outside your

State? (a) Refuse certification? Yes .... No .... (b) Require additional semester hours of college work? Yes .... No .... (c) Require evidence of unqualified admission to an accredited institution? Yes .... No .... (d) Other: ....

6. Do you partially waive this degree or graduation requirement for applicants (a) from accredited institutions within your State? Yes .... No ..... If yes, rarely? ...... Sometimes? .... Often? .... (b) From accredited institutions outside your State? Yes .... No ..... If yes, rarely? .... Sometimes? .... Often? ....

STATEMENT OF ACADEMIC REQUIREMENTS:

---

7. Is any course included in these academic requirements which must be taken in an institution in your State? Yes ...... No .... If yes, which course? ....
8. Do you certify people who have met these academic requirements in an institution outside your State on an EQUAL BASIS with people who have satisfied these requirements in an institution within your State? Yes ...... No ....
9. Are any phases of these academic requirements ever waived for a person who has received his training in an institution (a) within your State? Yes ...... No ...... (b) outside your State? Yes ...... No .... If yes, in either instance, under what conditions? ....
10. Must any subject in these academic requirements have a particular title or course name? Yes ...... No .... If yes, which one? ....
11. Would you waive any part of these academic requirements for a teacher who had met all other requirements, who had taught five years in secondary schools of another State, and who was deficient in these academic requirements by 3, 4, or 5 semester hours? Yes ...... No ....
12. Do you issue a one-year, temporary certificate to a person meeting all other requirements but is deficient by 3, 4, or 5 semester hours in these academic requirements? Yes ...... No ....

STATEMENT OF PROFESSIONAL COURSE REQUIREMENTS:

---

13. Must any course in the above professional requirements have an exact title or course name? Yes ...... No .... If yes, which course? ....
14. Must any part of the above requirement be satisfied by attendance at an institution of higher learning *within* your State? Yes ...... No .... If yes, which part? ....
15. Other qualifications being equal, would you certify a person who had met these above requirements in an out-of-State institution on THE SAME BASIS as the person who had met these requirements in an institution within your State? Yes ...... No ....
16. Excluding practice teaching, are any parts of the above professional requirements waived for applicants (a) from outside your State? Yes ...... No ...... (b) from within your State? Yes ...... No .... If yes in either instance, what part and amount would you waive? ....
Under what conditions would you waive this? ....

17. Must ALL these professional requirements be satisfied BEFORE an *inexperienced* teacher may begin teaching *in your* State? Yes ...... No .... Before an *experienced* teacher may begin teaching in your State? Yes ...... No ....
18. Do you grant a one-year temporary certificate to an inexperienced teacher who has met all other requirements but has a deficiency in some of these professional requirements? Yes ...... No .... To a teacher of five years' experience who has a deficiency only in these requirements? Yes .... No ....
19. Would you accept an equal number of semester hours in professional courses of *different content* to meet any of the above requirements if all other requirements had been met? Yes ...... No ....
20. Is the course content, not the title, the determining factor in your acceptance of courses to meet the above professional course requirements? Yes ...... No ..... Do you accept the statement of the registrar of the institution in which the course was taken as to the equivalency of the course to your requirement? Yes ...... No ....
21. If an inexperienced college graduate had a deficiency of one or two semester hours of practice teaching, or a deficiency of 20, 30, or 40 clock hours of actual practice teaching, what procedure would you follow: (a) Refuse certification ...... (b) accept another professional course to meet the deficiency .... (c) require deficiency made up before certificating ...... (d) waive requirement deficiency if all other requirements are met ...... (e) Other: (*Specify*) ....
22. Is exactly the same number of semester hours and clock hours of practice teaching required of out-of-state applicants as is required of applicants from your own State? Yes ...... No ....

STATEMENT OF MISCELLANEOUS CERTIFICATION REQUIREMENTS:

---

23. Does any phase of the above requirements, as administered, restrict in any way the free interstate movement of teachers coming into your State? Yes ...... No .... If yes, in what way? ....
24. Does any phase of the above requirement group differentiate in any way between applicants from outside your State and applicants from within your State? Yes ...... No .... If yes, in which way is this differentiation made?

OTHER INFORMATION REGARDING CERTIFICATION:

---

25. Do you certify persons who meet your written certification requirements without regard to the applicant's (a) race or color? Yes ...... No ...... (b) religion? ...... Yes ...... No ...... (c) political party or views? Yes ..... No ......
26. If a person had met your State certification requirements, would this person WITHOUT MEETING FURTHER REQUIREMENTS IN ANY WAY be entirely eligible for a teaching position in the general, academic subject matter fields in the secondary schools in ANY city or town in your own State? Yes ..... No ...... If no, what cities or towns have requirements? Kindly list: ....
27. Do you contemplate raising, within the next five years, these general secondary certification requirements in any of the following areas? Please check those areas to be increased:

(a) Degree requirements ....
(b) Academic course requirements .. ..
(c) Total professional course requirements ....
(d) Particular professional course requirements ....
(e) Practice teaching requirements .. ..
(f) Residence requirements ....
(g) Specific State requirements like.. ....
State School Law .... State History ....
State Constitution .... State Manual ....
State Course of Study .... State Program ....
(h) United States Constitution ......
(i) Other: (*List*) ....

28. If you have a requirement that the applicant for a certificate must have the promise of a position before being certificated, do you find that this requirement tends to restrict applicants coming into your State from other States? Yes ...... No .... If yes, in what ways? ....

29. Is it your opinion that a person may obtain employment more easily if he first has a certificate than if he first has the promise of a position before obtaining the certificate? Yes ...... No....... *If yes,* do you think this position requirement is restrictive in this way? Yes ...... No ....

30. Do you find that the employment policies of the cities and towns in your State tend to restrict the entrance of teachers from other States? Yes ...... No .... If yes, in your opinion, to what degree do you think these employment policies, in general, restrict out-of-state people from obtaining positions? Please check one of the following (a) Great restriction ...... (b) A restriction ..... (c) Barely a restriction ...... (d) Not a restriction at all ....

31. Must an applicant from outside your State meet FIRST the requirements in his own State before being certificated in your State? Yes ...... No ....

32. What is your own estimate as to the number of secondary school teaching positions filled each year in your State by people coming in from other States? (Estimate) ....

33. What three States provide you with the most teachers of those coming into your State from others?
(The most) .... (Next) .... (Third) ....

34. In your opinion, in general, if restrictions to the free interstate movement of teachers exist in certification practices, are they intimately connected with any or all of the following. Please check:
    (a) An over supply of teachers? Yes ...... No ...... (b) Poor economic situation in the nation? Yes...... No ....
    (c) Public bounty idea of home positions for home people? Yes .... No .... Other ....

35. What two factors of your own State certification requirements or community employment procedures are, in your opinion, most restrictive to the entrance of teachers from other States?
    (a) ....
    (b) ....

....
Your name

Kindly return this data sheet to:
Mr. William Stratford, Assistant to the Secretary,
Teachers College, Columbia University, New York City

APPENDIX B

DATA SHEET AND ACCOMPANYING LETTER SENT TO CITY SCHOOL SUPERINTENDENTS

TEACHERS COLLEGE
COLUMBIA UNIVERSITY
NEW YORK

The enclosed *Data Sheet on Employment Policies and Teacher Residence* is being sent to leading superintendents of schools throughout the United States. This constitutes an initial step in a series of research studies investigating the effect upon the employment of teachers of the factor of residence, consisting chiefly of the local teacher problem and restrictions to the free interstate movement of teachers.

While much has been written upon this subject, very little is known of the actual practices and attitudes of the men who are daily confronted with the practical problems arising out of the problem.

Any information which you may be kind enough to contribute will be very greatly appreciated. These data will be used solely by the undersigned and will be kept entirely confidential. The published reports will consist of tables and their interpretation so the identity of particular communities will not be revealed.

May we earnestly solicit your cooperation in this professional endeavor? The data sheet is so devised that it may be answered very rapidly. Will you please fill it out at your earliest convenience and return in the stamped; self-addressed envelope?

Yours very truly,
WILLIAM D. STRATFORD
Assistant to the Secretary
Teachers College, Columbia University
and
HAROLD E. SNYDER

DATA SHEET ON EMPLOYMENT POLICIES AND TEACHERS' RESIDENCE

(Note: This information will be kept strictly confidential. Please return to William Stratford, Teachers College, Columbia University)

I. CURRENT STATUS AND PRACTICES:

A. GENERAL INFORMATION

1. Name of city: ....
2. How many teachers are there at present in your school system? ....

3. Approximately how many of your teachers were, at the time of their initial employment in your system, residents of OTHER states? (Indicate by number) ....
4. Approximately how many of your teachers received their training in HIGHER INSTITUTIONS in OTHER states? (Indicate by number) ....
5. Approximately how many of your teachers are graduates of the secondary schools of your community? (Indicate by number) ....
6. Is there any HIGHER institution which trains teachers within your community? YES ...... NO ...... If YES, please check the type of institution as follows: Normal School ...... Junior College ...... Teachers College ...... Liberal Arts College ...... University ...... Others (Specify) ....

B. Employment Policies Relating to Residence of Teaching Candidates

1. Do you have a fairly CONSISTENT POLICY, NOT prescribed by any school board regulation, giving preference in the employment of new teachers to one or more of the following: (Please check) (a) Local residents? ...... (b) Residents of other communities? ...... (c) Residents of your state? ...... (d) Residents of one or more adjacent states? ...... (e) Residents of distant states? ...... (f) Other type of REGULATION concerning residence of teaching candidates? (Specify) ....
2. Do you have SPECIFIC SCHOOL BOARD REGULATIONS which give preference in the employment of a new teacher to any of the following: (Please check) (a) Local residents? ...... (b) Residents of other communities? ...... (c) Residents of your state? ...... (d) Residents of one or more adjacent states? ...... (e) Residents of distant states? ...... (f) Other type of REGULATION concerning residence of teaching candidates: (Please specify.) ....
3. Is it your practice in selecting teachers to give preference to graduates of one or more of the following: (a) Local institutions of higher learning? YES ...... NO ...... NO INSTITUTION IN CITY ...... (b) Institutions located within your state? YES ...... NO ......; ...... (c) Institutions located in other states? YES ...... NO ......; ....
4. Do you have any requirements for employment other than local or nonlocal residence, that would tend to handicap out-of-state applicants for teaching positions? Yes ...... No ...... If yes, kindly describe briefly the nature of these requirements: ....
....
....
5. Do your local minimum standards of training or other requirements for teaching positions EXCEED in any way the STATE certification requirements? YES ...... NO .... If YES, indicate by checking the areas in which your CITY requirements EXCEED the STATE requirements: (a) Amount of undergraduate training ...... (b) Graduate training ...... (c) Specific academic courses ...... (d) Specific professional courses ...... (e) Other unusual course requirements ...... (f) More practice teaching ...... (g) Teaching experience for all candidates ...... (h) Other requirements or standards of training: (Please specify.) ....
....

6. If you have indicated above that RESIDENCE is a FACTOR in the employment of teachers in your community, does this preference for local or in-state teachers apply EQUALLY to all groups or categories of teachers? YES .... NO ...... If NO, that is, if you make distinctions between certain groups in applying the restrictions or preference on residence, please check the groups for which there is NO RESIDENCE REQUIREMENT OR PREFERENCE FOR LOCAL TEACHERS. (a) Elementary teachers ...... (b) Junior High school teachers ...... (c) High school teachers ...... (d) Special teachers ...... (e) Men teachers ...... (f) Women teachers ...... (g) Married women teachers ...... (h) Other type (Specify) ....
....

II. ATTITUDES TOWARD THE PROBLEM OF TEACHER RESIDENCE

1. Are there, in your opinion, any significant differences among any of the following groups, taken as a whole, in their general efficiency as teachers in YOUR LOCAL SCHOOL SYSTEM: (a) local residents, (b) non-local residents, (c) residents of your state, (d) residents of other states? YES ...... NO .... If YES, which groups have you found to be superior or inferior as teachers, indicating your reasons? ....
....
....

2. DISREGARDING YOUR LOCAL SITUATION, do you think that in the TYPICAL SCHOOL SYSTEM there are likely to be significant differences among any of the following groups in their general efficiency as teachers: (a) local residents, (b) non-local residents, (c) residents of your state, (d) residents of other states? YES ...... NO ....
If your answer to this question was YES and your answer to the preceding question was NO, or, if you answered NO to this question and YES to the preceding question, kindly give your reasons for making a distinction between YOUR LOCAL PROBLEM and THE GENERAL PROBLEM of teacher residence. ....
....
....

3. Please check the following statement which best describes YOUR ATTITUDE toward the present proportion of LOCAL AND NON-LOCAL teachers in your school system:
   (a) Proportion ABOUT RIGHT in terms of local conditions ....
   (b) Favor MUCH HIGHER proportion of NON-LOCAL teachers ....
   (c) Favor SLIGHTLY HIGHER proportion of NON-LOCAL teachers ....
   (d) Favor SLIGHTLY LOWER proportion of NON-LOCAL teachers ....
   (e) Favor MUCH LOWER proportion of NON-LOCAL teachers ....
4. Please check the following statement which best describes YOUR ATTITUDE toward the present proportion of IN-STATE and OUT-OF-STATE teachers in your school system:
   (a) Proportion ABOUT RIGHT in terms of local conditions ....
   (b) Favor MUCH HIGHER proportions of OUT-OF-STATE teachers ......
   (c) Favor SLIGHTLY HIGHER proportion of OUT-OF-STATE teachers ......
   (d) Favor SLIGHTLY LOWER proportion of OUT-OF-STATE teachers......
   (e) Favor MUCH LOWER proportion of OUT-OF-STATE teachers ....

5. Does the prevailing attitude in your community differ fundamentally from your own views with respect to the desirability of employing local, non-local, in-state, or out-of-state teachers? YES ...... NO ....
Does the prevailing attitude of your Board of Education differ fundamentally from your own views on this matter? YES ...... NO ....
If you have answered YES to either or both of the above questions, will you state briefly what differences of opinion exist? ....
....
....

6. Have you noted any difference over a period of years in the extent to which pressure has been exerted on behalf of local or in-state candidates at various times, as a result of either local, state, or national conditions? YES ...... NO ......
If YES, please indicate below the years or groups of years during which the pressure was greatest and the years or groups of years during which the pressure was least noticeable:
(a) Greatest pressure in favor of employing local or in-state teachers (years) ....
(b) Least pressure in favor of employing local or in-state teachers (years) ....
Any comments which you may care to make concerning the nature and source of such pressure, or concerning any other phase of the problem will be helpful to the investigators. ....
....

APPENDIX C

ACCREDITING ASSOCIATIONS AND THEIR REQUIREMENTS

Middle States and Maryland Association

I. Completion of a four years' course in a college approved by the Association or in a college of equal rank, for a teacher of academic subjects.

II. Professional requirements: teachers should have had professional training or should have had successful teaching experience.

New England Association

I. Teachers of academic subjects should have completed at least four years of study in institutions of collegiate grade.

II. Professional requirements: training in semester hours—12.

North Central Association

I. Bachelor's degree from an institution approved by the Association.

II. Academic requirements: semester hours in the academic subject taught—English 15, Mathematics 15, Foreign Language 15 (in the subject taught), Science 15 (5 in the science taught), Social Studies 15 (including preparation in specific subjects taught). Deduction in fields of Foreign Language and Mathematics, 2 semester hours for each high school unit, not to exceed 6.

III. Professional requirements: semester hours in Education—15. The Association recommends the following types of courses: Educational Psychology, Principles of Secondary Education, Theory of Teaching, Special Methods (in subject taught), Observation and Practice Teaching, History of Education, Educational Sociology, and School Administration and Supervision.

Note: Until the professional courses are defined by the Association, it will accept as such only courses certified as Education by the institution in which they are earned.

Northwest Association

I. Graduation (Bachelor or equivalent degree) from a college or university approved by the Northwest Association of Secondary and Higher Schools, by a similar accrediting association, or by the educational authorities of the state in which the college is located.

II. All teachers in new schools and all new teachers in secondary schools must teach in the fields of their major and minor specialization in college preparation. A minor shall be interpreted to mean not less than 12 semester hours.

III. Professional requirements: semester hours in Education—15. This should include special study of the subject to be taught.

Southern Association

I. Degree from a college approved by the Southern Association.
II. Teachers should not teach outside fields of their college specialization.
III. Professional requirements: semester hours in Education—12. Courses in Psychology, Methods and Principles of Teaching, History of Education, Observation and Directed Teaching, Tests and Measurements, etc.

Western Association of Colleges and Secondary Schools

The Association is composed of institutions of the secondary and collegiate rank within the boundaries of the State of California and has no accrediting regulations for member institutions.

American Association of Junior Colleges

Academic requirements:
I. One year of graduate study majoring in the subject to be taught.
II. Successful experience or evidence of efficiency in teaching.

American Association of Teachers Colleges

Academic requirements:
I. Master's degree or its equivalent.
II. Twenty-four semester hours of undergraduate or graduate work in the field taught, and also professional courses in that field.

Note: Because of local conditions and because of difficulty of securing degrees in some special subject fields, an institution may be considered to have met this standard if not more than 15 per cent of the teaching faculty does not have the Master's degree or its equivalent.

Lists of States in Regional Associations

Middle States and Maryland Association

Delaware, District of Columbia, Maryland, New Jersey, New York, Pennsylvania.

New England Association

Connecticut, Maine, Massachusetts, New Hampshire, Rhode Island, Vermont.

North Central Association

Arizona, Arkansas, Colorado, Illinois, Indiana, Iowa, Kansas, Michigan, Minnesota, Missouri, Montana, Nebraska, New Mexico, North Dakota, Ohio, Oklahoma, South Dakota, West Virginia, Wisconsin, Wyoming.

Northwest Association

Alaska, California, Idaho, Montana, Oregon, Utah, Washington

Southern Association

Alabama, Florida, Georgia, Kentucky, Louisiana, Mississippi, North Carolina, South Carolina, Tennessee, Texas, Virginia.

APPENDIX D

LETTER TO THE FORTY-EIGHT STATE ATTORNEY GENERALS

TEACHERS COLLEGE
COLUMBIA UNIVERSITY
NEW YORK

A study is being undertaken which rests, in large part, on a point of law, in connection with which I should like much to have your assistance.

How long does a person need to reside in your State to become a legal resident there for voting and for educational purposes, assuming that the day he entered the State he intended to become a legal resident of your State?

How long would a person need to reside in a community in your State to become a legal resident of that community for voting and for educational purposes, assuming that the day he entered the community he intended to become a legal resident of that community?

Your answer at your early convenience will be appreciated.

Yours very truly,
William D. Stratford
Assistant to the Secretary
Teachers College, Columbia University

APPENDIX E

POLICIES OF COMMONWEALTHS ON RETIREMENT MONEYS

CREDIT FOR OUT-OF-STATE SERVICE GIVEN BY THE STATES TOWARD THE RETIREMENT QUALIFICATIONS *

System	Total Service Requirement	Number of Years Allowed Out of State
1	2	3
Arkansas	25	15
California	30	15 [a]
Connecticut	20/35	15 [b]
Illinois	25	10 [c]
Indiana	40	10 [d]
Kentucky	20	..
Maine	30	10
Maryland	..	[c]
Massachusetts	..	10 [c]
Michigan	25/30	15
Minnesota	30 (or age requirement)	[e]
Montana	15	10
Nevada	30	5 [f]
New Hampshire	30	10
New Jersey	..	10
New York	25/35	[g]
North Dakota	25	7
Utah	15/30	..
Vermont	30	10
Virginia	30	..
Washington	30 and/or age 60	10/15

* National Educational Association, Research Division and National Council on Teacher Retirement, *Analysis of the Statutory Provisions for State Teachers Retirement Systems*, January, 1939. Adapted from Table 2, p. 19.

[a] All service outside the state is credited for the purpose of determining the total contributions due, but contributions for not more than 30 years may be charged on service rendered to July 1, 1935.

[b] If a member before 1929, credit for all out-of-state service is given without payment by member, after 20 years' service in the state. If member joined after 1929, credit up to 10 years is given provided teacher pays to fund assessments for period of outside service and regular interest thereon.

[c] By making up deposits due, teacher may receive credit for prior service.

[d] Credit for outside service is not to exceed 10 years or one-fourth of service necessary before any benefits are payable; all prior service credited but teacher must make up deposits due, at 4 percent interest.

[e] After 15 years' service in state, teacher may get credit for out-of-state service by paying sum equal to 5 percent of average yearly salary (not exceeding $2000) received during 5 years previous to making payments multiplied by the number of years' service credit desired, plus interest at 4 percent.

[f] Fifteen allowed original members; 5 for new members.

[g] Out-of-state service credited in prior-service certificate, not to exceed 10 years.

REFUNDS OF TEACHERS' CONTRIBUTIONS TO RETIREMENT FUNDS BY THE STATES IN CASE OF WITHDRAWAL OF MEMBER BEFORE RETIREMENT *

All retirement laws considered in this analysis make some provision for refund of the teachers' contributions except Virginia whose law is silent on the subject. In 3 other laws the provisions are indefinite. That is, Louisiana, Maryland, and Montana stipulate that upon withdrawal, or upon death before retirement, the board shall refund "such part of amount as is demanded." In Maryland the board has ruled that this indefinite statement shall be interpreted to mean all deposits of the member.

In the following states, the refund to be payable in case of the teacher's withdrawal or in case of death to the beneficiary or to the estate is stated in the law definitely so that no legal contest is needed.

All deposits with interest (except for California) payable to beneficiary or to estate, or upon withdrawal to the teacher:

California (no interest), Connecticut,[1] Kentucky, Maine, Massachusetts,[2] Minnesota, Nevada,[3] New Hampshire, New Jersey,[4] New York, Ohio, Pennsylvania,[5] Texas, Vermont,[6] and Washington.[7]

Only part of deposits are returnable in either case:

Michigan	75 percent of deposits, without interest.
North Dakota	50 percent of deposits, without interest.

Provisions for refund in case of withdrawal differ from provisions in case of death:

	In case of withdrawal:	*In case of death:*
Arkansas	Total deposits, with interest	No interest.
Indiana	After 1 year, 25 percent of deposits are returnable; after 10 years, all contributions are returnable upon withdrawal	Contributions with 4 percent interest are payable to beneficiary or estate.
Utah	Total deposits with interest	Total deposits plus an amount equal to half the last year's contract salary.

* National Education Association, Research Division and National Council on Teacher Retirement, *Analysis of the Statutory Provisions for State Teachers Retirement Systems,* January, 1939, pp. 17–18.

1 Teacher withdrawing after 10 years' membership may elect to receive annuity based on contributions.

2 Teacher withdrawing after 10 years' membership may elect to receive annuity based on contributions.

3 For original members, amount refunded depends upon optional plan chosen at time of joining.

4 Three and one-half percent interest compounded annually.

5 Teacher upon withdrawal may elect to receive annuity actuarially equivalent.

6 For members who joined before July 1931, deposits are returnable with interest if member has less than 6 years' service. If teacher has more than 6 years' service, deposits and state's contributions are both returnable but without interest. For members who joined after July 1931, all own contributions are returned with interest, regardless of service. Same amounts are paid to beneficiary or estate in case of death of member.

7 With compound interest to withdrawing teacher or to beneficiary or estate in case of death of member.

No provision for payment to beneficiary or estate:

Illinois	If teacher withdraws before reaching the third classification (more than 15 years' service), he may withdraw 50 percent of contributions, without interest.
Nevada	Upon withdrawal, no provision for interest unless teacher elects to leave deposits to accumulate interest for annuity to be bought at a later date.
Wisconsin	Contributions are returnable as lump sum or as annuity, in case of withdrawal.

QUALIFICATIONS FOR VOLUNTARY RETIREMENT AMONG THE STATES *

State	Minimum Age	Years of Service		
		Total	In State	Immediately Preceding Retirement
1	2	3	4	5
Arkansas	60	25	10	5
California	..	30	15	10
Connecticut	60	20	20	..
	..	35	20	5
Hawaii	60	..	..	..
Illinois	50	25	15	..
Indiana	60	40	30	..
Kentucky	60	20	20	5
Louisiana	60	..	..	..
Maine	60	30	20	7
Maryland	60	..	..	..
Massachusetts	60	..	..	..
Michigan	60	30	15	5
	..	25	..	..
Minnesota	55	..	..	..
	..	30	..	..
Montana	60	15	10	..
Nevada	60 [a]	30	25 [b]	10
New Hampshire	60 (women) 65 (men)	30	20	5
New Jersey	62 [c]	..	..	..
New York	60	25	..	..
	..	35	..	..
North Dakota	..	25	18	5
Ohio	60	..	..	..
	..	36	..	..
Pennsylvania	62	..	..	..
Texas	60	..	..	..
Utah	60	15	15	..
	55	30	30	..
Vermont	60 (women) 65 (men)	30	20	5
Virginia	50 (women) 58 (men)	30	30	..
Washington	..	30	15 to 20 [d]	..
Wisconsin	50	..	..	..

[a] Original members who had 20 years of service prior to July 1, 1937, may retire upon completion of service requirements regardless of age.

[b] Fifteen years for original members.

[c] Present entrant members may retire before 62 after 35 years of service, the last 25 of which must have been in the state.

[d] Five years of Washington service must be membership in the retirement system.

* National Education Association, Research Division and National Council on Teacher Retirement, *Analysis of the Statutory Provisions for State Teachers Retirement Systems*, January, 1939. Adapted from Table 3, p. 20.

APPENDIX F

POPULATION CHANGES OF THE 48 STATES FROM 1920 TO 1940 *

State or Section	Total Population 1920	1930	Pct. Increase	Population ** 1940	Pct. Increase
NEW ENGLAND					
Maine	768,014	797,423	3.8	845,139	6.0
New Hampshire	443,083	465,293	5.00	489,716	5.2
Vermont	352,428	359,611	2.00	357,598	−0.6
Massachusetts	3,852,356	4,249,614	10.3	4,312,332	1.5
Rhode Island	604,397	687,497	13.7	711,669	1.5
Connecticut	1,380,631	1,606,903	16.4	1,710,112	6.4
MIDDLE ATLANTIC					
New York	10,385,227	12,588,066	21.2	13,379,622	6.3
New Jersey	3,155,900	4,041,334	28.1	4,148,562	2.7
Pennsylvania	8,720,017	9,631,350	10.5	9,891,709	2.7
EAST NORTH CENTRAL					
Ohio	5,759,394	6,646,697	15.4	6,889,623	3.7
Indiana	2,930,390	3,238,503	10.5	3,416,152	5.5
Illinois	6,485,280	7,630,654	17.7	7,874,155	3.2
Michigan	3,668,412	4,842,325	32.0	5,245,012	8.3
Wisconsin	2,632,067	2,939,006	11.7	3,125,881	6.4
WEST NORTH CENTRAL					
Minnesota	2,387,125	2,563,953	7.4	2,785,896	8.7
Iowa	2,404,021	2,470,939	2.8	2,535,430	2.6
Missouri	3,404,055	3,629,367	6.6	3,775,737	4.0
North Dakota	646,872	680,845	5.3	639,690	−6.0
South Dakota	636,547	692,849	8.8	641,134	−7.5
Nebraska	1,296,372	1,377,963	6.3	1,313,468	−.47
Kansas	1,769,257	1,880,999	6.3	1,799,137	−4.4
SOUTH ATLANTIC					
Delaware	223,003	238,380	6.0	264,603	11.0
Maryland	1,449,661	1,631,526	12.5	1,811,546	11.0
Virginia	2,309,187	2,421,851	4.9	2,664,847	10.0
West Virginia	1,463,701	1,729,205	18.1	1,900,217	9.9
North Carolina	2,559,123	3,170,276	23.9	3,563,174	12.4
South Carolina	1,683,724	1,738,765	3.3	1,905,815	9.6
Georgia	2,895,832	2,908,506	0.4	3,119,953	7.3
Florida	968,470	1,468,211	51.6	1,877,791	27.9
EAST SOUTH CENTRAL					
Kentucky	2,416,630	2,614,589	8.2	2,839,927	8.9
Tennessee	2,337,885	2,616,556	11.9	2,910,992	11.3
Alabama	2,348,174	2,646,248	12.7	2,830,285	7.0
Mississippi	1,790,618	2,009,821	12.2	2,181,763	8.6
WEST SOUTH CENTRAL					
Arkansas	1,752,204	1,854,482	5.8	1,948,268	5.1
Louisiana	1,798,509	2,101,593	16.9	2,355,821	12.1
Oklahoma	2,028,283	2,396,040	18.1	2,329,808	−2.8
Texas	4,663,228	5,824,715	24.9	6,418,321	10.2
MOUNTAIN					
Montana	548,889	537,606	−2.1	554,136	3.1
Idaho	431,866	445,032	3.0	523,440	17.6
Wyoming	194,402	225,565	16.0	246,763	9.4
Colorado	939,629	1,035,791	10.2	1,118,820	8.0
New Mexico	360,350	423,317	17.5	528,687	24.9
Arizona	334,162	435,573	30.3	497,789	14.3
Utah	449,396	507,847	13.0	548,393	8.0
Nevada	77,407	91,058	17.6	110,014	20.8
PACIFIC					
Washington	1,356,621	1,563,396	15.2	1,721,376	10.1
Oregon	783,389	953,786	21.8	1,087,717	14.0
California	3,426,861	5,677,251	65.7	6,873,688	21.1
UNITED STATES	105,273,049	122,288,177	16.1	130,621,728	6.8

* 15th Census of the U. S. Population, Vol. III. Part I, p. 24. Table 32, 1920, 1930.

** Figures are tentative. Released by the U. S. Census, 1940.